LOOSE LEAVES FROM A BUSY LIFE

A Da Capo Press Reprint Series

CIVIL LIBERTIES IN AMERICAN HISTORY

GENERAL EDITOR: LEONARD W. LEVY
Claremont Graduate School

LOOSE LEAVES
FROM A BUSY LIFE

BY
MORRIS HILLQUIT

DA CAPO PRESS • NEW YORK • 1971

A Da Capo Press Reprint Edition

This Da Capo Press edition of
Loose Leaves from a Busy Life
is an unabridged republication of
the first edition published in
New York in 1934.

Library of Congress Catalog Card Number 78-146160
SBN 306-70102-2

Published by Da Capo Press
A Division of Plenum Publishing Corporation
227 West 17th Street, New York, N.Y. 10011
All Rights Reserved

Manufactured in the United States of America

LOOSE LEAVES FROM A BUSY LIFE

LOOSE LEAVES
FROM A BUSY LIFE

BY
MORRIS HILLQUIT

NEW YORK
THE MACMILLAN COMPANY
1934

SET UP BY BROWN BROTHERS LINOTYPERS
PRINTED IN THE UNITED STATES OF AMERICA
BY THE FERRIS PRINTING COMPANY

CONTENTS

CONTENTS

BOOK III

THE SWING OF THE PENDULUM

LOOSE LEAVES FROM A BUSY LIFE

INTRODUCTION

THE ROOFS ON CHERRY STREET

Near the corner of Cherry and Montgomery streets on the lower East Side of New York, there still stand four uniform old tenement houses.

In 1888 they were new and were considered model dwellings. They had been built by a group of public-spirited citizens as a semi-philanthropic enterprise. The apartments, consisting mainly of one or two rooms, were small, dark, and cheerless. They were let by the week and were mostly occupied by Jewish immigrants from Russia.

The feature of the buildings was their roofs—four flat roofs with cement flooring and low parapets, all on an even level and communicating with one another through open gates.

In the hot summer nights the spacious and open roofs offered the one breathing place for the tenants of the stuffy and airless rooms in the buildings and their friends who lived in similarly stuffy and airless rooms in other buildings.

In favorable weather the roofs were crowded from the early evening to the wee hours of the morning.

It was an eager assemblage that forgathered there, mostly made up of young intellectuals, boys and girls ranging in age from eighteen to twenty-five, who had come here on the crest of the wave of mass immigration from Russia during the eighties of the last century. They were persons of high school or college education, who had been suddenly plucked from their studies and associations by persecutions and discriminations in their

1

cruel native land and found themselves transplanted in new and strange soil.

Some of them were recent arrivals, others had lived in the United States several years. Few, if any, had fully adjusted themselves to their changed surroundings and the unfamiliar ways of the country of their adoption. Their years of preparation for professional careers were of no practical value to them without a proper knowledge of English. They had not been trained for work at any trade and were impelled by economic necessity to engage in unskilled and unattractive occupations at which they earned a meager living.

They felt unhappy and forlorn in their workshops, but at night on the roofs they again lived in a congenial atmosphere. Once more they were students among students, forgetting the miseries of their hard and toilsome lives and enjoying the pleasures of freedom and companionship with the abandon and enthusiasm of youth.

Peals of gay laughter and voices of earnest and animated conversation would come from different groups on the roofs, while the melancholy and nostalgic strains of popular Russian folk songs would often resound in the still evening air. It was a slice of old Russian life that was thus transported to Cherry Street by the uprooted young immigrants.

But song and laughter were not the main pastime of the habitués of the roofs. Most of their evenings were spent in discussion. And what discussion! There was not a mooted question in science, philosophy, or politics that was not aired on the roofs in ardent, impassioned, and tumultuous debate. Politics was the favorite subject.

Some of these young people had received their political baptism in the underground revolutionary movement of Russia. All had definite social creeds and were ever ready to expound and defend them.

These creeds were almost invariably of a radical tincture and fell into three main categories.

Probably the most numerous group was that of the Socialists. The Socialist movement in those days was in its formative stages. It had not attained to political power and influence in any country, and nobody imagined that within a generation it would furnish prime ministers and cabinet members to the governments of the nations.

In Germany the forces of Social Democracy were making a valiant and winning fight against the notorious "exceptional laws" of the Iron Chancellor, which had practically outlawed the Socialist movement.

In the other countries of Europe the Socialist parties were weak, often divided and sometimes proscribed.

In Russia the movement had closed one epoch and was standing at the threshold of another. The romantic career of the famous revolutionary organization known as "The Will of the People" had practically come to an end. The intrepid band of terrorist idealists had succeeded in a spectacular but unequal duel with the heavy power of Romanoff absolutism. A new Socialist concept was being formulated by George Plekhanoff, Paul Axelrod and Vera Sassulitch from their Geneva exile, a concept based on the expected rise of an industrial working class in Russia and the possibility of a Socialist mass movement along Western European lines. The new program was eagerly discussed and widely accepted by the theoreticians of the roofs.

In the United States the movement was in its cradle. What there was of it was more like a foreign colony of Social Democracy in Germany than an indigenous American movement.

The Socialists of that remote period were not practical politicians. They were idealists and propagandists, who clung to their social creed with religious zeal. They were few in number, misunderstood and railed at by the multitude, and felt more than a mere political kinship with each other. They were comrades in a personal and intimate sense.

Almost rivaling the Socialists in numerical strength were the anarchists.

The anarchist movement was then at its zenith. The brutal suppression of Socialist propaganda in most countries of continental Europe had weakened the faith of many in the efficacy of peaceful methods and embittered them. Anarchism was a movement of reprisal and violence against the personal representatives of the capitalist system and its political rulers. The true anarchists disdained peaceful trade-union activities and all species of social reform. To them any improvement in the condition of the masses was a reactionary measure calculated to retard the final day of reckoning.

They rejected the Socialist concept of an ordered coöperative commonwealth. They were opposed to all forms of "authoritative and oppressive" government. Their own ideal was a world composed of a large number of small, autonomous and fluid communities, freely formed by voluntary association of congenial individuals. Their program was revolution, one big smashing revolution that would wipe out the forces of capitalism and establish the rule of the proletariat.

To pave the way for the final revolution the anarchists advocated and promoted all forms of political and economic revolts and individual "executions." This was the "propaganda of the deed," which they considered as at least equal in persuasiveness with the "propaganda by the word."

The doctrine made a special appeal to the Russian mind, largely because of the seemingly hopeless political conditions of Russia. It is no accident that the two great apostles of the creed, Michael Bakunin and Peter Kropotkin, were both Russians. In the United States the main supporters of the movement, like those of social democracy, were German immigrants. The fiery Johann Most was its high priest.

Communist anarchism, as it was then termed, was a simple creed and a romantic movement filled with thrilling conspiracies and acts of heroism and self-sacrifice. It had an irresistible attraction for the young and found many adherents on the Cherry Street roofs.

When I first met them, the memory of the judicial murder of the heroic anarchist leaders of Chicago in November, 1886, was still fresh in their minds and rankling in their hearts. They were full of bitterness.

It was amusing to hear these mild-mannered and soft-spoken boys and girls talk glibly about blowing up buildings and killing tyrants. But it was all theory with them, and many a night did we spend in heated discussion of the respective merits of the bomb and the ballot as agencies of social salvation. In later years the anarchist movement gradually declined. It has now practically disappeared as an organized force in this or any other country.

Another creed, now practically extinct, which was represented on the roofs, was Positivism.

This was a mixture of political and religious faith deriving its inspiration from the teachings of Auguste Comte (1798-1857). It was not so much concerned with the elaborate classification and hierarchy of sciences of the French philosopher as with his somewhat unrelated ethical doctrines and quasi-religious practices. The positivism of Auguste Comte was based on the conception of superiority of society over man and called for the subordination of individual rights to social duties. Not content with the abstract statement of ethical and social doctrines, the founder of the school erected his system into a formal religion— the Religion of Humanity, with the Great Being as the deity, a formal code of worship, a professional priesthood, and a calendar of saints. It was, to borrow the epigrammatic criticism of Huxley, "catholicism minus Christianity."

In the latter part of the nineteenth century positivism had gained considerable following among certain classes of intellectuals, notably in England, where several formal Churches of Humanity were organized with Comtist rituals. In the United States the creed had developed a limited following under the influence of the interesting and picturesque personality of William Frey.

Mr. Frey, whose real name was Vladimir Heins, was a Russian of noble birth, a military officer by training, mathematician by avocation, and revolutionist by conviction. In 1875 he emigrated to the United States, founding a Christian Communist colony in Kansas. There he was converted to the social philosophy of Auguste Comte. For a time William Frey lived in New York, where he was busy lecturing on the Religion of Humanity. The deep earnestness of his conviction and, above all, his nobility of character and purity of life made a profound impression on the youthful members of the Russian colony and gained him many followers.

In the days of the roofs the cult of positivism was already on the decline, but its surviving adherents were amply represented on them. They kept aloof from all political and industrial struggles and were wholly absorbed by their efforts to attain individual perfection, to lead "the good life." They were humanitarians, nonresistants, and mostly vegetarians.

The adherents of each of three dominant social creeds naturally gravitated towards a separate center, and in the end the dividing lines between the roofs of the four adjoining buildings became political as well as physical boundaries. But these boundary lines were not rigidly fixed or maintained, and incursions from hostile neighboring roofs for intellectual battle were not only tolerated but welcomed. It was into this enthusiastic, contentious, and overheated atmosphere that I happened to drift almost immediately after my arrival in the United States.

I did not fully fit into it. The young men and women that assembled on the Cherry Street roofs were a slice of old Russia. Although most of them were of Jewish birth, they had only a tinge of the Semitic temperament and were all Russians by education, culture, and habits, in manner, spirit, and ideology. I was only partly Russian.

The city of Riga, in which I was born and bred, is today the capital of Latvia, one of the small border states carved off from Russia by the Brest-Litovsk "peace" treaty. The little country is governed by the Letts, a unique and ancient race of the Aryan family, who constitute the vast majority of its population. In my day the Letts played a very subordinate part in the economic, political, and cultural life of Riga or of any part of the region which subsequently went to make up the Latvian republic. As conquered aborigines they were relegated to the status of peasants in the country and to menial occupations in domestic service and industry in the cities. They had no culture, history, or traditions of their own. Their national consciousness sprang up and was more or less artificially fostered towards the latter part of the last century in line with the general nationalist renaissance of that period. Riga was a geographical anomaly. Politically it was part of Russia. Culturally, linguistically, and even architecturally, it was a typical German city. It was founded eight hundred years ago by a group of Bremen merchants and almost immediately fell under the sway of the feudal Order of Teutonic Knights, who erected walls, fortifications, castles, domes, and churches. They and their descendants remained the ruling class of Riga throughout the centuries of its political vicissitudes, as a free member of the Hanseatic League and under the alternate rule of the Livonian bishops and of the conquering Poles, Swedes, and Russians. Until the closing decades of the nineteenth century, when the government of Alexander III inaugurated a ruthless policy of "Russification" in all its numerous non-Russian provinces, the official language of Riga, the language of its courts and administrative offices, its theaters and schools, the language of its business and social intercourse, remained German. My own mother tongue was German, and so was my early education. It was by mere chance that I later enrolled in the only Russian "gymnasium" (a middle school or college with an eight-year course of classical study). Henceforward my education was purely Russian. Russian literature and history were among the subjects of my most assiduous studies, and I was duly impregnated with the spirit of "Holy Russia," her institutions and traditions, her folklore and song, her fervid patriotism and "broad soul." But it was all book learning and theory to me. I had never been outside of Riga until I left it for good. I had never set foot on true Russian soil and really did not know Russia and the Russian people. Germany was closer to me in spirit, culture, and temperament, but I was not a German. Thus I grew up, a bilingual and cosmopolitan, without any marked national traits.

I was somewhat more reserved than the expansive habitués of the Cherry Street roofs and a little different from them in manner and habits. Yet I was strongly attracted to them. In the unwonted and uncongenial routine of existence into which I was thrown during my first period in America, they represented to me the real life. The fraternity on the roofs for a time was the main link between the idealism of my youth and the sordid realities of my new daily occupations. I relished the discussions of lofty problems and high themes which constituted the daily conversational fare of the roofs, the clashes of opinions and faiths, the ardor of controversy. I was deeply interested in the social philosophies represented by the rival schools of radicalism.

At that period I already considered myself a Socialist, but my Socialism was largely emotional and sentimental. My notions about the philosophy and practical program of the movement were quite vague. I had had no opportunity to study its theory and history. Here at least the finer points of the creed were discussed, analyzed, compared, attacked, and defended, and while it would have been unsafe to accept the haphazard and extemporaneous roof discussions as authoritative expositions of the social sciences, they were a tolerably efficient seminar.

To me these discussions were stimulating in the highest degree. I was an avid reader and eagerly studied all works on theoretical Socialism and allied subjects of which I could get hold.

Through some of my newly acquired friends on the roofs I got my first opportunity to make direct contacts with the organized Socialist movement. Many of them were members of a newly founded society called "The Russian Progressive Union." This was composed of adherents of all shades of radical and liberal thought. Its only practical activity consisted of organizing public lectures, which were held every Sunday afternoon. The lectures were mostly in Russian but sometimes also in English or German. As a rule they were delivered by guest speakers, exponents of all shades of contemporary social thought or abstract science; and they were invariably followed by lively discussions from the floor. Ultimately the Russian Progressive Union led to the organization of definite political groups, socialistic and anarchistic.

It did not take me long to choose between the rival social creeds that divided the constituency of the Cherry Street roofs and the Russian Progressive Union. I allied myself with the Social Democrats almost immediately.

It would be difficult for me at this time to define just what determined my choice. I am inclined to believe that political creeds and philosophies of life are as a rule formed by the imponderable elements of personal temperament, predisposition and mental affinities rather than by reasoned analysis of their merits.

But it seems to me in long retrospect that even in those early days I was guided by certain fundamental principles or, at least, leanings.

The selfish positivist cult of individual perfection and personal salvation did not satisfy my social instincts.

The romanticism of the anarchists held no attraction for me. I always had a certain sense of realism, which rendered me immune from the intoxicating effects of the hollow revolutionary phrase. I could not envisage a great social, economic, and moral world revolution accomplished by guerrilla warfare, dynamite bombs, and theatrical conspiracies. I could not take the violent anarchist thunder seriously.

I was on the other hand deeply impressed with the practical idealism of Social Democracy. Socialism has never become a religious dogma to me. I accepted its philosophy as convincing on the whole, without insisting on every article of the Marxian creed for myself or my comrades. I subscribed to the Socialist program and have ever since adhered to it with a full realization that it implies a long and laborious work of education, organization, and struggle, with slow progress and frequent setbacks. I fully measured the magnitude of the Socialist task in the incipient stages of the movement; the task of revolutionizing the minds of the passive millions of workers in all advanced countries of the world and galvanizing them into concerted action in their own behalf; the task of replacing the accumulated notions and prejudices of the ages by radically new social concepts.

As I recall it, the Cherry Street roofs lasted only two or three seasons as the social center of the Russian radical youth. With the development of practical organizational activities among its habitués and with the growing antagonism between the contending social creeds, the gatherings on the roofs lost their charm of unrestrained play and good-fellowship. They lagged and then died out.

I was a regular devotee of the roofs only one summer. The following one already found me busy with the everyday struggles of the life below. But that summer on the Cherry Street roofs will always remain one of the cherished recollections of my early American days.

BOOK I

EARLY DAYS

CHAPTER I

THE BIRTH OF THE JEWISH UNIONS

Aside from the roofs on Cherry Street our favorite gathering places were the East Side tea shops. There, particularly in the long winter nights, we would pass many hours talking and occasionally sipping weak tea served in tumblers, Russian style. A glass of tea and a "coffee twist" of ample proportions were, as a rule, the limit of a guest's consumption. The price of each was five cents.

I often wondered how the owners of the establishments could keep going on such meager income, and I suppose the owners were kept wondering harder than I. But they somehow managed. In some cases they were of the same kind and type as their guests, and they took it for granted that the tea shop was there not so much for drinking or eating as for discussions.

Of discussion there was plenty, but the purely vocal exercise did not long satisfy the enthusiastic young Socialists' yearning for action. They cast about for a promising field of practical work and inevitably discovered it among their own countrymen. The anti-Jewish riots or "pogroms" of 1881 and 1882 had set in motion a powerful stream of Jewish emigration from Russia and Poland. Thousands of immigrants arrived on the shores of this country every week seeking shelter and bread. By 1890 their number was estimated at no less than half a million. In New York they formed the largest Jewish settlement of the world, the largest, most congested, and poorest.

In two thousand years of homeless wandering among the

nations of Africa, Europe, and Asia, in centuries of outlawry and persecution, the Jewish people had been largely excluded from productive work and had become a race of traders and money lenders. In the new world they evolved for the first time a solid proletarian block.

In the early days of immigration, many of them turned to the lowest form of trade—peddling; but that occupation proved utterly inadequate when their numbers rose to hundreds of thousands. They were compelled to seek employment at manual labor. The great majority of the new arrivals found work in the different branches of the clothing industry. Others tried to eke out a precarious existence as bakers, cigar makers, house painters, and factory workers. Their conditions of life and labor were pitiful. Ignorant of the language and ways of the country of their adoption, mostly without technical training of any kind, penniless and helpless, they were left at the mercy of their employers, mostly men of their own race. Many of these "employers" were mere middlemen or contractors acting as intermediaries between manufacturers and workers.

There were hundreds of these middlemen in the clothing industry, and they operated in fierce competition with one another. A number of hired sewing machines set up in a tenement-house room, often connected with their own living quarters, constituted their whole capital and establishment. In these close, dark, ill ventilated, and unsanitary shops a welter of working and perspiring humanity, men and women, from three to twenty or thirty in number, were crowded together. Their pay was almost nominal, their work hours were unlimited. As a rule they were employed "by the piece," and as their work was seasonal and irregular, they were spurred to inhuman exertions in the rare and short busy periods.

Mercilessly exploited by their employers and despised by their American fellow workers as wage cutters, they completely lacked

self-assertiveness and the power of resistance. They were weak
from overwork and malnutrition, tired and listless, meek and
submissive. Tuberculosis, the dread white plague of the tenements, was rife among them.

Here was a situation that fairly cried out for sympathy and
help. Our group was quick to heed the summons. We resolved
to undertake the task of bettering the lives of our laboring countrymen, of educating them to a realization of their human rights,
of organizing them for resistance to their exploiters, and of securing for them tolerable conditions of labor and life.

It was a task beset with baffling difficulties. Several attempts
to organize the Jewish workers of New York had been made
before and had failed. A few spontaneous strikes had been
quickly quelled. A few nuclei of labor unions had been still-
born. The Jewish workers seemed to be unorganizable. They
had not been trained in any form of collective action in the
countries of their birth. They were dull, apathetic, and unintelligent. And worst of all we did not speak their language, both
figuratively and literally. Our language was Russian. The workers spoke Yiddish, a corrupted German dialect with several pro-
vincial variations. Few of us knew Yiddish well enough to embark on a campaign of propaganda. The only one among us who
could speak Yiddish and did it fluently, lovingly, and artistically
was Abraham Cahan, who subsequently made equally enviable
places for himself in the English and Yiddish worlds of letters.
Cahan was somewhat older than the rest of us. He was nearly
thirty at that time, and we looked up to him with envy and
respect, not only on account of his venerable age but also because
of his incomparable knowledge of the language of the people.

We all began perfecting our Yiddish. Those of us who happened to know German had a somewhat easier task than those
who spoke only Russian and had to labor at it word by word
and idiom by idiom.

The next problem was to make contacts with the workers. This also proved a highly elusive undertaking. There were so many of them, and they were hopelessly scattered.

It would have taken decades to build a Jewish labor movement from the bottom up, educating individual workers, forming them into organized trade groups and finally uniting them into one coöperating body. We were forced to reverse the logical process and to attempt to build from the top down.

Taking the bull by the horns, we founded the "United Hebrew Trades" in October, 1888. It was a central labor body without affiliated labor unions, a mere shell within which we hoped in time to develop a solid kernel. The idea originated among the Jewish members of the Socialist Labor Party, the political organization of American Socialism at that time.

The party had two Jewish branch organizations or "sections" in New York, one composed of Yiddish-speaking members, known as Section 8 and the other, Section 17, whose members spoke Russian. The task of setting the contemplated organization in motion was entrusted to a joint committee of the two sections, each electing two members. The Yiddish-speaking section was represented on the committee by I. Magidoff and Bernard Weinstein.

Magidoff, who may be termed the father of the idea, was very active in the initial stages of the Jewish labor movement, but later dropped out of it and devoted himself entirely to newspaper work. Bernard Weinstein was and remained one of the best types produced by the Jewish labor movement in the United States. A native of Odessa, in the southern part of Russia, he came here as a boy with the first wave of Russian emigration in 1882, and found employment in a cigar factory alongside Samuel Gompers, then also an obscure cigar maker.

He associated himself with the early Socialist and labor movements immediately upon his arrival and has remained wholeheartedly devoted to their cause for fifty years. Handicapped by a slight facial deformity, devoid of the gift of popular oratory and modest to the point of shyness, Bernard Weinstein was never very prominent in the leadership of the movement. But he did not seek prominence or even recognition. He served the cause for the sake of the cause, served it with simple and unwavering faith, steadily, unostentatiously, and with utter self-abnegation.

The "Russian section" was represented on the committee by Leo Bandes and by myself. Bandes was a somewhat maturer man than most of us. He had won his revolutionary spurs as a member of the redoubtable "Will of the People" and had served time in Russian prisons for his Socialist activities. He was a person of kind disposition and rare idealism and occupied a leading and authoritative position in our councils. But we were not long permitted to enjoy his companionship. He had contracted a tubercular affection of the lungs during his prison life, and the tenement air of New York was not at all conducive to recovery. He languished before our eyes and died in less than two years.

The organization meeting of the United Hebrew Trades took place at 25 East Fourth Street, the headquarters of the Socialist Labor Party, and the meeting place of the United German Trades (Vereinigte Deutsche Gewerkschaften). It was the latter organization that inspired the name of the newcomer in the field of organized labor.

The United German Trades was a powerful body in those days. It was a federation of labor unions composed of German workers, who practically controlled several important industries in New York. Originally called into being for the sole purpose of supporting the German labor press, it soon broadened its functions to include those usually exercised by central labor bodies in cities. It was a progressive organization and worked in close coöperation with the Socialist movement.

The United German Trades assisted in the formation of its

younger Jewish brother by practical advice and made a generous contribution of ten dollars to its war chest.

Before we called the organization meeting, Bernard Weinstein and I made a minute and painstaking search of all nuclei or remnants of Jewish labor unions in New York. There had been, we knew, unions of shirt makers, cloak operators, and bakery workers at one time or another. We thought them dormant. We found them dead.

The only Jewish unions that could lay any claim to existence were two in number, the Hebrew Typographical Union and the union of chorus singers. The typesetters' union was only a few months old. It was made up of employees of the struggling newspapers and job printing shops on the lower East Side.

The Chorus Singers' Union was somewhat of an anomaly in the labor movement. It was composed of members of the chorus of the two Yiddish theaters then operating in New York. In the daytime they were employed at other trades, the men mostly as cigar makers and the women as garment finishers. The work at rehearsals and in the nightly performances was strenuous, and the pay ranged from three to four dollars a week. But it was not so much the hard work and low wages that drove them to seek protection in organization as the brutal treatment to which they were subjected by the theater managers.

In membership the two "unions" together represented a grand total of forty. This was the modest beginning of the organization that in later years boasted of an affiliated membership of a quarter of a million workers.

Undaunted by the slim foundation, we proceeded to the formal organization of the "United Hebrew Trades," with Bernard Weinstein as recording secretary and myself in the somewhat vague post of "corresponding secretary." The triple aim of the new organization was declared to be: (1) mutual aid and co-operation among the Jewish trade unions of New York; (2) organization of new unions; (3) the propaganda of Socialism among the Jewish workers.

A somewhat humorous sample of the work ahead of us presented itself at the very first meeting of our newly formed body. Just before adjournment a delegation from an actors' union appeared and applied for affiliation.

The Jewish theaters of New York were in their infancy and had a hard struggle for existence. The members of the troupes were not paid fixed salaries but worked on shares. The lion's share of these "shares," however, went to the numerous stars, while the lesser lights of the stage were left with little more than the gratification of their artistic aspirations. The class struggle in this instance was between the minor parts and the headliners, and the former had just formed a union against the latter. The definite organization meeting of the new union was to be held in a few days, and we were asked to send a speaker to initiate the neophytes in the principles and practices of trade unionism.

Of course, we were eager to serve, but the spokesman for the theatrical proletariat was careful to attach proper conditions to his request. Actors are artists after all, he explained, and cannot be expected to receive instruction in coarse and common Yiddish. Our speaker would have to address them in German, the language of the poets and thinkers. All eyes turned on me. I nodded assent, and this part of the problem seemed to be solved. But not so with the next condition of our theatrical comrade. "To have the attention and respect of the audience," he calmly proceeded, "the speaker will have to appear in proper attire, i.e., dressed in frock coat and silk hat."

Again all eyes turned on me, but this time not with confidence but with consternation succeeded by irrepressible mirth. I was nineteen and looked younger. Frock coats and silk hats were not among the customary articles of my wardrobe and were generally not sported at our meetings.

This was our first taste of some of the difficulties of practical trade-union politics, and we just gave it up. The organization meeting of the actors' union was held without a representative of our group and seems to have gotten along quite well, for the Jewish Actors' Union was definitely and firmly organized and has remained in continued and effective existence ever since. For years one of the favorite and exciting subjects of our debates was, whether actors were wage workers and had a legitimate place in the labor movement. The final decision was in the affirmative.

Our work among the genuine and simon-pure proletariat began very soon. Our first effort was to reorganize the defunct shirt makers' union. This was accomplished within a few weeks after the foundation of the United Hebrew Trades. It was a comparatively easy task because this particular trade happened to employ large numbers of Socialist intellectuals.

The problem was infinitely more difficult in the other branches of the needle industry, but gradually a technique of organization was developed.

I remember most vividly the origin and early history of the Knee Pants Makers' Union, and shall rapidly sketch them because they were typical of all tailoring trades.

In 1890 there were about one thousand knee pants makers employed in New York, all "green" and most of them illiterate. It was a sweat-shop industry *par excellence.* The work was done entirely on the contracting system. A contractor employed about ten workers on the average and usually operated his shop in his living-rooms. His sole function consisted of procuring bundles of cut garments from the manufacturer and having them made up by the workers. He did not even furnish the sewing machines. The operator provided his own machine as well as the needles and thread. The work day was endless, and the average earnings of experienced operators ran from six to seven dollars per week. Often the contractor would abscond with a week's pay; often the worker would be discharged because he was not fast enough to suit the contractor, and often he would be compelled to quit his job because of maltreatment or intolerable working conditions. Every time a knee pants maker changed contractors, he was compelled to put his sewing machine on his back and carry it through the streets to his new place of employment. It was at this point that their patience finally gave out. In the early part of 1890 they struck. The movement was spontaneous, without program, leadership, or organization. It was a blind outbreak of revolt and was destined to collapse if left to itself, sharing the fate of many similar outbursts in the past.

In this case the United Hebrew Trades stepped in during the very first hours of the strike. Through a committee of five, of whom I was one, it took complete charge of the situation.

Our first step was to hire a meeting hall large enough to accommodate all the strikers. There were about nine hundred, and we gathered them in from all shops and street corners. In the hall we held them in practically continuous session, day and night, allowing them only the necessary time to go home to sleep. We feared to let them go, lest they be tempted to return to work, and we entertained them all the time with speeches and such other forms of instruction and amusement as we could devise.

While the continuous performance was going on in the main hall, we tried to bring order and system into the strike and to organize the strikers into a solid and permanent union.

In consultation with the most intelligent men and women from the ranks of the strikers we worked out a list of demands centering upon the employer's obligation to furnish sewing machines and other work tools at his own expense. Then we choose pickets, relief committees, and settlement committees, all operating under our direct supervision and guidance.

The men did not know how to conduct meetings or transact

business of any kind. They had never acted in concert. Our discourses on the principles of trade unionism and the philosophy of Socialism were interspersed with elementary lessons in parliamentary procedure and practical methods of organization. We tried to pick out the most promising among them and train them for leadership of their fellows. The strike was a course of intensive training and education, but it was of short duration. After one week without a break in the ranks of the workers, the contractors weakened; one Saturday night they became panicky and stormed the meeting hall of the strikers in a body, demanding an immediate and collective settlement on the workers' terms.

The United Hebrew Trades had scored a great victory and was encouraged to new efforts in other fields.

One of the most difficult tasks the pioneering group was called upon to tackle was the organization of the Jewish bakery workers. In the early days of Jewish immigration a limited number of bakeshops had sprung up on the lower East Side. They specialized in "Jewish" rye bread and other bakery products to which the Jewish consumers had been accustomed in the countries of their origin. These bakeries were in deep and dark subcellars, without ventilation or any hygienic accommodations. The walls and ceilings were moist and moldy. The shops were infested with rats and reeked with dirt. The air was pestilential. The bake ovens were primitive. No machinery was used. The work was all done by hand.

The new industry employed a total of a few hundred workers, mostly immigrants from Galicia, Hungary, and Poland. They were different from the bulk of the Russian Jewish workers, more stolid, unemotional, and irresponsive. They worked seventeen to eighteen hours a day except on Thursday, when their "work day" began early in the morning and lasted until noon on Friday. As a rule they boarded and lodged with their employers. They worked at the ovens naked from the waist up and slept in the bakery cellars. When they did not receive board and lodging, their wages averaged six to seven dollars a week.

Their only leisure time was between making the dough and its rising, and these hours they spent in their favorite saloons, drinking beer and playing cards.

The beer saloons, particularly one on the corner of Ludlow and Hester streets, provided the only romance in their drab lives. Here were their social clubs and also their labor bureaus. Here they would exchange information about jobs and here also employers would come in quest of "hands."

Pale-faced, hollow-chested, listless, and brutified, they seemed to be hopeless material for organization and struggle. In 1887 the newly organized Bakery and Confectionery Workers International Union of America had succeeded in enlisting a number of them into a Jewish local union, but the organization collapsed within a year, for a reason very characteristic of the workers' mentality.

Anxious to remove them from the demoralizing atmosphere of the Ludlow Street saloon, the secretary of the national organization of bakery workers had secured new headquarters for them. It was a room back of a beer saloon on Orchard Street. Meeting halls connected with saloons were the customary thing for labor unions in New York in those days. The saloon keeper would make no charge for the use of the room, expecting to be compensated in trade. In the case of the German and Irish unions the scheme worked well, but with the Jewish unions it mostly proved unprofitable from the saloon keeper's point of view.

The attempted removal of the organized Jewish bakers from the Ludlow Street saloon met with considerable opposition. They were used to their old gathering place and its ways, and many of them were suspicious of the proposed change. A severe factional fight broke out between the conservative adherents of Ludlow Street and the radical supporters of Orchard Street. To the

Jewish bakery workers of that period the class struggle assumed the form of a fight between two rival beer saloons. With the help of the proprietor and the support of the employers the anti-union Ludlow Street saloon won out. The union disbanded.

Undeterred by this miscarried attempt, the United Hebrew Trades launched a new campaign to organize the bakers in 1889. After some preparatory propaganda a strike was called. The principal demand of the workers was for the six-day week with one day of rest, on Saturdays, a radical demand in those days.

The strike call met with general response. The Jewish bakeshops were tied up, and within a few days their proprietors surrendered to the union.

As in the case of the knee pants makers, the strike was organized and conducted by a group of young Socialists acting in behalf of the United Hebrew Trades; and as in that case we tried to take advantage of the situation to give the workers an intensive course of instruction in the principles and methods of trade unionism. Our efforts seemed to be successful beyond our most optimistic expectations. Within a few months the organization numbered about four hundred members, constituting practically the whole body of Jewish bakery workers. The Union became their religion, and they zealously adhered to its tenets as they understood them.

A tragic incident which occurred shortly after the organization of the Jewish bakers' union served to call general public attention to the revolting condition in the bakeshops of New York's East Side and led to important consequences in the field of labor legislation.

One early morning the secretary of the newly organized union reported to Bernard Weinstein at the office of the United Hebrew Trades that a baker had collapsed while working at night and was still in the bakeshop, critically ill. The secretary, as well as the employer, was at a loss to know what to do. When Weinstein reached the bakery cellar, he found a most appalling condition of filth, with three emaciated and exhausted bakers continuing to work at the side of their agonizing comrade. He made arrangements to have the sick man taken to a hospital and reported the case to the labor department.

An investigation of the bakeshops on the East Side followed and resulted in a sensational report condemning the inhuman labor conditions in these shops and branding them as a standing menace to public health.

As a consequence of this investigation and report the New York State Legislature shortly thereafter enacted a law, limiting work in bakeries to ten hours a day. The law had an interesting career in the courts and largely served to determine the limit of protective labor legislation.

Contesting the constitutionality of the law, the employers fought it in all courts of the state and in the Supreme Court of the United States. It was upheld by the trial judge, whose decision was affirmed in the Appellate Division by the narrow margin of three to two votes and in the Court of Appeals by a vote of four to three. In the United States Supreme Court it was reversed by a vote of five to four.

"There is no reasonable ground for interfering with the liberty of person or the right of free contract, by determining the hours of labor, in the occupation of a baker," declared Mr. Justice Peckham, who wrote the prevailing opinion in the case of Lochner against New York. "There is no contention that bakers as a class are not equal in intelligence and capacity to men in other trades and manual occupations, or that they are not able to assert their rights and care for themselves without the protesting arm of the state interfering with their independence of judgment and of action."

The learned court held that the law curtailed both "the right of the individual to labor for such time as he may choose" and the right of the employer "to purchase labor" in such quantities as he may choose.

I have often wondered whether Mr. Justice Peckham and his four concurring associates would have felt quite so certain about the capacity of the bakers to assert their rights and to exercise "their independence of judgment and of action," if they had met the Jewish bakers in their hang-out in the Ludlow Street corner saloon, or gone through the numerous strikes with them, or accompanied Bernard Weinstein in his mission of help to the sovereign and independent baker who fell in the midst of his free labor like an overburdened beast. And I am still wondering why a few theorists, ignorant of the daily struggles and sufferings of the toiling masses, should be allowed to determine industrial relations, social conflicts, and human rights, irrevocably and regardless of public sentiment and the enactments of popularly chosen legislative bodies.

The bakers' union subsequently became one of the strongest, most progressive, and best disciplined organizations among the Jewish workers of America. But that development took many years of patient and persistent struggle punctuated by recurring disappointments, failures, and defeats.

In spite of its promising beginning the union founded by the United Hebrew Trades had a short life. With the immediate objects of their strike attained, the members lost interest in their organization and within a short time the union disbanded. The lack of organization led to a new deterioration of labor standards and to a new revolt, another strike, and a revival of the union, followed by an inevitable decline and eventual dissolution. The disheartening process was repeated at fairly regular intervals every two or three years, each new organization being a little stronger and lasting a little longer than its predecessor, until stability and permanence were at last achieved after a zigzagging course of fifteen to twenty years.

Such also was the history of the Knee Pants Makers' Union and of practically all other Jewish trade unions organized since the advent of the United Hebrew Trades.

I have dwelt at length on the organizations of the Jewish knee pants makers and bakers because they were typical instances of the accomplishments and problems of the United Hebrew Trades. But these organizations were by no means the only ones called into life by the United Hebrew Trades, nor the most important ones. In its early career the Jewish Hebrew Trades was incessantly busy organizing and reorganizing Jewish trade unions. During the first eighteen months of its existence it had increased the number of its affiliated bodies from two to thirty-two. These included practically all industries in which Jewish workers were engaged in substantial numbers. Heading the list were the different tailoring branches, such as the cloak makers, men's tailors, furriers, and cap makers, but included in it were also such occupations as musicians, retail store clerks, book-binders and soda-water workers. And in practically all cases the unions were short-lived. They came and went and had to be reorganized every few years. In the minds of the Jewish workers of that period unions were associated with strikes and were little more than instruments of strikes. They were mostly born in strikes and died with the end of the strikes. It took twenty years of patient and persistent work to educate the Jewish workers to a realization of the value of trade unions in peace as well as in war, and it was not until about 1910 that the Jewish labor movement was organized on a solid and stable basis.

One of the important factors that contributed to that result was the consolidation of the multifarious organizations of separate branches of the needle-trade crafts into large unions embracing all parts of a related industry, such as the International

Ladies' Garment Workers Union, whose jurisdiction extends to all branches of the manufacture of women's apparel and the Amalgamated Clothing Workers Union, which is composed of all workers in the men's tailoring industry.

At this time several hundred thousand Jewish workers are normally organized in national and local trade unions. They have been fully accepted by their fellow workers as an organic part of the American labor movement, and have made a distinct contribution to the general progress of the movement.

During the half-century of their struggles, trials, errors, and experiences the Jewish workers in America have been strikingly transformed, mentally, morally, and even physically. From a race of timid, submissive, cheerless, and hopeless drudges they have grown into a generation of self-reliant, self-respecting men and women, conscious of their social and industrial rights and ever ready to defend them.

CHAPTER II

MY EARLY BUSINESS CAREER

I WAS seventeen when I came to America with my mother, a younger brother, and two sisters. My father and an older brother had preceded us by about two years and established a "home" for us in a two-room apartment in a tenement house on Clinton Street.

It was the unanimous decision of the family that I resume my interrupted studies and prepare myself for a professional career. My first step in that direction was to enroll in a public high school on Fourteenth Street.

I had come to New York with a smattering of school English, which served me very well in Russia, but proved utterly inadequate and largely incomprehensible in New York. My prime object in attending public school was to learn some real American English.

I liked the school, its friendly atmosphere and free and easy ways. Most of my fellow students were younger than I, and I must have appeared to them queer with my foreign ways and quaint English; but the boys were kind and helpful, and the teachers took a sympathetic interest in my progress.

After a short time, however, I was again compelled to interrupt my studies.

My parents were frightfully poor. My elder brother and the older of my sisters were working. I felt uncomfortable in the rôle of the drone of the family and determined to go to work.

To decide to work was one thing, but to find work was, as I

soon discovered, quite another thing. Because of my fragmentary knowledge of English and total lack of business connections I could not look for anything but manual labor. I was frail and untrained for any trade and almost inevitably gravitated into a shirt shop. For some fortuitous reason, shirt making had become the favorite occupation of the circle of young Russian intellectuals in which I moved. It was a trade easy to learn principally because of the minute division of labor that prevailed in it. Nobody made a complete shirt. The task of each worker was confined to one small and uniform operation, such as making the front or the sleeve, the collar or cuff, hemming the bottom or sewing some parts together. The cuff was the simplest part and required least skill and training. The operation of the "cuff maker" consisted of stitching together two square pieces of cut material on three sides and attaching it to the sleeve. I started my career as a cuff maker and never advanced to a higher stage of the art.

The work was not exacting, and the surroundings were not uncongenial. The operators in the stuffy little workshop spent at least as much time in discussing social and literary topics as in turning out shirts, and the whir of the sewing machines was often accompanied by the loud and hearty sound of revolutionary songs.

But the monetary returns were distressingly slim. The "boss," i.e., the contractor who ran the shop, took no business chances. He practically paid no rent, since the work was done in one of the rooms of his living quarters. He had no outlay on machinery because every worker hired his own sewing machine, at a rental of two dollars per month. Wages were low and were paid "by the piece." Work was seasonal and irregular. The machine rent was the only constant element in the peculiar industrial scheme, so that a worker of my skill and productivity sometimes wound up the month with a deficit in earnings.

Disappointed with the financial aspect of the shirt industry, I turned my talents to waist making. For a short time I also held down a job in a picture frame factory. But in all of these occupations my earnings were highly precarious, to say the least.

Stability of employment and income came to me only with what I may term my first political job. That was nothing less than a clerkship in the national office of the Socialist Labor Party. The party at that time occupied a four-story building at 25 East Fourth Street. The ground floor was used as a beer saloon, while the upper stories were divided into meeting halls, editorial rooms of the two weekly publications of the party—*Der Sozialist* in German and *The Workmen's Advocate* in English—and the office of the National Secretary. In the same building the party also conducted a bookstore and publication department under the firm name of Labor News Company.

I was attached to the latter. My salary, as I recall it, was four dollars a week. I was very happy in my new occupation. There was no rigid dividing line between the different departments in the headquarters of the Socialist Labor Party, and my work offered me a fine opportunity to familiarize myself not only with the Socialist literature then extant but also with the practical problems and methods of the organized movement. The National Secretary of the party, William L. Rosenberg, was also the editor of its German paper and the titular head of the whole establishment at 25 East Fourth Street. He was a poet of some merit, a sentimental idealist, and the kindliest of companions and teachers. He had taken a liking to me the first time he noticed me at a party meeting, and it was he who picked me for the job.

But again my employment was destined to be of short duration. After a few months of peaceful and serene work at the party headquarters, I was called upon to assume more responsible duties in a different field.

From the very beginning of our efforts to organize and consolidate the Jewish trade unions we felt the crying need of a labor paper as an organ of the movement, as a medium of communication between the unions and their members, and, above all, as an instrument of progaganda and education.

There was at that time a well-edited German Socialist daily newspaper in New York, the *New Yorker Volkszeitung;* but the Jewish workers could not read German. Nor could they read English. They knew only Yiddish.

Plans for the publication of a Yiddish weekly labor paper were often discussed among the leaders of the movement and in the fall of 1889 several formal conferences were held on the subject.

The original idea was that the paper be "nonpartisan" in editorial policy, and the conferences were attended by representatives of anarchist groups as well as the Socialist Labor Party and the trade unions. But the fundamental differences of view between the two wings of the radical movement, which found heated, vociferous and continuous expression at the conferences, soon demonstrated the impossibility of the project. The social democratic and trade union organizations separated themselves from the anarchists and decided to go it alone.

Months of incessant and enthusiastic preparatory work ensued. Funds had to be raised, the paper planned, and its management organized. Among the most active promoters of the project were Abraham Cahan, one Louis E. Miller, and I.

Cahan's life always was an uninterrupted succession of enthusiasms. Whatever interest happened to take hold of him at the moment dominated his thoughts and actions to the exclusion of everything else. He now threw himself body and soul into the new enterprise and never tired of discussing the proposed paper and working for its realization. He had two advantages over the rest of us. He knew Yiddish well, and he had the instincts of a born journalist.

The other member of our trio, who went by the name of Louis E. Miller, was a brother of Leo Bandes mentioned in the preceding chapter. He was a few years older than I. He had left his native Russia at a very early age and spent several years in Switzerland working, studying, and associating with the numerous Russian Socialist émigrés in Geneva.

In New York he spent his first years working by fits and starts in shirt factories and editing and publishing a Russian Socialist weekly of very limited circulation. Later he was admitted to the bar and practiced law rather sparingly, preferring to give his time to the Socialist movement and newspaper work. He was a person of persuasive eloquence, indomitable energy, and fanatical devotion to the cause.

Together we set out soliciting contributions for the projected paper. Almost every night we visited one or more Jewish trade unions and friendly German labor organizations, making our plea and receiving donations.

Within a few months we raised the enormous capital of $800.

On the 6th of March, 1890, the first number of our *Arbeiter-Zeitung* (Workers' Paper) appeared. It was an event of first magnitude in the Jewish Socialist and labor movements and an occasion for boundless rejoicing. For hours a throng of eager sympathizers stood in front of the printer's shop waiting for the first copies to come off the press. As fast as they did, they were handed out to the waiting crowds and snatched up by them with reverence and wonder. Here it was "in the flesh," a four-page paper neatly printed in the familiar Hebrew characters, all written for them and about them. Their hopes and dreams of many months were finally realized.

The paper was an instantaneous success. For weeks and weeks we had carefully planned every detail of its contents. It was our aim to conduct the paper along broad educational lines rather than to confine it to dry economic theories and Socialist propaganda. The Jewish masses were totally uncultured. They stood in need of elementary information about the important things in life outside of the direct concerns of the Socialist and labor movement. Without a certain minimum of general culture they could not be expected to develop an intelligent understanding of their own problems and interest in their own struggles.

Alongside a weekly chronicle of the Socialist and labor movements, the *Arbeiter-Zeitung* printed simple expositions of the philosophy of the movements in their different phases, articles on popular science, descriptions of travel, good fiction, and even poetry. Abraham Cahan largely supplied the "human interest" features. I contributed editorials, historical sketches, and articles on Socialist theory and a variety of other subjects. Other contributions came from the editor-in-chief and a number of volunteer writers who gradually augmented our forces.

The paper soon reached a circulation of about eight thousand copies, an almost fantastic figure in view of all our handicaps and modest expectation. Its size was increased from four pages to eight.

The *Arbeiter-Zeitung* exerted a powerful influence on the course of the Jewish labor movement and contributed materially to the intellectual development of the Jewish laboring masses. It retained the field until it was succeeded by the Jewish *Daily Forward,* which, under the able editorship of Abraham Cahan, became one of the great Socialist newspapers of the world and probably the most prosperous.

As editor we chose one Jacob Rombro, who wrote under the nom de plume of Phillip Kranz. He was considerably older than most of us, had established some reputation as a contributor to Russian magazines and was at the time living in London, where he edited a small radical Jewish weekly paper known as the *Arbeiter Freund* (The Workers' Friend). We lured him to New York by the promise of a larger and more fruitful field of activity and the offer of a princely salary of seven dollars per week.

I was the rest of the staff, combining in my own person the offices of associate editor, business manager, bookkeeper, and official poet, for all of which I was paid five dollars a week.

As I look back on it in the calm judgment of sobering time, I rather think I was overpaid. I had no business experience. My bookkeeping system was reduced to the simple processes of addition and subtraction in one running account. The income of the paper I kept in a desk drawer, and the "petty cash" in my pockets. If there was a discrepancy between my accounts and my pocket, one or the other suffered the consequences. My weekly poems were a liability rather than an asset to the paper. As to my prose contributions I thought and still think they were tolerably good in substance, but Cahan severely criticized my language. "It is not Yiddish," he would assert, "it is German written in Hebrew characters." I did not and could not deny the charge, but attempted to justify the practice. There were practically no recognized authorities on written Yiddish at the time. The literary style of the language was in the making. What was it to be? Cahan advocated a faithful reproduction of the spoken Yiddish with all its crudities. I, on the other hand, argued that since Yiddish is nothing but a corrupted, illiterate, and ungrammatical German, the task of the Yiddish writer was to improve and purify the language with the ultimate aim of converting it into modern German.

I did not maintain my end of the interesting controversy very vigorously or very long and ultimately Cahan's views prevailed.

When the paper became more prosperous and could afford to pay more adequate salaries, I resigned my multiple business offices on it. Although I would not say that my resignation was forced, I have a distinct recollection that it was rather encouraged by my colleagues.

I continued writing for the *Arbeiter-Zeitung* from time to time as a voluntary contributor, but gradually drifted away from the Jewish labor movement.

In the first few years after the organization of the United Hebrew Trades, a number of capable leaders had developed in the Jewish trade unions. At the same time some organizations of English-speaking members began to spring up within the Socialist Labor Party. I was quick to perceive the superior importance of that branch of the movement to the ultimate success of Socialism in the United States, and transferred to it the greater part of my activities.

I had learned English in the meantime and was supplementing my meager income by teaching this language to some of my less advanced countrymen.

In those days of heavy immigration and slow assimilation the task of teaching English to foreigners was one of great public importance, particularly in New York. Evening classes for that purpose were organized in the public schools in ever growing numbers and pupils were eagerly sought.

One day I made the acquaintance of one Joseph Darling, a man of charming personality and liberal political views, a devout follower of Henry George. Mr. Darling was a school teacher and had just been appointed principal of a newly created evening school for foreigners in Public School No. 1, on Vandewater Street, towards the southern extremity of the city and within walking distance from the Jewish settlement. The course of instruction in these evening schools consisted of ninety nights in the year, and the teachers were paid three dollars a night. Half of a normal weekly wage for two hours' work, what a lucrative compensation! "Is your teaching staff complete?" I asked Mr. Darling. No, it was not. "Could I apply for the position of a teacher?" "Yes," Mr. Darling assured me, "but on two conditions: First, you will have to pass an examination and secure a teacher's license and, second, I shall have to have students for you. This fall will be our first experiment and I do not know how many, if any students, will enroll."

The problems did not seem difficult. I took the examination at the earliest possible date and induced my friends Louis Miller and Phillip Kranz to do likewise. We all passed the test satisfactorily and were given licenses to teach English to foreigners in the public schools.

As the opening of the school term approached we hired a hall in the vicinity of the Vandewater Street school and inserted a notice in the *Arbeiter-Zeitung* calling upon all workers desiring to learn English under Socialist tutelage to meet in the hall at seven o'clock. About one hundred and fifty prospective students responded to the call. I explained the situation to them in a brief speech and concluded with the request that all those who desired to enroll in the school raise their hands. All hands went up.

"Well, then, let us go," I commanded.

Fifteen minutes later I arrived at the school auditorium at the head of an army of one hundred and fifty men in regular march formation. Mr. Darling, who sat at a desk in front of an empty enrollment book, looked up, and his eyes widened with utter amazement.

"What is this?" he asked me.

"These are students coming to enroll for your evening classes," I quietly explained.

"How many are there?" the principal inquired with growing bewilderment. I mentioned their number.

"But what shall I do with them?" ejaculated Mr. Darling. "I cannot put more than forty or fifty into one class, and I have no teachers for three new classes."

"The teachers are here," I informed him, introducing Mr. Miller and Mr. Kranz to him.

Then the humor of the situation dawned on him, and he broke

out into hearty laughter. I was appointed a sort of foreman of the new crew and assigned the task of classifying and enrolling the students. The task was soon accomplished. I reserved the most advanced class for myself and divided the rest between my two colleagues.

I taught evening school for three years, and the recollection of these years is among the most pleasant in my life.

My pupils were about my age or a little older. Most of them had had a good education in the countries of their birth. They were intelligent and earnest and, with very few exceptions, of radical leanings. Our relations were comradely and cordial and sometimes, particularly at the close of the school terms, their demonstrations of genuine affection for me were touching. For many years thereafter, I would often meet men who had made their mark in liberal professions or in business, and who would smilingly remind me that I had taught them English in the Vandewater Street school.

During my leisure hours in these years I took up the study of law. Having passed the requisite "Regents' examination," I enrolled in the New York University Law School and was admitted to the bar in the spring of 1893.

I immediately settled down to the practice of the law and have remained active in it ever since.

CHAPTER III

THE BEGINNINGS OF AMERICAN SOCIALISM

I BECAME a member of the Socialist Labor Party as soon as I reached the required minimum age of eighteen.

The party was then eleven years old and had made no perceptible progress since its organization. Its membership oscillated between 2,000 and 3,000. Of these, about ten per cent. were estimated to be native Americans. The rest were Germans with a thin sprinkling of Scandinavians and Bohemians.

The German pioneers of American Socialism were persons of superior type. With few exceptions they were political exiles from their fatherland who had taken active part in the first struggles of the working classes under the leadership of that most brilliant of Socialist propagandists of all times, Ferdinand Lassalle or under that of the early Marxian protagonists, Wilhelm Liebknecht and August Bebel.

They were mostly skilled workers, solid and reliable. In political intelligence they far outranked their American fellow workers. My youthful mind was strongly attracted by their quiet idealism and steady purpose, and I believe my early and close association with them had a strong influence on the whole development of my Socialist outlook.

Among the many capable leaders of the movement the outstanding figures were Alexander Jonas and Serge Schewitsch. The two men were fast personal friends but very different in type.

Alexander Jonas, when I first met him, was in his fifties. He was a native of Berlin and possessed in a high degree the peculiar sense of humor of the typical Berliner. He was a man of education and culture, a logical thinker, lucid writer, and persuasive speaker. Always calm and serene, always sober and practical, he exerted a decisive influence in the councils of the party.

When the *New Yorker Volkszeitung* was founded in 1878, he was chosen its editor-in-chief, and with few and slight interruptions he worked on the paper until his death.

Serge Schewitsch was considerably younger than Jonas. He was a Russian by birth and came from a noble family in high favor at the court of the tsars. He had studied in Germany and England and knew French, German, and English as well as his native Russian. Having become involved in the revolutionary movement, like so many other young men of his class at that period, he had been compelled to flee from Russia. He settled in Germany for a short time and there met, wooed, and married Helena von Racowitza, the beautiful young countess for whom Ferdinand Lassalle had fought his famous and fatal duel.

He was powerfully built and strikingly handsome and although a Socialist and democrat by conviction and associating by preference with working people, he was an aristocrat to the finger tips in manner and bearing.

Generally reserved and somewhat indolent in demeanor, Schewitsch became a passionate and flaming orator when confronted by a crowd. He was one of the most effective campaigners for Henry George in the New York mayoralty election of 1886, and subsequently was made editor-in-chief of the *Leader,* a daily newspaper founded for the support of the George movement. When the *Leader* suspended publication, he became associated with Jonas on the editorial staff of the *Volkszeitung.*

In 1901 Serge Schewitsch, through the influence of his family, obtained permission to return to Russia. He lived in Riga for a short time, and, having arranged some affair of inheritance, he settled in Germany.

Germany at that time was to the Socialists of the world what Russia is today to the Communists, the chosen land and the Mecca of the faithful. The drastic anti-Socialist laws had proved a stimulus rather than a hindrance to the growth of the movement during the twelve years of their rigid application. They were repealed in the face of the overwhelming Social Democratic success in the Reichstag election of 1890, when the party polled 1,427,000 votes for its candidates, doubling its best previous record and returning thirty-five representatives to the Reichstag.

It was the understanding of Schewitsch's friends here that he intended to acquire German citizenship in the hope of eventual election to the greatest Socialist arena of the world, the Reichstag. If such were his hopes, they were rudely and tragically nipped in the bud.

One fine morning the Berlin *Vorwärts,* the central organ of German Social Democracy, carried a sensational story "unmasking" Serge Schewitsch as a spy in the pay of the Russian government and an *agent provocateur*. The charge was absurd. It was inspired by a rancorous party opponent in the United States and was accepted by the credulous and impulsive veteran leader of the German movement and editor-in-chief of the *Vorwärts,* Wilhelm Liebknecht, without investigation or verification.

The publication caused a storm of indignation among the Socialists of New York, who knew and trusted Schewitsch, but it was characteristic of their awe and respect for the German party and its venerated leader that they were reluctant to engage in an open controversy with them. It was left to me, a mere youngster, to introduce and advocate at the next general party meeting a resolution of protest against the outrageous libel and an expression of confidence in the loyalty and integrity of our maligned comrade.

Largely as a result of the American protest, the *Vorwärts'* charges were practically withdrawn by the editor; but the damage was done, and the political career of Serge Schewitsch was blasted. He and his wife remained living in Munich; having spent their fortune, they found themselves destitute and friendless and ended the misery of their lives by their own hands. They died in a mutual pact of suicide in 1912, the same year when their friend Alexander Jonas died in New York of old age.

The task which the valiant band of German Socialists had set itself was nothing less than the creation of an effective, indigenous Socialist movement in the United States. It was a difficult, almost hopeless undertaking. They had practically no support from the native workers; their knowledge of the laws, institutions, and very language of the country of their adoption was highly fragmentary, and their material means were more than limited.

But they never lost faith in their cause or courage in their battle. For almost twenty-five years they plodded away at their self-imposed task of "Americanizing" their movement, patiently, tenaciously, and relentlessly.

During one brief period success seemed to beckon them. The widespread industrial unrest of the late seventies and early eighties had attracted a number of American workers to their banner and they even achieved several local electoral victories. But heavy desertions to the camp of anarchism, which was beginning to flourish at that time, again thinned their ranks.

When I joined the party, the net result of its Americanization efforts was represented by the publication of one English weekly, the *Workmen's Advocate*, which had a circulation of less than fifteen hundred, mostly among self-sacrificing German comrades. Subsequently an "American Section" of the party was formed in New York. In our zeal for the cause, we did not even appreciate the exquisite humor of a political party of the United States establishing a solitary "American Section" in the metropolis of the country. As soon as I judged, rather leniently I believe, that my

English could pass muster, I transferred my membership from the Russian Section to the "American."

The first nomination for public office on a straight Socialist ticket in the city of New York was made in 1888, when Alexander Jonas was chosen as the party's candidate for mayor. He accepted the proffered honor reluctantly and only upon our emphatic representation that a knowledge of English was not among the required constitutional qualifications for the office. About sixteen hundred citizens of New York signified their endorsement of our opinion by casting their votes for him.

A definite change in the policies and methods of the Socialist Labor Party came with the advent of Daniel De Leon, who joined the party in 1890.

De Leon represented a new type of leadership in the Socialist movement of America.

Born in Curaçao, in the Dutch West Indies, he came to the United States as a young man. He studied in Holland, Germany, and at Columbia Law School in New York, and later lectured at Columbia University on international law and diplomacy. He had actively supported Henry George in his mayoralty campaign and subsequently developed a growing interest in the Socialist and labor movements. For a decade he exerted a determining influence in the Socialist Labor Party. In fact he was the first and probably the only man who occupied the position of the traditional political boss in the Socialist movement of America.

Daniel De Leon was intensely personal. Almost immediately upon his entry in the Socialist arena he divided the movement into two antagonistic camps—his devoted admirers and followers and his bitter critics and opponents. Now, almost twenty years after his death, it is still not easy to formulate a just and objective evaluation of his personality and of the part he played in the history of American Socialism.

De Leon was unquestionably a person of great erudition, rare ability, and indomitable energy. He served the cause of Socialism, as he saw it, with single-minded devotion. He had unshakable faith in Socialism and its future, but his greater faith was in himself. He never admitted a doubt about the soundness of his interpretation of the Socialist philosophy or the infallibility of his methods and tactics. Those who agreed with him were good Socialists. All who dissented from his views were enemies of the movement. He never compromised or temporized outside or inside the Socialist movement. "He who is not with me is against me" was his motto and the invariable guide of all his political relations and practical activities.

Daniel De Leon was a fanatic. A keen thinker and merciless logician, he was carried away beyond the realm of reality by the process of his own abstract and somewhat Talmudistic logic.

Of small stature, mobile features, and piercing black eyes, he was a distinctly southern type. He was a trenchant writer, fluent speaker, and sharp debater. For his opponents he had neither courtesy nor mercy. His peculiar traits and methods were not due entirely to his personal temperament and character. In part at least they were the logical expression of his social philosophy. De Leon was not a social democrat with the emphasis on the "democrat." He was strongly influenced by the Blanquist conception of the "capture of power," and placed organization ahead of education, politics above economic struggles, and leadership above the rank and file of the movement. He was the perfect American prototype of Russian Bolshevism.

Having unsuccessfully attempted to "capture" the Knights of Labor and the American Federation of Labor, he organized a rival trade-union body under the name of Socialist Trade and Labor Alliance, thus provoking an open breach with the organized labor movement of the country.

His policy of antagonizing the trade unions and his régime of despotism and intolerance resulted in a strong and organized opposition to him. The final breach came in 1899, when the party split into two antagonistic factions, each claiming title to the party name and property.

The split was preceded by a long and bitter fight within the party, in which the administration faction of Daniel De Leon was supported by the official party papers, *The People* in English, and the *Vorwärts* in German, while the opposition rallied around the daily *Volkszeitung*.

I was chosen by my comrades for the strenuous task of leading the opposition. There was never much love lost between Daniel De Leon and me. I was repelled by his dictatorial demeanor, so utterly misplaced in a voluntary and democratic movement, and I considered his trade-union policy as suicidal to the party. When the Socialist Trade and Labor Alliance was organized and officially sanctioned by the party at its national convention in 1896, I could not accept it and for a time retired from active party work. But I soon realized that retirement was no solution and returned to the harness determined to make an open fight on the spirit and practices that had come to be known among us as Deleonism.

I was given ample opportunity to fight. In the columns of the party papers, at the meetings of the "Sections," and in numerous private conferences, the battle raged on both sides with ever-growing asperity, and I took part in all of it. Daniel De Leon proved a formidable antagonist. He excelled any person I ever knew in unscrupulousness of attack, inventiveness of intrigue, and picturesqueness of invective. But in spite of his vigorous methods of combat, or perhaps because of them, the opposition grew constantly. While the official title to the party name was awarded by the courts to the De Leon faction, the secessionists clearly represented the numerical majority.

In the meantime reinforcement came to American Socialism

from unexpected quarters. In the Middle West an indigenous though somewhat vague Socialist movement sprang up as a sort of cross breed between certain surviving radical elements of Populism and the remnants of the American Railway Union shattered by the ill-fated Pullman strike. The movement crystallized in the organization of the "Social Democracy of America" in 1897. One year later the new party split in two. The organization remained in control of a group of romantics, who proposed to introduce Socialism by the spread of coöperative colonies, while the followers of the modern Socialist program formed the "Social Democratic Party of America."

It was to this party that the insurgent faction of the Socialist Labor Party turned for unity and coöperation.

Formal negotiations for the merger of the two organizations were opened at the national convention of the Social Democratic Party held in Indianapolis in March of 1900.

I attended the convention as a member of a committee delegated by the organization opposed to De Leon to offer our hands and hearts to our Social Democratic comrades. Associated with me on the committee were Job Harriman, a California lawyer of rare eloquence, deep sincerity and irresistible personal charm, and Max Hayes, a printer of Cleveland, equally prominent and popular in the Socialist and trade-union movements.

It was on this occasion that I first met the two main leaders of the new party who were destined to play such important parts in the later history of American Socialism, Eugene V. Debs and Victor L. Berger.

The two men were a study in contrasts; each in his own way was a powerful figure, and both made a deep impression on me.

Debs was a man of striking appearance. Tall and lanky, with an air of infinite kindliness shining through his limpid gray eyes and emanating from his whole being, he immediately attracted and fascinated. Books, pamphlets, articles, and poems have been written about this unusual man and his interesting career, his early days as grocery clerk and railroad worker, his later position as well-paid trade-union official, his voluntary abandonment of the job for the hard and unremunerative work of organizing the unorganized railroad workers, his bold leadership of the most spectacular strike in the United States, his conversion to Socialism, his opposition to the war, and his repeated imprisonment for his convictions.

Almost everything written about Debs is couched in superlative terms. Almost all his biographers are enthusiastic and uncritical.

There was not much to criticize about Gene Debs. He may not have been an original thinker or effective organizer. He may have contributed little, if anything, to the development of Socialist theory or the establishment of the practical methods of the movement. Yet he was beyond a doubt the outstanding leader of American Socialism. His power and influence emanated entirely from his own personality, and their source sprang from his boundless love of man. I never knew any person so deeply, completely, almost physically permeated by love of his kind.

Among all the character analyses of Eugene Debs and attempted explanations of his peculiar personal magnetism, there is probably none keener and truer than the characterization by the Hoosier poet, James Whitcomb Riley, in the oft-quoted four lines:

> *And there's Gene Debs—a man 'at stands*
> *And jest holds out in his two hands*
> *As warm a heart as ever beat*
> *Betwixt here and the Judgment seat.*

Holding out his heart in his two hands—that was the secret of his popularity and the source of his power. But Debs was not an indiscriminate lover.

Because he was so deeply and thoroughly imbued with the love of his fellow men, he was a good hater. He hated all forms of injustice and oppression with a burning hate and castigated their perpetrators with passion. Like the gentle Nazarene, Gene Debs was ever ready to chase the Pharisees and money changers from the temple by physical force.

He was a crusader and a fighter, and nothing delighted his loving soul so much as a stiff fight for a good cause. A humorous incident illustrative of this trait of his character comes to my mind.

Gene Debs had just been pardoned by President Harding after serving two and a half years of a ten-year sentence on a conviction under the Espionage Law. The pardon did not include a formal restoration to the rights of citizenship, and Debs was under the impression that he had forfeited his citizenship, that he was "a man without a country." Here then was a fine opportunity for a good fight, not for himself, but for the thousands of unfortunate victims of a heartless and relentless "justice," condemned to remain pariahs and outlaws after having fully expiated their alleged crimes. Debs was to inaugurate a vigorous campaign against this barbarous condition and was coming to New York to confer with me about his plans. Walking into my office one morning, I found his long figure slumped in a chair waiting for me. It was the old Gene Debs. The years in the Moundsville and Atlanta prisons had not broken the spirit of the old fighter. He was alert and eager and almost immediately plunged into a discussion of his contemplated campaign.

I had in the meantime carefully examined the law and convinced myself that the popular notion that a conviction of felony entails loss of citizenship was wrong. A person convicted of crime remains a citizen for all purposes, except that his right to vote and to hold public office is often curtailed by state laws. The laws of Indiana, Debs's home state, are quite liberal on that point.

I felt that my juridic discovery would not please my client over-much, and I communicated it to him with some hesitancy.

"The weakness of your case," I observed, "lies in the fact that you have not forfeited your citizenship at all. You are still a citizen of the United States."

Debs flared up. "What do you mean, I am still a citizen?" he exclaimed indignantly. "All newspapers assert that I have lost my citizenship and the United States Attorney General has confirmed the statement."

I handed him a memorandum on the law, which I had prepared for the purpose. He read the document with a frown and returned to me the formidable array of authorities with an air of keen disappointment.

I felt guilty and somewhat lamely suggested: "If you feel like testing your rights, Gene, you might offer to register and vote in the next election; and if the local election board interferes with you, we will take the case into the courts."

But my plan was cut short by Debs. "Oh, they will not question my right to vote in Terre Haute," he said in a tone of utter disgust. There was a perfectly good fight gone to waste.

Eugene V. Debs and I did not readily adjust ourselves to each other. In the first years of our acquaintance we had several clashes on questions of party policy. Debs could be quite vehement in quarrels with his fellow Socialists, but he never nursed his grudges and nobody could bear him a grudge for any length of time. In later years we became close friends, and no party differences were permitted to disturb the harmony of our personal relations.

Victor Berger was a different type from Eugene Debs and occupied a different place in the Socialist movement. In one of his recent novels Sinclair Lewis has characterized Berger as the St. Paul of American Socialism and Debs as its St. John. With the traditional conception of St. John as the inspired prophet, preacher, and poet of early Christianity and St. Paul as its practical propagandist and builder, the likeness is quite apt.

Victor Berger had none of the ecstatic fervor and ardent idealism, nor the sentimental nature and expansive manner of Eugene Debs. He came from different soil and stock and was of different temperament and make-up.

Born in Austria in 1860, he studied at the universities of Vienna and Budapest and came to the United States at the age of eighteen. After a while he settled in the city of Milwaukee, whose political destinies he was later to influence so profoundly.

In 1896 he was still connected with the Populist movement, although he had already been a convinced Socialist for some years. When the Social Democracy of America was formed he immediately joined the organization. From that time and until his tragic, accidental death in 1929 he was one of the leading spirits of the Socialist movement in the United States. His principal and most direct field of activity was his home city, in which he built up a powerful organization. In 1910 he was elected to the House of Representatives as the first Socialist member of that body. He was again elected in 1918, but denied a seat in the house on account of his opposition to the war. Twice reëlected by increased majorities, he was kept out of Congress until 1922, when he was finally seated. He was elected again in 1924 and 1926.

It was while serving in Congress as the lone Socialist representative that Victor Berger made a national reputation for himself as a consistent and persistent advocate of social reform and labor legislation and as a lucid exponent of the Socialist philosophy.

He was not an orator and disdained eloquence in speech and writing, but he had a thorough mastery of the Socialist theory and an abundant fund of knowledge in the spheres of social science and history. He had strong convictions on every subject and a rare gift of clear and simple exposition. In party councils he was inclined to be self-assertive and domineering and utterly intolerant of dissenting views.

He was sublimely egotistic, but somehow his egotism did not smack of conceit and was not offensive. It was the expression of deep and naïve faith in himself, and this unshakable faith was one of the mainsprings of his power over men.

Berger and I clashed often and violently on questions of Socialist policy, and in these clashes we rarely spared each other's feelings; but we were always friends, and the bond of friendship between us tightened with advancing years.

But to return to 1900 and our "unity" convention in Indianapolis. The message of good will and coöperation which we of the seceding wing of the Socialist Labor Party brought to the assembled delegates of the Social Democratic Party was greeted by the latter with tumultuous applause and exuberant enthusiasm. The principle of unification was adopted on the spot, and committees of the two organizations were appointed to work out the technical details. The convention adjourned in a spirit of exaltation and joy, which, alas, soon proved premature.

It appeared that the leaders of the Social Democratic Party, including Debs and Berger, were by no means as enthusiastic for unity as their followers. They had misgivings about the character and motives of the insurgent offshoot of the hated Socialist Labor Party. In the convention they bowed to the irresistible sentiment of the delegates, but when the finishing touches were left in their hands they changed front and decided against any form of merger. The immediate effect of the decision was to divide the Social Democratic Party into two separate factions, the "unionists" and the "antiunionists."

Chaos now reigned supreme in the ranks of the organized Socialist movement. Both the Socialist Labor Party and the Social Democratic Party were torn in two. The administration factions of the two parties maintained headquarters in New York and Chicago respectively, while the united insurgent wings of both, also operating under the name Social Democratic Party, established headquarters in Springfield, Massachusetts; and each of the parties made bitter war on the others.

The Socialists were then, as they are now, in the habit of expressing their sentiments in vigorous language, particularly in their own internal quarrels, and never did they make fuller use of the privilege than in those agitated days. I shudder to think of the reams of paper and quantities of printer's ink consumed in the pamphlets, newspaper articles, manifestos, appeals, charges, and counter charges which came in incessant torrents from all parties against all other parties and of the picturesque epithets in which they abounded. Be it confessed here that I contributed my full and honest share to this belligerent "unity" literature.

But I realize now that our seemingly childish quarrels had sense and meaning. They marked the passing of the phase of the Socialist movement which was largely based on academic propaganda and ushered in an era of active social and political struggle. It was the older and narrower movement that had matured within its loins the broader movement of modern Socialism and was reluctant to yield the field to its own rebellious child.

The logic of the situation finally prevailed over temporary unreason and personal passion. In the summer of 1901 another unity convention was held in Indianapolis with full representation of both warring wings of the Social Democratic Party and this time lasting unity was actually accomplished. The present Socialist Party was born.

CHAPTER IV

THE GOLDEN AGE

ALMOST immediately after the organization of the Socialist Party it became evident that Socialism was beginning to take root in the United States. The first years of the party's existence were years of steady and uninterrupted growth.

Unlike other American political parties, the Socialist Party is composed of a body of members formally initiated and paying regular monthly dues. The party began its career with an enrolled membership in the neighborhood of 5,000, mostly foreign-born. In five years the number exceeded 30,000 and the majority were native Americans.

During the same period the Socialist vote grew from about one hundred thousand to well-nigh half a million. The party had 1,500 local organizations in all parts of the country and no fewer than fifty periodical publications in different languages to support it. In the following decade the high point of Socialist strength was reached.

During the early years the body of organized Socialists in America was largely made up of working people, with only a sprinkling of "intellectuals" in its leadership. After about 1905 the movement began to attract ever-growing numbers of men and women in literary and academic circles. Socialism became popular, almost a fad.

The ground was prepared by the crusade of political and economic reform of the first years of our century, which found expression in the "literature of exposure."

Lincoln Steffens was castigating the shame and brazenness of municipal political rings. Ida Tarbell was publishing a compiled register of industrial sins of John D. Rockefeller and the Standard Oil Company. Thomas W. Lawson revealed the iniquitous inner workings of high finance; Charles Edward Russell attacked the unscrupulous practices of the beef trust; Ray Stannard Baker dealt with the scandalous histories and methods of the railroad corporations, and a host of journalists of lesser fame turned the searchlight of investigation upon the various social, economic, and political institutions of the country and found them wanting. Every popular magazine exposed something. "Muckraking," as Theodore Roosevelt contemptuously baptized the literature of exposé, was the fashion.

But the vogue of the purely critical and negative movement could not endure forever. Thoroughly convinced of the evils, many thoughtful persons began to look for the remedy, and there was Socialism offering a ready and constructive program of radical change. It was inevitable that the critics and doubters should turn with interest to the new creed. Socialism became a favorite topic of discussion among New York's intelligentsia, and the intelligentsia were always strong on discussion.

I remember particularly one talk-fest which proved of almost historic importance for the Socialist movement. It was organized by Robert Hunter and lasted three days and three nights. Mr. Hunter was then a young man of twenty-eight years. He was a settlement worker imbued with radical views and had just written a book, *Poverty,* which had attracted some attention. The book went considerably beyond the point of mere critical exposure, but stopped short of a comprehensive social program. The young settlement worker was still looking for the light. He was married to Caroline Phelps Stokes, daughter of the wealthy Anson Phelps Stokes.

Mr. Hunter invited some twenty-five reformers of different stripes to an informal and general discussion at the spacious house of his father-in-law in Noroton, Connecticut, and thither we pilgrimaged in quest of Dame Truth or at least of controversy about her. The conference opened on the 3rd of March, 1906.

Besides Robert Hunter our hosts were J. G. Phelps Stokes, Rose Pastor Stokes, his wife, and Helen Stokes, his sister. Mr. Stokes was a few years older than Hunter. He was a physician by training but not by profession, had traveled widely, and had spent years in social and philanthropic work and developed radical political leanings. In 1904 he was a presidential elector on the Populist ticket, and the following year the candidate of the Municipal Ownership Party for the office of President of the Board of Aldermen of New York as the running mate of the party's nominee for Mayor, William Randolph Hearst. Like the latter he was probably elected but counted out. He was ascetic in appearance and habits and deeply earnest in his convictions, whatever they happened to be. About half a year earlier he had married Rose Pastor, a Jewish factory worker of rare charm, who in the aristocratic surroundings of the Noroton "Brick House" looked and acted more to the manner born than almost any other member of the assembly. Helen Stokes was then little known in radical circles, but immediately captivated the hearts of her guests by her gentle manner, broad-mindedness, and spirit of tolerance and understanding.

Among the invitees I recall Arthur Brisbane, brilliant and cynical, who held a particular interest for me as the son of one of the first American Socialists, Albert Brisbane, apostle of Fourier-ism and one of the founders of the famous and romantic Brook Farm colony; Charles Edward Russell, the muckraker, who disguised a tender heart under the gruff appearance and manner of a bear; David Graham Phillips, the popular novelist, polished and reserved; John Brisben Walker, editor and owner of the *Cosmopolitan Magazine;* Everett Colby, progressive politician of New Jersey; George Fred Williams, liberal Democrat and former Congressman from Massachusetts; Finley Peter Dunne, the jovial philosopher, known to the reading public as Mr. Dooley; Tom Watson, editor of *Watson's Magazine,* twice presidential candidate of the People's Party and later United States Senator from Georgia, and Alfred J. Boulton, prominent in the local labor movement and in Hearst's Independence League, and the sole representative of the proletariat in the radical gathering.

Senator La Follette, Lincoln Steffens, Edwin Markham, and Eugene Debs were also expected, but did not arrive.

The Socialist Party was represented by Victor Berger, John Spargo, and myself.

The debate was lively and continuous, interrupted regularly by three meals a day and irregularly and fitfully by sleep. It covered a large range of subjects, with Socialism always in the background. All phases of the Socialist philosophy and methods were expounded, analyzed, attacked, and defended. It was on this occasion that I received a valuable lesson about the importance of manner in propaganda.

It was a late evening hour and the spirits were somewhat overheated by discussion. Victor Berger was holding forth. He spoke loudly and emphatically in condemnation of the existing social order, property rights, and system of law. "They are your laws," he exclaimed, turning to the group of his listeners. "We abhor them. We obey them because you have the power to force them on us. But wait until we have the power. Then we shall make our own laws and, by God, we will make you obey them!" He was red in the face. His eyes flared and he reinforced his conclusion by striking the table with his clenched fist. An embarrassed silence fell on the gathering. The discussion came to an abrupt end.

The next morning one of the conferees cornered me. "What do you think of Berger's violent speech?" he asked anxiously. "Surely you do not share his views?"

"Well," I replied in my mellowest tones and suavest manner, "we Socialists believe in democracy. Under any democratic system the majority of the people, of course, have the right to make laws and the power to enforce them. The minority must submit, but may continue to advocate a complete change of the law. When it has succeeded in persuading a sufficient number of people, the minority becomes the majority, empowered to make new laws, to which the new minority must bow with equal grace. Is not that your conception of democracy?"

"Oh, yes," said my relieved interlocutor. "Nobody can quarrel with that theory, but Berger spoke like an anarchist rather than a Socialist."

"Has he not practically said the same thing?" I queried.

My friend thought awhile, then laughed, "C'est le ton qui fait la musique."

Of those present at the Noroton conference, Robert Hunter, Charles Edward Russell, Helen Stokes, J. G. Phelps Stokes, and Rose Pastor Stokes soon thereafter became members of the Socialist Party and rose to high rank in its councils. Hunter developed a clear conception of the Socialist philosophy and a sound view on practical policies. He was a student and wrote some valuable books on Socialism. He and Mr. Stokes were several times elected to membership on the party's National Executive Committee. Mr. Russell proved an eloquent speaker and incomparable propagandist and was frequently nominated for high public office.

After our entry into the World War, Russell, Hunter, and Stokes withdrew from the Socialist Party because of its anti-war position and joined the short-lived Social Democratic League of America, organized for support of the war. Rose Pastor Stokes, on the other hand, threw her political lot with the Communist Party, when the latter was organized.

It was at that early period also that two important institutions for the promotion of cultural activities in the Socialist movement were organized, the Intercollegiate Socialist Society and the Rand School of Social Science.

The godfather of the Intercollegiate Socialist Society was Upton Sinclair, then a young man of twenty-seven years and a struggling writer little dreaming of the international fame that was to come to him a year later with the publication of *The Jungle.*

Together with one George Strobell, a jewelry manufacturer and enthusiastic Socialist, he prepared a call for the organization of an association "for the purpose of promoting an intelligent interest in Socialism among college men and women, graduate and undergraduate, through the formation of study clubs in the colleges and universities, and the encouragement of all legitimate endeavors to awaken the interest in Socialism among the educated men and women of the country."

The call was signed by ten sponsors, including several persons of eminence in public life. Heading the list was Thomas Wentworth Higginson, pioneer of American Socialism in the days of the Fourierist creed, ardent abolitionist and veteran of the Civil War, author, philosopher and humanitarian. The "grand old man of Harvard" was then in his eighty-third year, but his mind remained alert, receptive, and youthful. When called to task by the conservative press for his aid and comfort to the threatened invasion of the sacred institutions of learning by the subversive doctrines of Socialism, he pointed out the steady growth of socialization in modern public life. The Intercollegiate Socialist Society, he observed, was formed to encourage the study of Socialism, not necessarily to make Socialists, and he likened his critics to the medieval grammarian who met the arguments of his opponent with the pious wish, "May God confound thee for thy theory of the irregular verb."

Among the other signatories were Oscar Lovell Triggs, editor of *Tomorrow's Magazine,* president of the People's Industrial College and author of *The Changing Social Order;* Jack London, at twenty-nine years already famous as the author of *The Call of the Wild* and *The People of the Abyss;* Clarence Darrow, constitutional rebel and iconoclast without fixed social and political convictions and unfailing champion of unpopular causes, and Charlotte Perkins Gilman, author, lecturer, and prominent woman suffrage advocate.

The organization meeting of the Intercollegiate Socialist Society was held on the top floor of Peck's restaurant, 140 Fulton Street, New York. It was an enthusiastic gathering and included many persons unattached to the organized Socialist movement.

William J. Ghent, who had just come to the notice of the radical fraternity by the successive publication of his two noteworthy books, *Our Benevolent Feudalism* and *Mass and Class,* presided. Jack London was unanimously chosen the first president of the Society.

I attended the meeting by invitation and took an active part in its interesting deliberations. I was elected a member of the board of directors and served on the board for ten consecutive years, during seven of which I also discharged the duties, by no means too onerous in those days, of the Society's treasurer. With me on the first board were Upton Sinclair, J. G. Phelps Stokes, Robert Hunter, George Willis Cook, author and lecturer, Katherine Meserole, George Strobell, and Harry W. Laidler. The latter, who was then an undergraduate at the Wesleyan University, was destined to become in later years one of the leading spirits of the organization.

During the first two or three years of its existence the Intercollegiate Socialist Society remained an idea and symbol rather than an active factor in the Socialist movement, but from about 1908 it made rapid progress. In 1917, the year of our entry into the war, the Society had undergraduate "chapters" in sixty or seventy of the leading colleges and universities of the country and about a dozen organized alumni groups.

After the war, it changed its name to League for Industrial Democracy and continued its career of growth and expansion under the joint direction of Harry W. Laidler and Norman Thomas.

The Rand School owes its existence mainly to that extraordinary figure who flashed on the horizon of American Socialism like a meteor in the early years of our century, George D. Herron.

Dr. Herron was a Congregational minister of rather unorthodox views and radical leanings. Presiding over a congregation in Des Moines, Iowa, he attracted the attention and won the friendship of Carrie Rand, a wealthy elderly widow of advanced views and strong character, who endowed for him a chair of Applied Christianity at Iowa College.

There was at the time a struggling organization in the United States known as the Society of Christian Socialists. The Rev. William D. P. Bliss and Prof. Richard T. Ely were its leading spirits. It preached a vague Socialist doctrine based on ethical and religious concepts and proclaimed its creed in the following language: "We hold that God is the source and guide of all human progress, and we believe that all social, political and industrial relations should be based on the fatherhood of God and brotherhood of man, in the spirit and according to the teachings of Jesus Christ.

George D. Herron enlisted in the movement of Christian Socialism and soon became one of its most zealous propagandists. He expounded the new creed in numerous pamphlets, public lectures and from his college chair. Growing opposition to his radicalism finally forced him to sever his connection with the church and to resign his professorship. A few years later he discarded the special brand of Christian Socialism, announced his full acceptance of the philosophy and program of working-class political Socialism and formally joined the Socialist Party. His striking appearance, charm of manner, polished eloquence, and deep earnestness soon won for him a place of prominence in Socialist circles, but his political career was cut short by an important event in his personal life.

George D. Herron, who was a married man, fell in love with the youngest daughter of his patroness and benefactress, like the latter named Carrie. His sentiments were fully reciprocated. After years of mental struggle Professor Herron obtained a divorce from his wife and married Carrie Rand.

Then the wrath of public opinion as represented by the yellow press broke upon the heads of the couple. The elder Mrs. Rand had enabled her future son-in-law to make generous provision for his first wife and the children of his first marriage. The fact leaked out and the newspapers, eager for a ground of attack on the apostate minister and radical revolutionist, launched a relentless campaign of persecution against him. "The rich Mrs. Rand has bought the professer from his first wife for her daughter," was the burden of the charge, and it was reiterated with endless variations and elaborations in stories, editorials, and cartoons. The newly married couple were followed at every step by hordes of newspaper reporters and photographers. Their union was publicly denounced from the pulpits. They were socially ostracized.

They bore the ordeal with fortitude, hoping that their persecutors would finally tire of the game; but there was no let-up. Every time the name of George D. Herron appeared in print in connection with his most unrelated activities the story of his "barter of wives" was rehashed with juicy detail and ornamentation.

It must have been a period of keen suffering for Carrie Rand

Herron, who concealed a deeply sensitive nature beneath a serene and smiling countenance. Mrs. Herron had rapidly become a favorite among her Socialist comrades. Simple, unassuming, always cheerful and sympathetic, she assisted her husband in the countless tasks and activities, large and small, prominent and obscure, gratifying and thankless, which go to make up the life of the Socialist propagandist.

At last they could stand it no longer. They forsook their cruel fatherland and spent the remainder of their lives in voluntary exile in Italy. Carrie Herron died in Florence in 1913. Her husband survived her by twelve years.

Almost the last act of the Herrons in America was to create a fund for the establishment and maintenance of the institution that became known as the Rand School of Social Science.

The need of a school for the systematic study of the Socialist philosophy and related subjects was felt keenly by the Socialist leaders. The rapidly growing movement called for trained organizers, speakers, and writers. There was no dearth of qualified teachers among the Socialist intellectuals; but the movement was poor, and a regular school, no matter how economically managed, meant a substantial initial outlay in the establishment and comparatively large expenditures in operation.

Mrs. Rand, who died in 1905, had created by her will a somewhat vague trust fund "to carry on and further the work to which I have devoted the later years of my life." The income from the fund was about $5,000 to $6,000 a year at the start, but was to decrease gradually as the grandchildren of the testatrix reached a certain age. To allay any misapprehension on the part of the generous friends who may feel an urge to support the Rand School, I hasten to add that the endowment has been exhausted.

The fund was to be managed and its uses determined by two trustees with the provision that any vacancy among them be filled by the surviving trustee. At the date of Mrs. Rand's death her daughter Carrie Herron was the sole acting trustee. She designated me as her co-trustee, and together we decided that the cause to which the testatrix had devoted the later years of her life was or should have been the Socialist movement, and that the best use to which the fund could be put was to establish a Socialist school. But the other children of Carrie Rand had no sympathy with their mother's radical attachments and threatened to contest the particular provision of her will.

It was then that Mrs. Herron gave sublime proof of her idealism and nobility of character. Quietly, almost secretly, she adjusted the claims of the contestants at a very substantial personal sacrifice. The trust fund was saved. The Rand School of Social Science came into life.

The organization in charge of the school was incorporated under the name of American Socialist Society. The board of directors named in the certificate of incorporation included, besides George D. Herron, Mrs. Herron, and myself, Algernon Lee, Job Harriman, Benjamin Hanford, William Mailly, Leonard D. Abbott and Henry Slobodin.

In addition to the Herrons, three of these are no longer among the living. Job Harriman died in 1925 at the age of sixty-four years. From early manhood he had been afflicted with an advanced case of pulmonary tuberculosis, and it was only his iron will and exuberant enthusiasm that kept him alive and active. His last years he spent building up a socialistic community known as the Llano Colony, first in California, then in Louisiana.

Benjamin Hanford is little remembered by the present generation of Socialists. He died in 1910, after a long and painful sickness. But in his day he was a tower of strength in the Socialist movement. A printer by trade, he occupied a position of prominence and respect in the Typographical Union. He enlisted in the Socialist movement in the days of the old Socialist Labor

Party, when American-born workmen were exceedingly scarce in its ranks, and immediately attracted attention by his deep earnestness, almost religious devotion to the cause, and a certain rough and ready style of eloquence. In the Socialist Party he was twice nominated for the Vice Presidency as the running mate of Eugene Debs and several times he was the party's candidate for governor of New York.

It was he who created the character of the fictitious "Jimmy Higgins," the modest and self-effacing worker in the ranks of the Socialist movement, who carries platforms for street-corner meetings, distributes party literature, watches the polls on election day and does the numerous prosaic and obscure chores of the movement, regularly and tirelessly, unheeded, unacclaimed, and unrewarded, the unknown soldier of Socialism. "Jimmy Higgins" is still a household word in the Socialist movement, while the memory of the man who coined the name has largely faded away.

William Mailly died young. He was only forty-one years old when death terminated what promised to be a most fruitful career in the Socialist movement. As one of the first national secretaries of the party he accomplished miracles in welding the new and raw Socialist recruits into an orderly and effective organization. His winning personality, almost naïve faith, and boyish enthusiasm made him a prime favorite in the Socialist movement. His premature death was a severe blow to his many friends.

Alongside the board of directors we appointed an advisory committee composed of Charles A. Beard, the distinguished historian, then an instructor at Columbia University; Dr. P. A. Levine, member of the Rockefeller Institute of Medical Research, and Hermann Schlueter, a veteran of the Socialist movement on two continents and editor-in-chief of the *New Yorker Volkszeitung*.

The first secretary of the Society, who acted as school principal, was W. J. Ghent. When he resigned after three or four years of service, his place was taken by Algernon Lee, who has ever since remained the guiding spirit of the institution in his successive capacities as educational director and president. To him and to Bertha H. Mailly, widow of William Mailly and for many years secretary of the Society, the school owes its growth and progress in the first instance.

From the outset, the founders of the school agreed on a broad curriculum to include not only the theory of Socialism but a liberal range of general cultural subjects. We expected to recruit the body of students from the ranks of the workers, many of whom had been deprived of the advantages of even an elementary education, and we realized that they could not be trained for effective work in the Socialist and labor movement by a mere study of dry economics. The program of the first year of instruction included, besides the history, philosophy, economics, and methods of Socialism and trade unionism, such subjects as Social Evolution, the Arts, Composition and Rhetoric. Later the curriculum was extended to all conceivable subjects of general information beginning with elementary classes in English for foreigners and running through the whole gamut of history, philosophy, sociology, psychology, popular science, literature, music, the drama and foreign languages besides the more practical and direct subjects of instruction for which the school was primarily organized.

The courses are given after work hours, and hundreds of workingmen and workingwomen take advantage of them to satisfy their thirst for knowledge and to fit themselves for effective service to their fellows. The attendance, however, is not confined to workers, but includes a number of young students and persons of good general education who come for instruction in some of the special courses offered by the school.

Another interesting institution that sprang up and flourished in those days of social effervescence was the "X Club." This was not an out-and-out Socialist organization, although perhaps, most of its members were avowed Socialists.

The club was organized towards the end of 1903 mainly upon the initiative of W. J. Ghent. It had no program and no object except to unite a group of chosen spirits for periodical talk-fests. The club started with a membership of fifteen, which gradually rose to thirty or forty.

The X-ers assembled every two or three weeks in a private room of a midtown Italian restaurant, dined together, sparingly and expeditiously, then talked. It was the task of the secretary, the sole officer of the organization, to select a timely topic of discussion and the person to open it. Then each member, in the order seated around a long table, would make his contribution to the discussion. Nobody was excused. Nobody wanted to be excused.

The membership of the club could be roughly classed in four groups:

Literary persons like Lincoln Steffens; Norman Hapgood, then editor of *Collier's Weekly;* Eugene Wood, the popular author of "back-home" stories; Samuel Moffett, one of the editors of *Collier's Weekly;* Hamilton Holt, then managing editor of the *Independent,* now college president and leading advocate of America's adherence to the League of Nations; Edwin E. Slosson, associate editor of the *Independent;* Charles Edward Russell, and Leroy Scott, the novelist.

University professors like John Dewey, the leading psychologist; Franklin H. Giddings, one of the outstanding sociologists; James T. Shotwell, the historian; William P. Montague; professor of philosophy, and Charles A. Beard.

Social reformers such as Owen R. Lovejoy, secretary of the National Child Labor Committee; John B. Andrews, secretary of the American Association for Labor Legislation; Raymond

Ingersoll and George W. Alger, both of whom were later to play such important parts in the turbulent cloak and suit industry as arbitrators and pacifiers; Walter E. Weyl, John Martin, and Alfred J. Boulton.

The fourth group consisted of "just Socialists" and included at one time or another, besides myself, Leonard D. Abbott, Robert W. Bruère, W. J. Ghent, Edmond Kelly, Algernon Lee, Darwin J. Meserole, William Noyes, J. G. Phelps Stokes, William English Walling, and Rufus Weeks, a fine old gentleman who was actuary and vice president of the New York Life Insurance Company.

No subject was too abstruse or too frivolous for our discussion. Politics, science, religion, literature, and art, each had its turn; and on all of them we had decided though by no means harmonious views. On rare occasions we would invite outsiders as guest victims. I remember particularly the visits of H. G. Wells, who subsequently described the X Club as one of the few worth-while things in America; George Lansbury, now leader of the British Labor Party, who startled the club by his peculiar mixture of evangelism and revolution, and Emile Vandervelde, who came here shortly after the outbreak of the war.

The discussions, if not always instructive, were generally interesting and stimulating; and at any rate they had the merit of not being taken too seriously by the participants.

On the occasion of the hundredth meeting of the club, held on the 10th of October, 1911, Edwin E. Slosson, journalist, chemist, mathematician, exponent of Einstein, and general wit, read a humorous paper pretending to record the proceedings of the two hundredth meeting, nine years hence. The satire is so illustrative of the spirit of the club and of the manner and point of approach of some of its members that I cannot resist the temptation to share it with my readers. I append the delightful parody to this chapter.

The club functioned irregularly but continuously until 1917. America's participation in the war divided its membership into two opposite camps, and it was no longer a good-natured and tolerant division on abstract social or political views. Our club succumbed to the bitterness which was invariably engendered between supporters and opponents of the war, a sort of personal hostility that caused people to shun one another. It disbanded almost automatically. Years after the war, in 1925, an attempt was made to bring the X Club back to life, and a meeting of the surviving members was called by Mr. Ghent for that purpose; but the attempt failed signally. The spirit of rancor had not entirely subsided in the erstwhile hostile camps. The charm of friendly companionship was broken. The whole atmosphere was changed. A few more meetings were held with a somewhat one-sided attendance. They were cold and uninteresting. In 1929 the club was formally dissolved.

If I have conveyed the impression that Socialism in the first decade of our century was largely a movement of intellectuals, the impression is entirely erroneous. The Socialist "intelligentsia" was largely confined to the leadership in New York. The body of Socialists, particularly in the West and Middle West, was overwhelmingly proletarian, with a considerable admixture of farmers, who began to come into the movement in increasing numbers.

The Socialist movement began to register practical political victories. By 1910, when the first Socialist member of Congress was elected in the person of Victor Berger, the party had already representatives in several state legislatures and had gained control of a number of municipalities.

By 1912 the Socialists had elected mayors in not less than fifty-six American cities and towns. The most noteworthy of these was the city of Milwaukee, which the Socialists carried by a landslide in 1910. Emil Seidel, the party's candidate for mayor, won by a clear plurality of 7,000 votes over his Democratic opponent and beat his Republican rival for office by more than 15,000 votes. With him were elected the Socialist candidates for city attorney, comptroller, two civil judges and twenty-one aldermen out of a total of thirty-five. With only one interruption since then the Socialists have headed the city government during all the varying fortunes of the movement and the party. Daniel W. Hoan, lawyer and Socialist propagandist, has been mayor of Milwaukee continuously since 1916. While the Socialists have not been in full control of the city government during that period, they have largely influenced its policies and brought about such measures of social and fiscal reform as the limited functions and powers of a municipality would permit. The administration of Milwaukee has become a model for American cities.

The political surprise of the period, however, was the Socialist victory in the city of Schenectady, in central New York.

Schenectady at the time had a population of about 75,000. In it the General Electric Company maintained its headquarters, its laboratories, and its largest plant. Employees of the company constituted a large portion of the city's population. They were skilled workers and well organized industrially. For some time the Socialist propaganda had begun making rapid headway among them. The movement was stimulated by two prominent, but very dissimilar residents of Schenectady, Charles P. Steinmetz and George R. Lunn.

Steinmetz was consulting engineer to the General Electric Company and one of the outstanding electrical geniuses of the country. Born in Germany, he studied in Breslau, Zurich, and Berlin. His participation in the Socialist movement of his native country led him into repeated difficulties with the authorities and finally forced him to emigrate. He came to the United States in 1889. Physically deformed and crippled, he was prevented from engaging in public Socialist propaganda, but he retained his ardent faith in Socialism and proclaimed it in unmistakable terms whenever and wherever he had the opportunity. His great prestige in the community went far to help the cause of Socialism. He died in 1923 at the age of fifty-eight years.

George R. Lunn was a Presybterian minister. He came to Schenectady in 1904 and served as pastor of one of the regular local churches for five years. When his radical sermons and somewhat unconventional demeanor brought him into conflict with the church authorities, he resigned and founded an independent congregation under the name United People's Church. He was immensely popular with the advanced sections of the city's population and with the workers on account of his liberal views, blunt expression, and democratic manner. He was the ideal type of the minister politician.

Having joined the Socialist Party, he was nominated for the office of mayor in the fall of 1911 and was elected by a comfortable plurality, carrying with him the principal candidates on the Socialist Party ticket, including a majority of the city council.

The unexpected victory presented a serious and perplexing problem. In Milwaukee the Socialists had had substantial preparatory training in municipal affairs before they were called upon to assume the government of the city. Some of their members had served on the board of aldermen and were thoroughly familiar with the practical problems of administration. In Schenectady the elected Socialist officials found themselves utterly unprepared for the big task ahead of them and with less than two months remaining in which to organize the city government, adopt an administrative program, and train themselves for the proper discharge of the duties of office. In their anxiety to make good, the Schenectady Socialists turned to some of their comrades in other places for help and guidance. I was invited to act as a sort of special counsel and foreign adviser to the administration, and retained that somewhat indefinite post throughout the entire two-year term of Mayor Lunn's first administration. It meant perpetual traveling between New York and Schenectady, but the work was interesting and seemed important. I felt that the Socialist administration in a good-sized New York town would be keenly watched by the opponents of the movement, that its mistakes would be magnified and exploited, and that failure might prove fatal in an era of incipient Socialist control of local governments.

We organized an informal cabinet composed of the principal city officers, elected or appointed, and of a few representatives of the party organization, to pass in joint conclave upon appointments and all administrative measures of importance. Often we invited into our councils men of experience in some specialized field of municipal government from other parts of the country, Socialists, liberals or non-partisan experts. One of the first principles we adopted was that all appointments to technical posts be made strictly on merit, with total disregard of party affiliation and even of residence. The Commissioners of Charities and Public Works as well as some other important city officials were imported from other cities where they had established good records of performance. Patronage and favors were to be strictly eschewed. Service was to be the test in all appointments and the watchword of the new Socialist administration. As his secretary, and incidentally secretary to the cabinet, Mayor Lunn upon my recommendation appointed a young Harvard graduate, who had organized the first Socialist club among his fellow students. His name was Walter Lippmann. He was then twenty-three years old and discharged the duties of his office for two years without, I am bound to admit, giving any indication of the brilliance of mind and style which was later to make him one of America's foremost publicists.

Walter Lippmann did not long continue in his Socialist faith. Nor did George R. Lunn. Defeated in the following election and irked by the strict rules of political conduct which the Socialist Party imposes on its members, he transferred his allegiance to the Democratic Party, where he was forthwith admitted to leadership. On the Democratic ticket he was elected mayor for three additional terms, member of Congress, and lieutenant governor of the State. He now serves as one of the Public Service Commissioners of New York.

In spite of occasional desertions the Socialist Party thrived and grew. In 1912 its dues-paying membership had risen to 118,000. It had active and effective organizations in every one of the forty-eight states, was supported by about one hundred and fifty periodicals, newspapers, and magazines, and reached the record vote of almost one million for its presidential candidate—about 6 per cent of the total cast.

THE X OF FUTURITY

By E. E. SLOSSON

When our worthy secretary and founder and statistician went to Washington to save his country his mantelpiece fell upon Professor Noyes. His record book was then for the first time opened to other eyes, and it was discovered that the secretary was possessed of more forethought than had been suspected. He had written up not only the minutes of previous meetings, but also of meetings far in the future. This to him was an easy matter, for it is a well known fact—or if it is not a fact it is equally well known—that it is possible to predict the conduct of human beings with as much accuracy as the movements of the planets if the necessary data are given in advance. This is particularly the case with the members of the X Club, whose minds follow well defined grooves—not to use a shorter and an uglier word. Even those of us who have less mathematical ability than our secretary and have been less constant in attendance are able to tell in advance just what would be the attitude of a given member on any new topic which might come up and to predict with considerable accuracy the words with which he would express his opinion and the gestures and facial expression with which he would enforce it and give it bodily beauty. The voluminous figures and notes which the secretary had taken were not merely for historical purposes. They enabled him to extend the Cartesian curve of each individual by extrapolation and so to solve the equation and obtain the value of X for any desired date in the future. As an example, I will give a paraphrase of the minutes of the two hundredth meeting of the X Club, October 10, 1919.

The Club met at the usual hour of 8:45 at a downtown restaurant on the corner of Broadway and 181st Street, the Chop Suey of Wun Lung, the Club having exhausted its credit with caterers of all other nationalities represented in New York.

The statistical report of attendance read by the Secretary, I will omit except to note that the average of Mr. Ghent was 99.98, the same as the standard of purity of Royal Baking Powder, while Mr. Ely's had been raised from two-tenths of one per cent. to three, as he had come into a recent meeting too late for the discussion but in time to pay his share of the dinner assessment.

The Secretary announced that the dinner tonight cost as usual, $3.50, including the customary 75 cents to waiter. The members accordingly threw paper and silver at the Secretary until he pronounced himself satisfied.

The topic which served as a point of departure for the discussion of the evening was the question of the adoption of a duodecimal system of notation and numeration as a substitute for the present decimal system.

Professor Giddings was first called upon to speak, and although he had not received a notification of the question he unlimbered and opened fire with his customary promptness and effect. The subject, he said, was one of profound importance and far-reaching significance, and one in which he had been absorbingly interested from childhood. It could only be understood by reference to the fundamental principles of sociology. The decimal system, common to most primitive races, owed its origin to the custom of counting on the fingers, which normally number ten. But since the Babylonians adopted a duodecimal system it is an obvious deduction that they must have been possessed of six fingers on each hand like certain mutants in our own race. The question of which system should be adopted could never be a matter of legislation since it depended upon the physiological constitution of individuals and could only be decided by a recognition of consciousness of kind.

The next speaker was Mr. Holt, who was wearing the jade button of a mandarin of the thirteenth degree with which he had recently been decorated by the Emperor of China. He said he agreed absolutely with 99 per cent. of what Professor Giddings had said but thought the question should be referred to The Hague as soon as the Federation of the World was established.

Mr. Hillquit, who had returned for the purpose of attending the meeting from Washington, where he was serving his second term in Congress, was then called upon. He said there was no use in discussing the question now. The Party had spoken and the case was closed. At the Tokyo meeting of the International Socialist Congress, at which he was a delegate, it was decided that the movement for a duodecimal notation was due to a conspiracy of the capitalists of the world to get 20 per cent. more work out of their employees without their knowing it.

Professor Noyes, who followed, said that he had hitherto favored the change because it would simplify instruction in manual training if the divisions of feet corresponded to the division of hours, but if it was going to be detrimental to the Party he could not longer countenance it.

At this point Mr. Ghent interjected the remark, apropos of feet, that the absolute asininity of the *Sun* became daily more appalling to him. One of yesterday's editorials contained a quotation from Twelfth Night, Act II, Scene III, with two syllables left out and a semicolon substituted for a colon.

Following, according to the invariable rule of the X Club, the course of the sun from left to right, the next in order was Mr. Meserole, who spoke briefly but with feeling on the relation of the question to the problem of the unemployed. He hoped that the duodecimal system would have a good effect, but he did not think it would make things any better if it did.

Mr. Slosson, next called on, did not have any opinion on the subject, but he expressed it at some length. He thought that there was a good deal to say on both sides, and he said most of it.

Mr. Lee expressed the fear that enumeration by twelves instead of tens would reduce the magnitude of the Socialist vote. Now that the party had won the election in Seattle by a majority of 2,000, it was no time to take such a step.

Here it was noticed a cloud of displeasure was gradually settling down over the face of the Secretary. When it had descended to his mouth he opened it and said, "You must have taken those figures from the top of the third column on the second page of last Monday's *Call*. They are grossly exaggerated and their publication will injure the standing of the party in the mind of every intellectual man. The Socialist majority in Seattle was not 2,000 but 1,999."

Mr. Wood thereupon told a funny story which the Secretary for some unexplained reason did not think proper to transcribe upon the record book.

Mr. Martin feared that the country was going to the dogs. He had quite lost patience with it since ten of the Western states had adopted woman suffrage. The only hope of salvation now lay in the adoption of an upper house modeled after the English House of Lords and the appointment as Viceroy of the Republic of one of the younger sons of George V.

Professor Montague was called upon as a representative of the militant wing of the realist syndicalists,* to which position he had been led by his prolonged study of the Bergsonian philosophy. He explained the causes of the failure of the recent strike of the faculty in Columbia University when the Amalgamated Union of Professors and Instructors had struck for an eight-hour month but had been beaten through the introduction of scabs from Harvard under the leadership of ex-President Eliot, manager of the Scholastic Strikebreakers Trust. Professor Montague said that the employees of President Butler had since adopted the policy of sabotage and had succeeded in surreptitiously ruining a large proportion of the output of Columbia College. Many of last year's graduates were unable to spell or to add correctly; they had the most absurd notions of their own importance; they had been completely deprived of religious principles; and their morals were such as to unfit them for any profitable career.

Professor Beard followed, and also spoke encouragingly of the success of educational sabotage in Columbia. His share in the work had been to instill into the minds of the students erroneous ideas of political science. He was happy to be able to inform the Club that the university was now turning out Ph.D.'s who were ignorant of the

---

* It should be remembered that this was written in the heyday of the syndicalist movement, when revolutionary syndicalism held a fascination for certain intellectuals similar to that which Communism holds today.—M. H.

first duties of citizenship and even looked upon them with distaste, amounting to aversion. This form of sabotage had already discredited the colleges of the country in the minds of the *bourgeoisie* and would in time lead to their ruin. Syndicalism would thus be enabled to accomplish its aim, whatever that aim might be supposed to be.

Judge Alger discussed the subject in its political aspect and told of the progress being made toward a union of all the respectable and responsible parties to check the rising tide of syndicalism. The leaders of the Republican, Democratic and Socialist parties had met and agreed to combine their party organizations into one under the name of Conservative Coalition as the only hope of saving the country from anarchy.

Mr. Boulton here inquired where Hearst came in, to which Judge Alger wittily retorted that Hearst had not come out yet.

After this the discussion drifted somewhat from the subject and the conversation became more general. This is not recorded in detail and what is given is hard to interpret, owing to the use of unfamiliar terms. Members of the Club who were commuters had slipped away to take the late suburban trains to Philadelphia and Boston. The Club does not seem to have formally adjourned that evening but merely to have dissolved. When Wun Lung came in to put out the light he found the room filled with the smoke of debate and the débris of an intellectual cataclysm.

CHAPTER V

SPEAKING AND WRITING

My first public speech was made without anticipation or preparation. I was almost trapped into it.

In our search for potential members of the United Hebrew Trades, then in the process of formation, we discovered a society of journeymen tailors composed of German and Austrian Jews. It was a fraternal benefit society rather than a trade union.

Leo Bandes and I were delegated to visit the society in an effort to enlist its coöperation and appeared at one of its regular meetings.

The men who made up the rather large gathering were physically and mentally well above the level of the Russian Jewish workers with whom I was acquainted.

We were received very cordially and were assured that our request would get proper consideration. Pleased with the result of our mission, Bandes and I were about to take our leave, when the chairman quietly announced: "The gentlemen of the committee are invited to address the meeting on the general subject of the Labor Problem (*Arbeiterfrage*)."

I was stunned. The language of the society was German. That barred my older and maturer co-delegate. The "gentlemen of the committee" were reduced to myself, and I was eighteen years old and had never made a public speech. It is a far-cry from appealing to a body of men to join an organization and delivering a lecture on the comprehensive subject of the Labor Problem. I had just about ten seconds to arrange my thoughts, if any, before facing my audience.

My decision was quickly made. I had just finished reading Friedrich Engels' booklet, *Development of Socialism from Utopia to Science*. This concise and lucid exposition of the Marxian philosophy captivated my imagination. The conception of the modern machine as a revolutionizing agent in the social, industrial, and political relations of men, the emergence of the "proletariat" as a class of workers deprived of their tools and the "capitalists" as a tool-owning, non-productive class, the resulting conflicts between them and the inevitable working-class program of socialization of the instruments of wealth production—all this was new to me and stood out vividly in my mind. I gave my hearers the full benefit of my recently acquired information.

As I spoke on, I warmed up to my subject. I soon forgot my audience and overcame my stage fright. I was attempting to restate in simple language and largely for my own benefit the lesson I had just learned.

Apparently my auditors had not read Engels. The social theories I expounded were as delightfully new and original to them as they had been to me a few days earlier. They were interested and followed my argument with close attention. I spoke about half an hour, which seemed to be an eternity, and was warmly applauded at the conclusion. Thus began my career as a public speaker. It has never ended.

How many speeches have I made in my life? I should prefer to leave the delicate question unanswered. But this book is in the nature of a confession, and I should not be honest with my readers if I attempted to minimize my offenses. I have, of course, kept no record of all my public addresses, but if I assume a minimum of fifty a year, an average of one a week, I am responsible for at least two thousand speeches. As a matter of fact the number of discourses I have inflicted on the long-suffering American public is probably much larger.

Most of the speeches were made under Socialist auspices, but many were delivered before non-Socialist audiences, in colleges and churches, before various discussion groups and social clubs. In the first years of Socialist popularity particularly, requests for Socialist speakers came from most unexpected quarters.

I have before me a clipping from the *New York Times* of April 2, 1908, which describes a meeting of the highly exclusive Economic Club in this language:

"The influence of the Socialistic doctrine upon industry and legislation was the topic discussed last night at the annual dinner of the Economic Club at the Hotel Astor. The Grand Ballroom was overcrowded, and an adjoining room had to be opened for the overflow of members and guests who desired to hear the discussion of the topic.

"Morris Hillquit was the dominant speaker of the evening. There were many speakers to combat his views and to argue against them. The members and guests were nearly all anti-Socialists.

"The President of the Economic Club is A. Barton Hepburn, President of the Chase National Bank. The Vice-Presidents are Francis Lynde Stetson and E. R. A. Seligman. In the company at tables were scores of captains of industry.

"Mr. Hillquit had abundant opportunity to preach Socialism to a gathering which represented wealth and financial interests."

Such sorties into the camp of the enemy were by no means rare. On numerous occasions I was called upon to expound the gospel of Socialism with its scathing indictment of the existing social and economic order to the very pillars of that order. In regular lectures or in symposia with speakers of other views I talked Socialism before most conservative audiences in political and social clubs, such as the Republican Club and the select Colony Club, before Chambers of Commerce and even in young ladies' finishing schools.

Typical of the interest in Socialism in high places at that

period was a "Socialist tea" given by Mrs. Rita Lydig. The beautiful and popular society matron invited a veritable galaxy of notables, bankers, brokers, high public officials and Supreme Court Justices to listen to my exposition of the Socialist philosophy and program. It was, as I recall it, a rather high-brow talk that I made to the distinguished gathering and left it wholly unimpressed.

But these sermons to the "gentiles" were more or less in the nature of diversions. I did not expect to convert the rich *en masse*, although I always found some individual idealists who rose above the prejudices and interests of their class.

My message was mostly addressed to the poor. Just two weeks after I had the honor of addressing the fashionable audience of the Economic Club I had the pleasure of talking to the dregs of New York's slum population at the Bowery Mission, and I must confess the meeting was infinitely more gratifying to me than the discussion before the Economic Club or Mrs. Lydig's tea.

The Mission, then located at 55 Bowery, in the heart of the most disreputable quarter of New York, was managed by J. G. Hallimond, a wise and broad-minded man with deep sympathies and understanding for the unfortunate, the weak and the low.

"Every evening," he wrote to me in his invitation to speak, "we have in our large Mission Hall a crowd of men who form one of the most interesting and appreciative congregations in the world. They are mostly men who have been unfortunate, and some, but by no means the majority of them, have been dissipated, improvident and reckless. There are, however, amongst them many bright intellects, and a large portion of them are capable of being raised into a splendid manhood."

When I came, I found the big hall crowded with an aggregation of men such as I had never seen before. Clad in rags and tatters, unshaven and unkempt, they looked like the kind of persons one would instinctively avoid meeting on a lonely street in the dark. Mostly emaciated and hungry-looking they stared vacantly into space or cast furtive glances around them. And there were hundreds of them. It was a weird spectacle reminiscent of one of Victor Hugo's fantastic conventions of beggars.

I felt embarrassed about speaking to them. I knew that most of them had not come to listen to a lecture. They had been attracted to the hospitable room of the Mission for its light, warmth, and cheer and, above all, for the cup of coffee and roll of bread that awaited them at the close of the meeting. I felt that it was an imposition to force them to listen to what they would probably regard as an irrelevant sermon, as a condition for obtaining small physical comfort. And then, what message did I have for them? Socialism appeals to the spirit of self-reliance, courage, and fight of active working masses. The crowd before me apparently were completely crushed by failure. Their spirit was broken. They had neither desire nor will and were passively resigned to their precarious animal existence.

But I was there to speak. I carefully avoided any appearance of preachment or assumption of superiority. I talked to them about the injustice of the capitalist system, the struggle of the workers for a better life and the Socialist ideal of human equality. I spoke in the simplest language, short sentences and words of one syllable.

Every experienced speaker knows almost at once whether he really establishes contact with his audience or leaves it cold. An unerring feeling in the atmosphere tells him whether he talks to his hearers or at them.

Somewhat to my surprise, I felt immediately that my Bowery audience was listening. My surprise was increased in the discussion period. Some questions came haltingly and clumsily, evidencing the labor of a sluggish brain struggling with a vague and hazy idea, but there were also questions and discussion from the floor in fluent and polished English, and some of these were keen and incisive, mostly with a flavor of bitterness and cynicism. They were obviously men of widely different education, origin, and antecedents, all reduced to the same depth of physical degradation by the merciless forces of misfortune and social iniquity.

A favorite form of Socialist propaganda in those days was public debate.

Out in New Rochelle Martin J. Keogh, one of the most popular judges of the Supreme Court, maintained a public forum largely for the political education of his fellow townsmen. He early recognized the power of attraction of controversial discussion and frequently organized debates in his forum. It fell to my lot to participate in several of them, but I best remember the first of the series. It was held in January, 1907. The subject was "Individualism *vs.* Socialism," and my opponent, who defended the principle of sturdy individualism against the insidious onslaughts of the Socialist doctrine was Jacob G. Schurman, president of Cornell University and later ambassador to Germany and other countries. It was Mr. Schurman, I understood, who had suggested the debate. He was obviously alarmed at the growth of subversive Socialist sentiment and determined to slay the red dragon in public view.

The debate attracted unusual public interest.

"From noon yesterday up to the time for the debate to begin," reported the *New York Times* the following morning, "every train and trolley car running to New Rochelle from this city was crowded with men and women, who discussed systems of government and trusts. They were all loyal supporters of Hillquit, confident of his triumph in the passage at arms with the college president. Long before three o'clock, the hour set for the debate to begin, the doors were closed and no more persons were admitted to the hall."

Mr. Schurman came prepared with an elaborate opening

speech, which he read from manuscript, and all went well while the manuscript lasted. His difficulties began with the rebuttal. I had not taken the line of argument my opponent apparently expected me to follow. Instead of belittling the merits of individualism, I cheerfully admitted them, but maintained that the system of capitalism tends to throttle true individual development, which could flourish only under an equitable Socialist economic order. I also pointed out that the modern industrial organization had long ceased to be individualistic.

Mr. Schurman was not ready to discuss these viewpoints. He had with him an ample brief case filled with anti-Socialist ammunition, probably collated in the economics department of his university, but the requisite material for his rebuttal was either lacking or improperly arranged. At any rate my opponent discarded the formidable brief case with disgust, and launched into a brilliant but rather irrelevant patriotic oration of the Fourth of July type, expressing his earnest conviction that ours was still "the best country on the face of the globe" and winding up with a "Hurrah for the Republic." The audience, including the Socialists, cheered lustily. The United States had come out with flying colors, but hardly the college president.

Years later Judge Keogh asked me whether I would not engage in another debate with Mr. Schurman on the same subject. Mr. Schurman had asked for it. He admitted that he had not been sufficiently familiar with the subject when we crossed swords the first time, but he assured the judge that he had since made a thorough study of Socialism. I did not accept the invitation.

Debates have the advantage of presenting both sides of a controversial topic and subjecting the opposing theories to the immediate test of adverse criticism. But above all they attract by the sportive element of combat, the battle of wits between the disputants. I am not at all certain of their educational value.

Public controversies on social or political subjects run the danger of dividing the audience into antagonistic camps and confirming existing preconceptions and prejudices. However, they are always apt to attract more attention than straight and one-sided discussion, and hold out the hope of convincing the hypothetical "open mind."

I have taken part in many interesting public debates on all phases of the Socialist philosophy and program with many eminent opponents, university professors, ministers, public officers, conservative labor leaders, and even fellow Socialists of divergent views on some questions of method; but my most notable debate did not take place behind the footlights of a public hall amid partisan shouts of approval or disagreement of an excited audience. It was quietly conducted in the pages of a monthly magazine.

In 1913 *Everybody's Magazine* was at the height of its popularity and influence. It had reached a fabulous circulation with the serial publication of Thomas W. Lawson's *Frenzied Finance,* and acquired a unique standing among the popular magazines of the country by its enterprising policy and the live quality of its contents.

It is significant of the public interest which the movement aroused at the time that the alert and sensational magazine chose the subject of Socialism for full and elaborate discussion in its pages. This discussion took the shape of a formal debate conducted in six consecutive numbers of the magazine, and covering the most salient phases of the Socialist doctrine.

I was asked to defend the Socialist position in the debate. My opponent was John A. Ryan, a Roman Catholic priest, then professor of moral theology and economics at St. Paul Seminary and later professor at the Catholic University of Washington. He is the author of several distinguished books on social problems.

The editor of *Everybody's* introduced the debate with a note, from which I quote:

"Here begins one of the most distinguished series of articles ever published in this or any other magazine: a joint debate upon the rights or wrongs of Socialism.

"The opposition to this world-wide movement comes not only from those who have qualified to speak, but also from many ill-equipped with information to justify their attacks. Moreover, such criticisms are usually addressed to audiences already in sympathy with them.

"Socialism, too, has its half-equipped apostles. And Socialist arguments are offered, for the most part, to people already attached to the cause.

"The importance of this series is twofold: For the first time the opposing arguments are to be presented with the highest competence, and side by side, in a form available for the immediate comparison of arguments.

"Our readers will be interested in the personnel of the authors and the circumstances that brought them into debate.

"The comment that the 'Catholic Church is the chief bulwark against Socialism' is familiar to many, in and outside the Church. For a long time this church has warred against Socialism, but during the past few years this campaign has become more general and systematic, and is the most highly organized attack on the Socialist doctrines.

"Yet it was a long step to that point, where, at the request of *Everybody's,* men distinguished in the church councils finally assented to an open discussion of the subject in the pages of a secular magazine. Naturally, it would be out of the question to ask of the Church or of the Socialists that they should choose an authoritative representative. This would be staking the cause on one spokesman, and would inevitably fail of perfection.

"The unique thing is that there could have been an approach

to the authority which *Everybody's* has received in the chosen opponents. Men eminent in both these world-wide groups have lent their good will, shared in the selection, and welcomed the conflict as one certain to be of the utmost value."

It was the desire of the editors as well as of the debaters to give to the readers a careful and reasoned presentation of both sides of the argument without allowing either to be caught by surprise or cut off from proper explanation. Accordingly, it was arranged that the debaters alternate in the introduction of the subjects, and that they exchange and reëxchange manuscripts with the right to each to introduce revisions in the light of what the other had written, until both should be content.

This was a perfectly fair procedure from the point of view of the reader, but it often proved provoking to the writers in actual operation. Many a time a passage of which the author was particularly proud had to be changed or discarded in view of a modified position taken by the other side. At one stage of the debate, for instance, Dr. Ryan made the assertion that a Socialist state could not offer the people substantially greater material benefits than our present order does. He arrived at the conclusion by the simple process of dividing the total wealth and income in the United States by the total number of inhabitants, and argued that on the basis of an equal division the wealth and income of each individual would still be comparatively small. This was a favorite argument against Socialism in those days, particularly in academic circles, and I was glad of the opportunity to meet it. I pointed out that the Socialists did not contemplate a state of wealth and income limited as under the present system; that a Socialist state would immensely increase the productivity of labor and the sum total of national wealth and income by eliminating all unproductive work and duplication of plants and efforts inherent in a system of competitive industries, and by operating at full capacity without the artificial curtail-ments due to the exigencies of the capitalist "market." I spent days in gathering facts and figures in support of my contention and prepared my answer with care and love. I was particularly satisfied with this piece of writing. My argument seemed to me quite convincing. But so it apparently also seemed to my candid opponent. When he read my reply he quietly eliminated the whole point in controversy from his manuscript and I was regretfully compelled to follow suit.

Dr. Ryan was probably the most formidable and at the same time the most gratifying opponent it ever was my good fortune to meet in public debate, well informed, painstaking, broad-minded, and scrupulously fair.

Our debate was subsequently published in book form under the title *Socialism, Promise or Menace?*

Everybody's Magazine was not the first important periodical to recognize the growing popular interest in the Socialist movement.

One year before the publication of my debate with John A. Ryan the *Metropolitan Magazine* printed a series of six articles from my pen under the title: *Socialism Up to Date.* The ownership of the magazine had changed and was reported to have passed to the Whitney family. The new management under the enterprising leadership of H. J. Whigham, editor-in-chief, improved and enlarged the publication and was casting about for a suitable subject around which to launch an effective circulation campaign. With a fine sense of public curiosity it hit upon the subject of Socialism, and I was given *carte blanche* to write the first series of articles without any editorial censorship or interference. The series was to be accompanied by full discussions of the pros and cons in the columns of the magazine by its readers. It was widely announced in newspapers, in copious and elaborate posters in the street cars, elevated railroads, and subways and by all other known methods of modern advertising.

The shrewd management had calculated well and wisely. Within the six months of the publication of my articles the circulation of the magazine was reported to have increased from a purely nominal figure to about three hundred thousand. The articles were later reprinted as a booklet under the title *Socialism Summed Up,* which was widely used by the Socialist Party for propaganda purposes.

The *Metropolitan Magazine* remained friendly to the Socialist movement during several years. My series of articles was followed by one from George D. Herron, and William Mailly was for a time a regular member of the editorial staff of the magazine. After the outbreak of the war and before our entry into it, the *Metropolitan* transferred its allegiance and affections to Theodore Roosevelt, of all men, who became a regular "contributing editor" of the magazine and made his headquarters in its office.

My writings during that period were not confined to magazine articles. When the Socialist movement began to make progress in the United States, it found itself badly handicapped by lack of appropriate literature. All we had was a few booklets, mostly translated from the German and often too technical and abstruse for consumption by American workers. A group of us, including Robert Hunter, John Spargo, Charles H. Vail, W. J. Ghent, William E. Walling and A. M. Simons, set to work to create an American Socialist literature.

My first contribution to this effort was a *History of Socialism in the United States.* It was largely pioneering work, and I enjoyed it thoroughly, particularly when I was able to demonstrate the falsity of the charge that Socialism was an exotic product by relating the fascinating story of the numerous native socialistic movements and experiments in the United States in the first half of the last century.

A few years later I published a work on the philosophy and

methods of the movement under the title *Socialism in Theory and Practice.*

Of course, my literary efforts were not limited to the books I have mentioned. They included magazine and newspaper articles, pamphlets and propaganda leaflets too numerous to mention. The life of a Socialist propagandist is one continuous feast of speaking and writing.

CHAPTER VI

A TILT WITH SAMUEL GOMPERS

AMONG my most interesting controversies was an impromptu debate with Samuel Gompers.

Samuel Gompers was beyond question the most picturesque and forceful figure produced by the American labor movement. Born in London in 1850, of Jewish-Dutch parents, he came to the United States at the age of thirteen and immediately went to work as a cigar maker. He joined the union of his trade one year after his arrival and remained active in the labor movement to the end of his life.

In the period of revival and growth of the trade unions following upon the Civil War, the enthusiastic and tireless young cigar maker gained a position of recognized leadership.

In 1881 the Federation of Organized Trade and Labor Unions of the United States and Canada was founded, and five years later it was reorganized as the American Federation of Labor. Samuel Gompers was elected the first president of the organization and held that post till his death in 1924, with only two breaks of one year each.

Throughout his long tenure of office he was not only the undisputed chief of the Federation, its brains and soul, but the recognized spokesman of the whole organized labor movement in the United States. It is safe to assert that no American labor leader before or after him has ever attained to the same high degree of authority among his fellow workers. To them his opinion was law, his word command.

In appearance he was almost grotesque, with a short-legged,

stocky figure, a massive head, big and mobile features, wide mouth, piercing gray eyes, and a broad forehead, terminating in a large skull, all bald except for a few isolated and unrelated tufts of disorderly hair of an undeterminable color. Yet, in spite of his unprepossessing physical make-up, he gave the impression of immense reserve strength and easily dominated every assembly in which he took part.

I shall never forget a characteristic scene in the annual convention of the American Federation of Labor held in Cincinnati in 1922.

The American labor movement was facing an acute legal situation. Within the preceding year there had been a veritable epidemic of adverse decisions in labor litigation. In four successive cases (American Steel Foundries *vs.* Tri-City Trades Council, Truax *vs.* Corrigan, Duplex Printing Co. *vs.* Deering, and United Mine Workers Union *vs.* Coronado Coal Co.), the Supreme Court of the United States drastically limited the right to picket, denied the right of state legislatures to legalize peaceful picketing, outlawed secondary boycotts, and made unions liable for unauthorized unlawful acts of their members. On May 15, 1922, the Court set aside as unconstitutional the Child Labor Law, which had been enacted by Congress after years of intense agitation. At the same time the federal and state courts seemed to be engaged in a race with each other in issuing the most sweeping and drastic injunctions in labor disputes.

The main task of the Cincinnati Convention of the Federation was to cope with these alarming developments. For this purpose President Gompers appointed a special committee composed, as he stated, of the best minds of the Convention. The committee was reinforced in its deliberations by eight lawyers of known labor sympathies from all parts of the country. I was one of the lawyers thus invited.

We had been in session many hours, grappling with all angles of the perplexing situation without getting anywhere in particular. It grew late; the conferees were weary, and the discussion ambled along informally and somewhat aimlessly. Then Samuel Gompers suddenly entered the room. In a trice the atmosphere changed. Every man present rose to his feet and remained standing until the big chief was seated. Mr. Gompers took complete charge of the meeting. Informing himself about the progress of the deliberations, he summed up the problems, threw out suggestions, and directed and dominated the gathering until the adjournment of the session late at night.

And yet, when the chief retired, followed by the "best minds" of the convention, and we lawyers were left alone to continue grappling with the intricate problem before us, we found that Mr. Gompers had done very little to give us direction or to lighten our task. A few apt but well-worn phrases and an undefinable spirit of defiance were the sum total of his contribution to the discussion. Through a process of delegation and subdelegation of the work Donald Richberg, counsel to the railroad workers, and I found ourselves charged with the task of drafting a report and program and relegated to our own resources and inspiration.

The superiority of Samuel Gompers sprang from a moral rather than intellectual source. He combined a wealth of accumulated experience with a fund of hard common sense. He had gained a stock of information about the numerous social problems directly and indirectly involved in the practical work of the labor movement, although he was not a student and never fully overcame the handicaps of a neglected early education. But what he lacked in book learning he amply made up in personal character, integrity, will power, and single-minded devotion to the cause of labor.

"I am a workingman," he proclaimed, "and in every nerve, in every fiber, in every aspiration, I am on the side which will advance the interests of my fellow workingmen. I represent my side, the side of the toiling wage-earning masses in every act and in my every utterance." *

This profession of faith was substantially true. Samuel Gompers, who flatly refused to accept the Marxian doctrine of the class struggle and the Socialist concept of class-consciousness, was inherently class-conscious to the point of religious fervor.

To these qualities should be added a profound and unshakable belief in himself, emphasis in speech often bordering on pompousness, and histrionic talents of no mean quality on the public platform. With all his self-appreciation and sense of superiority, however, he remained intensely human. His relations with labor leaders of inferior rank were those of true camaraderie and he was fond of smoking a cigar, taking a drink, and swapping stories with "the boys."

Samuel Gompers' political creed was somewhat vague. It probably came nearest to old-fashioned individualistic liberalism, not to say anarchism. He had a deep-seated distrust of governmental interference in economic matters, particularly in the affairs of labor and trade unions. He attached little importance to practical politics except as a possible and occasional aid to trade-union activity.

In the late seventies and early eighties Socialism was almost as popular among American trade-union leaders as it was among their European comrades. Some of the organizers of the Federation of Trade and Labor Unions were also leading members of the recently formed Socialist Labor Party.

I have often heard it said that Gompers also held membership in the party, but of this I find no proof, although he once admitted to me personally that he was strongly influenced by Socialist thought at that period. In later life he developed a

* Quoted in *Causes and Their Champions*, by M. A. De Wolfe Howe.

keen and abiding antagonism towards the Socialist movement. There were several reasons for this growing animosity on his part.

In the early days of the American Federation of Labor there was a considerable group of Socialist leaders in the organization. These constituted the "progressive" block as against the "conservative" forces headed by Mr. Gompers. In the annual conventions of the Federation the Socialist group regularly opposed his election.

The antagonism reached its climax with the organization of the Socialist Trade and Labor Alliance sponsored by the Socialist Labor Party under the leadership of Daniel De Leon.

The disavowal of the policy of antagonism to the American Federation of Labor by the subsequently formed Socialist Party did not appease Samuel Gompers, who continued viewing the Socialist trade-union activities with suspicion.

These suspicions soon found new nourishment in the formation of another rival labor body. In 1905 the Industrial Workers of the World (I.W.W.) was organized in Chicago. The movement sprang up within a number of dissident labor unions, national and local. The Socialist Party as such took a rather critical view of the new organization, but among the sponsors and founders of the latter were several prominent Socialist leaders, including Eugene V. Debs. Mr. Gompers invariably characterized it as a Socialist organization.

Personally I met Samuel Gompers on many and varied occasions, sometimes as opponent, more often as an ally. Our relations were a peculiar mixture of personal cordiality and political opposition. To the end of his days we remained "friendly enemies."

The controversy to which I alluded at the opening of this chapter took the form of a three-day debate before the famous Commission on Industrial Relations.

This commission was created by Act of Congress in 1912 "to inquire into the general conditions of labor in the principal industries of the United States . . . into the growth of associations of employers and wage earners and the effect of such associations upon the relations of employers and employees, and . . . into the methods which have been tried in any state or in foreign countries for maintaining mutually satisfactory relations between employees and employers."

The Commission was charged with the task of seeking to discover "the underlying causes of dissatisfaction in the industrial situation" and directed to "report its conclusions thereon."

It was one of the most striking measures of modern legislation, involving, as it did, an official recognition of the existence of industrial unrest and representing the first attempt at a general stock-taking of economic conditions and relations in the United States.

The act specified that the Commission "shall be composed of nine persons, to be appointed by the President of the United States, by and with the advice and consent of the Senate, not less than three of whom shall be employers of labor and not less than three of whom shall be representatives of organized labor."

On June 26, 1913, President Wilson named the following persons as members of the Commission. On the part of the public: Frank P. Walsh, the well-known lawyer, to serve as chairman; Professor John R. Commons, the noted economist; and Mrs. J. Borden Harriman. On the part of the employers: Frederic A. Delano, railway president, of Chicago; Harris Weinstock, merchant, author, and social worker, of Sacramento, California; and S. Thruston Ballard, capitalist, of St. Louis, Missouri. On the part of organized labor: John B. Lennon and James O'Connell, both officers of the American Federation of Labor; and Austin B. Garretson, president of the Order of Railway Conductors.

The Commission was given power to hold public hearings in

all parts of the United States and to compel the attendance of witnesses.

It held many interesting hearings in the principal cities of the country covering almost every conceivable phase of the labor question and related social problems. It heard seven hundred and forty "witnesses" summoned from many fields of industrial, social, and philanthropic endeavor and "reported its findings and conclusions" in eleven bulky volumes with a total of 11,250 large and closely printed pages.

The report is a rich mine of valuable material, now largely historical, which very few persons read. Congress never acted on it, and the "underlying causes of dissatisfaction in the industrial situation" remained undiscovered and unremedied.

On May 21, 1914, the Commission began a series of hearings in the city of New York intended to bring out the aims and methods of the mutual relations between the main divisions of organized labor, economic and political.

The American Federation of Labor, the Industrial Workers of the World and the Socialist Party, were all requested to designate spokesmen. Samuel Gompers was chosen by the Federation, Vincent St. John by the I.W.W., and I by the Socialist Party.

Vincent St. John's statement was a formal exposition of the organization, aims, and methods of the I.W.W. and rested there. Gompers' testimony and mine developed into a protracted and rather amusing verbal duel.

Called as a "witness" in the forenoon session of May 21st, I explained rather fully the Socialist philosophy and program and the structure, activities, and methods of the Socialist Party.

Under the procedure adopted by the Commission it was customary for its counsel, William O. Thompson, to examine and cross-examine the witnesses. Members of the Commission would also occasionally take a hand in the inquiry.

Samuel Gompers followed my exposition carefully and made copious notes. When I left the stand at the noon recess, we fell to chatting in a light vein about our business before the Commission.

"Your statement sounded very plausible," Gompers remarked, "and I suppose you can get away with it before the members of this Commission, but I know the situation better than they. I wish I could cross-examine you instead of Mr. Thompson."

The remark was made in a spirit of banter, but the rich possibilities of the idea flashed through my mind like lightning. "Do you really mean it?" I asked eagerly, and upon his emphatic affirmance I suggested that we join in a request to the Commission to dispense with the formal procedure and to allow us to cross-examine each other.

The Commission was quick to see the humor of the situation and after a brief and amused consultation acceded to it. From that point on the battle raged uninterruptedly during three consecutive sessions.

Mr. Gompers' cross-examination covered a wide range of subjects. He brought out the stock objections to the Socialist philosophy, its alleged confiscatory program, suppression of individual liberty, belief in a violent cataclysmic social change, etc., but with all that his questions were centered on an attempt to show that the Socialist Party had done little to aid in the practical struggles of organized labor, and that it was antagonistic to the American Federation of Labor. He was particularly insistent on the latter point and incessantly quoted from articles and speeches of Socialist supporters of the I.W.W. in unmeasured terms indicting the leadership of the Federation and criticizing its "craft" form of organization. His pet aversion in this connection was Eugene V. Debs, who always was extremely forceful and outspoken in his attacks on the Federation in general and Mr. Gompers in particular.

Time and again he would quote some picturesque language of the Socialist leader and ask me whether it represented the attitude of the party. This I invariably denied, referring Mr. Gompers to the official declarations of the party on the subject of trade unionism adopted at its various conventions. This long line of examination terminated in the following colloquy:

"Mr. GOMPERS: Do you regard that as the individual expression of opinion, when a man thrice the candidate of a political party, urges that a movement be inaugurated to dissolve the only general federation of organized workmen that ever existed for a period of time, such as the American Federation of Labor?

"Mr. HILLQUIT: I regard it purely as the individual expression of the man. The Socialist Party never puts its program or views into the hands of an individual candidate. It speaks for itself in conventions.

"Mr. GOMPERS: And the candidate for the Presidency of your party does not express, then, the sentiments and the views of the Party itself. Is that the inference to be drawn from your answer?

"Mr. HILLQUIT: You may draw this inference, that, whenever a candidate of the Socialist Party for the Presidency or otherwise, deviates from the declared principles of the Socialist Party, he does not speak for the Party, but speaks entirely on his responsibility.

"Mr. GOMPERS: Would you hold the same line of conduct to apply to, say, Mr. Taft, who was the candidate for President of the United States, nominated by the Republican Party?

"Mr. HILLQUIT: No, sir. The Republican Party has no declaration of general principles; no expressed attitude toward labor unions; no general social philosophy, and no social views of any kind. Its candidate for President therefore necessarily acts as the spokesman of his party. The Socialist Party is entirely different in this respect.

"Mr. GOMPERS: Would you say the candidate of the Prohibitionists, the candidate for President, if he were to make a declaration that was inconsistent with what his party would hold, would you regard that as simply his individual expression of opinion?

"MR. HILLQUIT: If the candidate for President of the Prohibition Party were to take a drink, I would not say that the Prohibition Party was committed to the drink evil."

At this point Samuel Gompers, who was known to be fond of an occasional libation, suddenly broke off with the indignant and somewhat irrelevant declaration:

"I prefer not to bring in the personal habits of any man."

When it came my turn to cross-examine Mr. Gompers, the failure of our minds to meet gave rise to an amusing situation.

Mr. Gompers assumed that I would criticize the methods or question the effectiveness of the A. F. of L.

Nothing, however, was farther from my purpose than to belittle the achievements of trade unionism or to claim any superiority over it in behalf of the Socialist movement. What I endeavored to demonstrate was the direct opposite of the proposition; namely, that trade unionism and Socialism sprang from the same economic conditions and necessities, that their ultimate goals were consciously or unconsciously identical, that one complemented the other and that both would gain by mutual understanding and practical coöperation.

My plan of procedure was to take up the main planks of the Socialist program, without labeling them as such and to establish Mr. Gompers' approval of them.

I proceeded accordingly to read the economic, political, and social planks as formulated in the last platform of the Socialist Party, in each instance prefacing the question with the phrase: "Does the American Federation of Labor advocate?"

In each instance Mr. Gompers, suspecting an implied doubt or denial on my part, emphatically and heatedly affirmed the acceptance of the plank by the Federation. This line of examination was concluded as follows:

"Mr. HILLQUIT: I have read to you point by point the working program of the Socialist Party with reference to economic and political measures, and I have asked you in each instance whether your Federation approves of such measures. Your answer has been in the affirmative, uniformly, except on the questions of the minimum wage and the maximum workday. As to those questions we agreed on the principle, but you would secure it by purely economic action and the Socialist Party by legal enactment. This is in the nature of a summary. I want it on the record. You may answer or not, as you please.

"Mr. GOMPERS: What did you want me to answer?

"Mr. HILLQUIT: Is it or is it not so?

"Mr. GOMPERS: I say that these demands which you have enumerated have been promulgated, declared and fought for, and in many instances accomplished, by the American Federation of Labor and the organized labor movement of the country. Your question would indicate that you claim the adhesion of the American labor movement to original propositions when, as a matter of fact, they have been put into your platform simply as vote-catchers."

Historically, Mr. Gompers' assertion was quite wrong. The principal planks I enumerated in my examination had been formulated by the Socialist movement in the days of the first International, i.e., in the seventies of the last century and long before the organization of the American Federation of Labor. But I was not concerned with the question of priorities. I was satisfied with having established the identity of the practical and immediate aims of both movements.

My next line of questioning aimed to prove that the two movements also led to similar conceptions of an ultimate social goal or ideal.

"On the witness stand," I had made the following statement under Mr. Gompers' cross-examination about the nature of the ideal Socialist state:

"Mr. Gompers: In the event that the Coöperative Commonwealth should be established, taking it for granted for the sake of the question, that it is possible, it would have for its present purpose the highest material and social and moral improvement of the condition of the workers attainable at that time, would it not?

"Mr. Hillquit: I think so.

"Mr. Gompers: And would there be any higher aim after that is established?

"Mr. Hillquit: Oh, there will be plenty more. There will be new aims coming every day.

"Mr. Gompers: Still more?

"Mr. Hillquit: Still further.

"Mr. Gompers: Still higher?

"Mr. Hillquit: Still higher.

"Mr. Gompers: Now, if that is so, isn't it a fact that it is not at all a goal, but simply a transitory ideal?

"Mr. Hillquit: Sure. It is our goal today. It is a transitory goal. There will be a movement towards a higher goal tomorrow."

Mr. Gompers seemed very pleased with my answers in the belief that they established the utopian and indefinite character of the Socialist movement as contrasted with the practical and definite aims of trade unionism.

In my examination of Mr. Gompers I approached the subject inductively. The result may be judged from the following colloquy:

"Mr. Hillquit: Now, Mr. Gompers, to take up another subject, is it your conception that workers in the United States today receive the full product of their labor?

"Mr. Gompers: In the generally accepted sense of that term, they do not.

"Mr. Hillquit: In any particular sense, yes?

"Mr. Gompers: No.

.   .   .   .

"Mr. Hillquit: Then one of the functions of organized labor is to increase the share of the workers in the product of their labor. Is that correct?

"Mr. Gompers: Yes, sir. Organized labor makes constantly increasing demand upon society for reward for the services which the workers render to society, and without which civilized life would be impossible.

"Mr. Hillquit: And these demands for an increasing share of the product of labor continue as a gradual process all the time?

"Mr. Gompers: I am not so sure as to gradual process. Sometimes it is not a gradual process, but it is all the time.

"Mr. Hillquit: All the time?

"Mr. Gompers: Yes, sir. . . . The aim is to secure the best conditions obtainable for the workers.

"Mr. Hillquit: Yes, and when these conditions are obtained——

"Mr. Gompers (interrupting): Why then we want better——

"Mr. Hillquit (continuing): You will still strive for better?

"Mr. Gompers: Yes.

"Mr. Hillquit: Now, my question is, will this effort on the part of organized labor ever stop before the workers receive the full reward for their labor?

"Mr. Gompers: It won't stop at all at any particular point, whether it be that towards which you have just stated, or anything else. The working people will never stop in their effort to obtain a better life for themselves, and for their wives and for their children and for humanity.

"MR. HILLQUIT: Then the object of the organized workmen is to obtain complete social justice for themselves and for their wives and for their children?

"MR. GOMPERS: It is the effort to obtain a better life every day.

"MR. HILLQUIT: Every day, and always——

"MR. GOMPERS (interrupting): Every day. That does not limit it.

"MR. HILLQUIT: Until such time——

"MR. GOMPERS (interrupting): Not until any time.

"MR. HILLQUIT: In other words——

"MR. GOMPERS (interrupting): In other words, we go farther than you. You have an end; we have not."

Theoretically the close kinship of aims and interests between the Socialist and trade-union movements was thus once more strikingly established.

It was nothing startling or even new. In practically all other industrial countries of the world the Socialist parties and labor unions invariably coöperate as two divisions of the same movement. The political efforts of the one and the economic struggles of the other are considered by the workers of those countries as nothing more than a practical separation of functions within the organized labor movement.

The main weakness of American Socialism and American trade unionism lies in their failure of mutual coöperation. The same condition prevailed in England up to the beginning of the present century with the same results.

I am inclined to believe that recent economic and political developments in the United States tend to break down the self-imposed barriers between the two movements and that eventually, perhaps shortly, they will reach the same degree of mutual understanding that characterizes the relations of their fellow workers on the other side of the ocean.

When that day comes the Socialist movement of America will attain to the same degree of political strength as the Labor Party of England, and the trade-union movement will infinitely gain in effectiveness.

CHAPTER VII

RUNNING FOR OFFICE

YEAR after year the Socialists name candidates for public office. From the point of view of immediate results their campaigns are often hopeless. Socialist candidates run for office primarily because electoral contests offer excellent opportunities for propaganda, and because they hope to build up an eventual political standing by steady and persistent effort, undiscouraged by slow growth and undismayed by occasional setbacks.

Running for office is an almost inescapable part of the work of the active Socialist propagandist, and I did my full share of it.

Aside from some minor and now forgotten candidacies in my early days, I was twice nominated by the Socialist Party to lead in mayoralty campaigns in New York, and five times I attempted to win a seat in the House of Representatives.

My congressional campaigns were not of the mere formal variety. They were serious fights for election conducted with vigor and hope, but I was never destined to enter the august portals of Congress.

Twice I failed of election by narrow margins. Once I was doubtlessly elected but counted out. Two times I was defeated by Democratic-Republican coalitions against me.

My first run was made in 1906 in what was then the Ninth Congressional District of New York. The district comprised the most congested section of the lower East Side. It was inhabited almost entirely by Russian-Jewish immigrants. The bulk of the population consisted of workers. Its petty "bourgeoisie" was represented by pushcart peddlers. Its upper strata were made up of small shopkeepers and professionals—physicians, dentists, and lawyers.

Ever since the advent of Tammany Hall, that organization had reigned supreme in the lower East Side. The Ninth Congressional District was a sort of feudal fief of the notorious Tammany chieftains, Christie and Timothy Sullivan, "the Sullivans" for short. Politics in the district was frankly and boastfully corrupt. On election days votes were openly purchased in front of polling places at the established price of two dollars each. "Floaters" and "repeaters" did a thriving business, and the count bore but a remote relation to the vote cast.

The local Republican organizations worked in cynical complicity with the Tammany machine. Only when the Socialists began developing appreciable political strength were the shameless practices somewhat curbed.

It was in this district that I was nominated by the local Socialist organization to run for Congress. In my letter of acceptance I thus described it:

"Our district covers a territory of barely one square mile, and it contains a population of over 200,000! It is a cold, cheerless existence that its people lead. For them there is but little light or sunshine, mirth or joy, pleasure or play in life. The men are careworn, tired, sullen; the women ragged, morose, and irritated; the children anemic, sickly, and sad; all are overworked, underfed, ill-clad, and miserable.

"The Ninth Congressional District is the home of the tenements, pushcarts, paupers, and tuberculosis. It is the experimental laboratory of the sentimental settlement worker, the horrible example of the pious moralist, and the chosen prey of the smug philanthropist. Geographically it is located in the slums; industrially it belongs to the sweat-shop system; politically it is a dependency of Tammany Hall."

The campaign kindled an indescribable fire of enthusiasm on the East Side. The Socialist Party had already gained a political foothold in the district. In the preceding campaign Joseph Barondess, the popular leader of the cloak makers, running on the Socialist ticket, had polled over 3,000 votes, about twenty per cent of the total. In 1906 the prospects seemed to be particularly promising because the district faced a four-cornered fight. In addition to the three parties who had contested the Congressional election in 1904, William R. Hearst's Independence League entered the arena with a full ticket of its own. Hearst had proved very popular on the East Side in the mayoralty campaign of the preceding year, and it was confidently expected that his candidate would seriously cut down the normal Democratic vote.

My chances of election were considered excellent, and the whole working East Side threw itself into the campaign with almost religious fervor. The trade unions organized a demonstration in the form of a street parade, which the newspapers described as "the largest ever staged by the Socialists in this city, if not in the country." The women, then not yet entitled to vote, organized a committee of three hundred to help in the campaign. Young boys and girls between the ages of thirteen and seventeen constituted themselves into a Juvenile Workers' League. Doctors, dentists, and lawyers formed a Professional League in support of the Socialist ticket. The principal contribution of the latter was a public dinner attended by a large number of well-known men and women outside of the district. Among the distinguished guests who spoke in support of my candidacy on that occasion were Edwin Markham, Professor Franklin H. Giddings, Hamilton Holt, Eugene Wood, and Charlotte Perkins Gilman.

A picturesque touch was given to the campaign by the appearance of Maxim Gorky as one of our "stump speakers." He made two speeches in support of my candidacy in Bowery theaters. This was in the early part of October, in the midst of the heated contest and a few days before the end of the tragic visit of the famous Russian novelist in the United States.

Under the tsarist régime literature, particularly in the abstract and elusive form of fiction, was practically the only outlet for the expression of liberal and revolutionary sentiment. Authors like Chernyshevsky, Tolstoy, Tourgeniev, Goncharoff, and later Chekhoff and Gorky, were the spiritual leaders of the Russian youth and the better part of the country's "intelligentsia." None of the others probably attained the height of popularity of Maxim Gorky. He had risen on the literary horizon with the suddenness and brilliance of a meteor. He was forceful, deep, and true, and, above all, he was thoroughly proletarian in origin and interest. Gorky was the first among the great writers of Russia to transfer the attention of the reading public from the decaying middle classes and the struggles of the young intellectuals for a new order to the dark masses of the people, the tramps and social outcasts, the "lower depths" of society. He wrote with a bold realism not devoid of a touch of romantic idealization of his humble subjects, and with a strong undercurrent of social revolt and defiance. Almost overnight he became the idol of revolutionary Russia.

Early in his career he enlisted in the underground organization of the Social Democratic Labor Party. He took an active part in the short-lived and abortive Russian revolution of 1905.

Maxim Gorky came to the United States in April, 1906. The real though unavowed object of his visit was to raise money for the revolutionary movement in his native land. Rarely did a man have greater opportunities to advance his cause, and rarely were they so utterly wasted and spoiled.

Gorky was received in New York with a spontaneous enthusiasm and acclaim hardly ever before accorded to a foreign visitor. Thousands of his compatriots had gathered in the vicinity of the pier to welcome him. The cheering crowd covered many solid blocks. A swarm of newspaper reporters and photographers and delegations of all conceivable liberal and radical movements met him at quarantine. Persons high in all fields of public life called to pay their respects to him. A committee of prominent writers, headed by Mark Twain, was organized to arrange a public banquet in his honor. Then one day there came an abrupt change. The popular guest suddenly became an object of scorn and persecution.

The newspapers discovered that Mrs. Gorky, who accompanied the illustrious Russian on his visit, was not in fact his lawfully wedded wife. The discovery was blazoned in screaming and shocked headlines and created a storm of indignation among the righteous people of New York. The hotel in which the Gorkys lived evicted them without ceremony. Other hotels closed their doors to them. They found themselves homeless and outlaws, and the newspapers reported their plight with glee. The prominent men of letters called off their planned dinner. Respectable society shunned the irregular and unlicensed couple.

H. G. Wells, who happened to be in New York at the time, thus describes the inglorious episode: *

Gorky arrived and the éclat was immense. We dined him, we lunched him, and were photographed in his company by flashlight. I very gladly shared the honor, for Gorky is not only a great master of the art I practice, but a splendid personality. He is one of those. persons to whom the camera does not do justice, whose work in English translation, forceful as it is, fails very largely to convey his peculiar quality. He is a big, quiet figure with a curious power of appeal in his face, a large simplicity in his voice and gesture. He impressed me as a peasant and except for a few common greetings in English he has no other language than Russian. So it was necessary that he should bring with him some one he could trust to interpret

* From *The Future in America*, by H. G. Wells. Copyright, 1906, by Harper & Brothers. By permission of the author.

him to the world. And, having, too, much of the practical help-
lessness of his type of genius, he could not come without his right
hand, that brave and honorable lady, Madame Andreiva, who has been
now for years in everything but the severest legal sense his wife. . . .

Although his wife had since found another companion, the Orthodox Church in Russia has no divorce facilities for men in the revolutionary camp. . . . I suppose the two of them forgot the technical
illegality until it burst upon them and the American public in a
monstrous storm of exposure.

. . . .

I do not know what motive actuated a certain section of the
American press to initiate this pelting of Maxim Gorky. A passion
for moral purity may perhaps have prompted it, but certainly no
passion for purity ever before begot so brazen and abundant a torrent
of lies. . . . The Gorkys were pursued with insult from hotel to
hotel. . . . They found themselves at last, after midnight, on the
streets of New York City with every door closed against them.
Infected persons could not have been treated more abominably in a
town smitten with a panic or plague.

The change happened in the course of twenty-four hours. On one
day Gorky was at the zenith, on the next he had been swept from
the world. To me it was astounding—it was terrifying.

The cause of the sudden and mysterious change of sentiment
that puzzled H. G. Wells soon became quite clear to me. Gorky
was the victim of poor advice from well-meaning friends. He
was surrounded by a few Russians who had come with him and
knew nothing about American psychology and conditions, and
by some amateur American radicals, who knew little about the
Socialist movement. By these advisers the candid and simple-
minded "peasant" was persuaded to adopt a "diplomatic" course
of conduct, which led to his undoing.

I was the international representative of the Socialist Party at
the time, and Gorky carried two messages to me, an official letter
of introduction from the Executive Committee of the Russian
Social Democratic Labor Party and a personal note from Nicolai

Lenin. Although I met him on his arrival, he did not mention the letters. When I asked him confidentially about the object of his visit and his plans of action, he was reticent and evasive. I did not feel like forcing my attentions on him and left him in the hands of his friends.

Later, when he was abandoned and in disgrace, I sought him out. He and his companion had found hospitable refuge in the Staten Island home of John Martin, a social reformer, who had once been associated with the Fabian Society of England.

It was only then that the disillusioned victim of high diplomacy handed his letters and opened his heart to me. Among other things I learned that the guileless novelist had been led to make a contract with one of the sensational and somewhat unscrupulous metropolitan dailies, giving it the exclusive right to all his writings while in America. The newspaper did not even assume the reciprocal obligation to print and pay for a stated minimum of articles.

It was immediately after the execution of the one-sided contract that the rival newspapers awoke to the realization of the appalling fact that the famous writer was living in sin in our puritanical midst. The absence of a formal marriage certificate in the union of Maxim Gorky with the charming, cultured, and high-minded actress had, of course, been generally known long before their arrival. It had been freely commented on among the newspaper reporters in the little tugboat that met the Russian visitors at Quarantine.

During the latter part of Gorky's stay in New York we saw a good deal of each other and became close friends.

The exposure of his marital status did not detract from Gorky's popularity in the Ninth Congressional District, largely inhabited by his own countrymen. If anything, his "lynching," as Professor Giddings called it, increased their affection for him as a hero and martyr. The theaters in which he delivered his campaign speeches were taxed to capacity by crowds frenzied with enthusiasm.

Gorky's appearance was but one incident in the stirring and busy contest on the East Side.

Street meetings were held by the score every night. Campaign literature was distributed by hundreds of volunteers. Our headquarters hummed with activity. It was, in the unanimous testimony of neutral newspaper observers, "the liveliest thing" in the campaign of 1906.

My election was practically conceded at the height of the campaign, and I did in fact poll a larger number of votes than any other congressional candidate in the district on any party ticket, but I was beaten by an unexpected eleventh-hour combination.

The incumbent in office and my Democratic opponent was one Henry M. Goldfogle, a typical Tammany politician of the lower order. There was no love for him in the Hearst camp. In the preceding election the Hearst newspapers opposed his candidacy and the *Evening Journal* wrote about him editorially:

"What impression is such a man as Goldfogle apt to make upon his fellow-citizens in Congress? How can a Congressman deficient mentally and physically be of use in fighting the battle that requires brain, character, and the respect of other men?"

In 1906 Goldfogle had by some devious means managed to secure the nomination of the Independence League in the Ninth Congressional District. The nomination was contested and the Appellate Division of the Supreme Court barred his candidacy on the ticket of the League, holding that the law, as it then stood, did not permit of a nomination by two parties. The road thus seemed clear, when the Court of Appeals in the last hour reversed the decision and allowed Goldfogle to remain on both tickets. That meant that under the form of ballot then in use every straight vote marked for the Independence League, headed by William R. Hearst for Governor, would also count for Goldfogle.

A public demand was made on the editor to disavow the candidate whom he had so recently and so bitterly castigated in the columns of one of his papers and who represented the worst political elements Mr. Hearst pretended to fight. But the crusader for political purity refused to move. He was a candidate for office and considerations of practical expediency outweighed the slender claims of principle.

The combined votes of Henry M. Goldfogle on the tickets of the Democratic Party and the Independence League exceeded mine.

Disappointed but not discouraged, I returned to the charge two years later, when the situation and prospects appeared even brighter. The fight was again between four parties. The Hearst Independence League was again in the field and Henry M. Goldfogle again had its endorsement in addition to his regular candidacy on the Democratic ticket.

On the other hand the Socialist organization in the district had grown stronger since the preceding campaign. Robert Hunter and J. G. Phelps Stokes, who had in the meantime become members of the Socialist Party, were nominated for the Assembly in two districts comprised within the Ninth Congressional District.

The campaign attracted greater interest than the preceding one among Socialists and sympathizers outside the district. Hordes of young intellectuals came down daily to speak at street corners, distribute campaign literature, canvass voters, and make themselves generally useful at headquarters.

Support of the Socialist candidates in the district came from persons in high places in the literary and academic worlds. We were particularly proud of the endorsement of William D.

Howells, the dean of American letters, then in his seventy-ninth year, who sent us a warm letter of encouragement with a campaign contribution.

The red-letter day of the campaign was when Eugene V. Debs appeared in the district. The whole East Side seemed to be on its feet as the Socialist presidential candidate, seated in an open car, made laborious progress from one speaking place to another through the dense, cheering, and excited crowds.

Once more my election was confidently predicted. Once more I failed. In the closing days of the campaign the Democratic camp became thoroughly panicky. A deal was speedily made with the local Republican machine, which openly urged its supporters to vote for Henry M. Goldfogle. In spite of the fact that the year was one of a presidential election, with William Howard Taft running against William Jennings Bryan, the Republican candidate polled a purely nominal vote. Mr. Goldfogle received all the votes of the Democratic Party and the Independence League and most of the Republican votes.

This was the last of my campaigns on the lower East Side. Later the boundaries of the congressional districts of New York were changed, the greater part of the Ninth District being incorporated in the Twelfth. The battle in the district was taken up where I left it off by Meyer London, a young Socialist lawyer and one of the best loved men on the East Side. He made the run for Congress in three successive campaigns and in 1914 he was elected—the first Socialist member of Congress from the East.

Meyer London was an idealist and a dreamer. He was endowed with a peculiar unadorned eloquence, and his moral earnestness and deep sincerity earned for him the attention and respect of his fellow members in the House. When he died in 1926, oddly enough through an accident similar to that which took the life of the only other Socialist Congressman, Victor

Berger, the whole East Side was in mourning. Not less than 50,000 persons marched in the funeral procession, while hundreds of thousands of men and women with tear-stained faces lined the streets through the long route of the cortège.

Eight years after my last run on the lower East Side I accepted a nomination for Congress in the Twentieth District, located on the upper East Side. This was a comparatively new but typical working-class district. In the continuous shift of New York's population, particularly during the period of heavy immigration, the trend of the movement was towards the north. The new arrivals would first settle on the lower East Side, and as they became more "Americanized" and better established they would move to the less congested "uptown" sections of the city.

In 1916 the Twentieth Congressional District was very similar in ethnic composition and social character to my old Ninth ten years earlier, except that it contained a larger element of Irish, Italian, and German workers, and that the people were somewhat better situated economically.

In that year Meyer London ran for reëlection, and the Socialists of New York concentrated their efforts on the two districts in the hope of electing both of us.

It was a lively campaign and was conducted largely in the same spirit of enthusiasm and hope as my earlier congressional campaigns.

On the night of the election the party headquarters and the sidewalks in front of it were thronged with an eager and expectant crowd. As our watchers returned from the polling places reporting the results of the count, which in most instances showed a comfortable lead over my opponents, cheer after cheer went up and joy was unbounded. By midnight we had unofficial returns from all but two election districts. They gave me a plurality of about 500 votes over my nearest opponent, the Republican candidate Isaac Siegel. The two unreported districts were known to be favorable to us, and victory thus seemed assured. But hour after hour passed, and no returns came from the missing election districts. It became obvious that the count was held up for a purpose. While the two tardy election boards were marking time, the local Republican and Democratic bosses were making a deal. We learned of their conference and sensed danger. We stormed the recalcitrant election officials demanding that they proceed with the count and announce the result. Vain effort. They sat there impassively and cynically, chinning, smoking, spitting, doing anything but counting the vote. When we appealed to the police officers stationed in the polling places, they merely shrugged their shoulders. They were powerless to act. Complaints to a city magistrate produced similarly negative results. The petty ward heelers in the "bipartisan" election board calmly waited for orders from their respective bosses, and there seemed to be no authority in the city of New York able or willing to interfere with the flagrant and flaunting lawlessness. No crimes are treated in our republic more indulgently, even humorously, than crimes against the elective franchise.

It was late in the afternoon of the next day that the bargain was closed, the returns properly doctored, and the count completed. It gave me 4,192 votes to 4,542 for my Republican opponent and 3,907 for the Democratic candidate. My plurality of about 500 had turned into a shortage of 350 votes.

I shall never forget the manifestation of grief and indignation in our headquarters that day. Scores of men and women had stayed up with us all night, alternately hoping and despairing. When I finally announced the official figures to them, there were tears in many eyes. For days there was a spirit of general mourning in the district. Then the indomitable Socialists began girding for the next battle, determined to pile up such a huge majority in the coming election that no corrupt combination of the old parties would be able to steal it.

The old parties, on the other hand, had had their fright and learned their lesson. In the following two congressional campaigns in the district they quietly laid aside all pretense of rivalry and united on one candidate. It happened to be the Republican in this case, while the Democrats were compensated by minor offices within the district.

After my mayoralty campaign of 1917, which is described in a later chapter, I ran again for Congress in the Twentieth District in 1918 but did not conduct an active campaign. The condition of my health compelled me to stay away from the city. In 1920 I made my final fight for the congressional seat of the district. In each of these elections I polled more than forty per cent of the total vote.

After that the district underwent another radical and rapid change in character and composition. The bulk of the Socialist workers moved farther north, mostly to the Bronx, and their place was largely taken by Porto Rican immigrants.

I did not run again for public office until 1932, when I was nominated for Mayor of New York to fill the one-year vacancy caused by the enforced resignation of James J. Walker, and received a quarter of a million votes.

CHAPTER VIII

THE PEOPLE VS. JOHANN MOST

My first *cause célèbre* was a criminal prosecution against Johann Most. Few figures as picturesque as the founder and leader of "Communist Anarchism" have been produced by the modern revolutionary movement.

His whole mental and temperamental make-up, his physical deformity, his bitter experience in life, his very birth, illegitimate or, as he himself was fond of expressing it, "contrary to police regulations," predestined him for a career of irreconcilable warfare against the existing social order and relations.

Johann Most was born in Augsburg, Germany, in 1846. At the age of seven years he contracted a gangrenous affliction which necessitated a radical facial operation. As a result his lower jaw remained wrenched out of position. His hideous appearance made him the butt of ridicule of his playmates, and his joyless childhood early embittered him against the world.

At fourteen he was apprenticed to a bookbinder, and upon the completion of his apprenticeship he spent several years in different parts of Germany, Switzerland, Italy, Austria, and Hungary as a traveling artisan in keeping with the custom of the time.

During the period of his work and wanderings he became acquainted with the literature of Socialism, and in 1868 he formally enlisted in the movement, joining the Swiss section of the First International at Zurich. Almost immediately the young bookbinder rose to a position of leadership.

He was a born orator with a rare power to sway the masses by his torrential eloquence, in turn caustic, humorous, emotional, and fiery. It had been his ambition in early life to become an actor. His physical deformity stood in the way of the coveted stage career, but the lecture platform amply compensated him for the disappointment. Theatrical, vain, and domineering, he stood out conspicuously in any group with which he associated himself. His pen was as trenchant as his tongue was sharp.

In 1869 we find him in Austria leading a revolutionary demonstration before the House of Parliament. For this offense he was sentenced to five years' imprisonment, of which he actually served more than a year. This was the first of a series of arrests and imprisonments that were to become part of the regular routine of his life. As he had studied the social conditions of different countries in his earlier years as a wandering artisan, so he explored their jails in later life as a traveling agitator.

Expelled from Austria, he went back to Germany, where he became editor of a Socialist daily paper. In 1874 he was elected to the Reichstag and in the same year he was prosecuted for a seditious speech and sentenced to imprisonment for eighteen months.

On the passage of the anti-Socialist laws Johann Most, like so many other Social Democrats, was compelled to leave Germany. He settled in London, at that time one of the last European citadels of free speech and press, and established there a weekly Socialist paper under the title *Freiheit* (Freedom).

The suppression of the Social Democratic organization in Germany and the impossibility of openly and systematically carrying on the work of the movement had given rise to a complex of new problems as to methods and tactics. The policy adopted by the leaders of German Socialism was to organize an underground propaganda and to conduct it on a large scale, but with a degree of caution so as not to deliver the movement and its followers into the hands of the watchful Bismarck spies.

Johann Most, who had always been at loggerheads with the other party leaders, decried their "timidity" and advocated methods of forcible resistance and terrorism. The controversy waxed acrimonious and personal, and resulted in the expulsion of Most from the Social Democratic party. Then he turned anarchist. His was not the philosophic anarchism of Peter Kropotkin or Elisée Reclus, but a gospel of violence and guerrilla warfare. His attack was directed not only against the existing social, economic, and political order, but also against the personal representatives of that order, the heads of governments and the big capitalists.

Violence played a triple rôle in the Mostian philosophy. It was to pave the road to freedom by the physical attrition of despots, to spread terror and demoralization in the ranks of the ruling classes, and to fan the smoldering sentiment of revolt among the masses into a powerful flame of active revolution.

When Alexander II of Russia was killed by nihilists in March, 1881, Johann Most glorified the event in his *Freiheit* and expressed the hope that "all tyrants would soon be served in like manner."

This earned him a term of sixteen months in a London jail. After his release he came to New York, arriving in December, 1882.

In the United States Most immediately assumed leadership of the anarchist movement, which made rapid progress under the inspiration of his writings and extended lecture tours. In 1883 a well-attended national convention of anarchists was held in Pittsburgh and issued the famous "Pittsburgh Proclamation," the political credo of Communist Anarchism drawn up by Most.

For five years the anarchist leader managed to continue an active propaganda in the United States and to keep out of jail, but in 1886, on the occasion of the execution of the Chicago anarchists, he made an incendiary speech in New York, for which he was arrested, tried, convicted, and sentenced to serve one year in the Blackwell's Island jail.

After his release Most continued his propagandist activities, including the publication of the *Freiheit*. He was a ready and prolific writer and largely filled the columns of his paper with his own articles. Occasionally, however, particularly when out on a propaganda tour or indulging in a protracted "beer session" of which he was extremely fond, the paper would have to be made up in a hurry. For such emergencies Most had a ready stock of "fillers-in," old articles of his own or of other revolutionary writers. A favorite among such "fillers-in" was an essay written by Karl Heinzen under the interesting title "Murder Against Murder."

Heinzen was a professional revolutionist of the old school, whose career was not unlike that of Johann Most. A German by birth and an active participant in the revolution of 1848, he fled from his native country, found temporary asylum in several other countries of Europe, from all of which he was eventually expelled, until he settled in the United States, where he continued his revolutionary propaganda at different times in New York, St. Louis, Cincinnati, and Boston.

The article "Murder Against Murder" was written about 1850 and was couched in the approved exultant and bombastic language of the period. Its main theme was that all power rests on violence and murder, and that these may be more legitimately used for the liberation of the people from the rule of despots than for the subjugation of the people by the despots.

"A bandit with several accomplices makes some district unsafe," Heinzen argued by way of illustration. "Power is employed to pursue him and to insure respect for the 'law.' He is captured and is hung as an expiation for the past and as a warning for the future. But suppose that he succeeds in beating the armed power, in overturning the law, in obtaining possession of the land, and becoming its lord. His band, of robbers become an 'army,' the bandit chief becomes a 'general,' the bandit becomes a 'king,' and a plundered population become loyal subjects who enthusiastically shout 'Long live our most gracious king.' . . .

"To conquer and destroy the enemy, that is the only object. History will only judge us according to this."

And again:

"The despots are outlawed. They are in human society what the tiger is among animals. To spare them is a crime. As despots permit themselves everything, betrayal, poison, murder, etc., so all this is to be employed against them.

"Let murder be our study, murder in every form," proclaimed the liberal revolutionist of 1848. "In this one word lies more humanity than in all our theories."

And he concluded:

"We say murder the murderers. Save humanity through blood, poison and iron."

The blood and thunder tone of the article struck a responsive chord in the heart of Johann Most, who reprinted it in his paper several times. He printed it once too often.

On September 5, 1901, the *Freiheit* appeared featuring Heinzen's "Murder Against Murder" on its front page. The next day President McKinley was shot in Buffalo by a professed anarchist of Polish extraction named Leon Czolgosz, and sustained injuries from which he died eight days later.

There was no traceable connection between Johann Most and Leon Czolgosz, and the latter probably never read the *Freiheit*. But the publication of the provocative article of the fiery German "forty-eighter" and the anarchist attempt on the life of the American President followed each other in such close sequence as to constitute a very embarrassing coincidence to say the least. Even Most realized it and immediately ordered the withdrawal of the paper from circulation. Unfortunately for him, a few copies of the issue had already been sold, one of them to a member of the secret service department of the New York police force. It was this solitary copy of the *Freiheit* on which the prosecution against the hapless editor was based.

There was at that time no anti-anarchy statute in New York. The charge against Johann Most was framed under a vague section of the penal code, which made it a misdemeanor "to commit an act which seriously disturbs or endangers the public peace or openly outrages public decency."

In the Police Court, Most appeared as his own counsel. The committing magistrate did not seem to attach much importance to the case. Almost perfunctorily he held him for trial before the Court of Special Sessions, a criminal court of inferior jurisdiction, and released him on the modest bail of five hundred dollars.

The three judges of the Special Sessions, however, took a more serious view of the case. When the defendant appeared before them, still disdaining the services of a lawyer, they curtly informed him that they considered the charge against him to be of a grave nature and directed him to retain counsel.

It was at this juncture that Johann Most and two of his friends called on me. The unexpected visit took me completely by surprise. There was no love in the anarchist breast for the "reactionary" Social Democrats. In fact the practical daily fights of the American anarchists were directed with infinitely greater vim and vigor against their Socialist stepbrethren than against the "political tyrants" and "capitalist despots." Only bitter necessity could have induced the anarchist leaders to apply to a Socialist for help. Our interview accordingly took a rather amusing turn. Johann Most acted as spokesman of the committee, and from his very first words it became abundantly clear to me that my enthusiastic would-be client would like nothing better than to have me refuse his case. When I expressed my readiness to serve, he made little effort to conceal his displeasure and tried to bully me into changing my mind.

"I deem it my duty to warn you," he announced, "that I have seen several lawyers and that every one of them has refused to undertake my defense." I assured him that I had not flattered myself into the belief that I headed his list of eligible lawyers, but that I was quite ready to undertake his defense anyhow.

"Do you realize," admonished my solicitous client, "that a case like mine may ruin the career of any young lawyer?"

I suggested that I be allowed to take care of my own career and reiterated my willingness to take up his defense.

Most looked disgusted, but he had yet one trump card to play. "You are ready to take the case," he said. "That is all good and well, but how about the fee? Ours is a very poor organization."

"I am not interested in the fee," was my tart rejoinder. "I am ready to take up your case because I believe it involves the important principle of freedom of press and speech."

With all defenses thus cut off the anarchist leader surrendered none too graciously. I noticed an almost imperceptible twinkle in his eyes as he finally placed his fate in my hands with this encouraging statement: "Well then, go ahead and try to defend me."

I tried. I tried very hard, but without success. I argued that the flamboyant tirade of the inveterate German republican was clearly directed against the crowned heads of European monarchies and was never intended to apply to elected officials in a political democracy; that the author of the article had been dead a long time and that the political struggles which inspired it had passed into history. I pointed out that the article had been allowed to be printed and reprinted innumerable times in this country in newspapers and as part of Heinzen's collected works, and that it did not contain a direct incitement against any living

person. I invoked the constitutional guaranty of the freedom of
the press and contended that the section of the Penal Code under
which Most was prosecuted was so general and vague as to be
meaningless.

I emphatically denied the right of the courts to create and
punish crimes not clearly and specifically defined as such by
statute or by common law precedents.

I combed the law books for support of my contentions and
buttressed my arguments with a formidable array of authorities.
I felt convinced, and I still feel now that we had a complete defense in law. But it was not a question of abstract legal rights.
President McKinley had died by the hand of an anarchist assas-
sin. The country was aroused against all anarchist agitators, and
the courts were fully responsive to the general popular sentiment.

The case was tried in the Court of Special Sessions and was
argued on appeal before two high judicial tribunals, including
the Court of Appeals, the court of last resort in the state. I
have in later years defended many unpopular causes, but at no
time did I feel such a dense atmosphere of cold hostility as descended upon the courtroom every time the ominous title of the
case, "The People *v.* John Most," was pronounced.

Most was convicted not so much because of the fortuitous and
ill-timed reprint of the hoary Heinzen article as for his general
anarchist propaganda.

In the Court of Special Sessions the judges gave counsel the
maximum praise "for the able manner in which he conducted
the defense and for his able brief" and gave the defendant the
maximum penalty allowed by law—imprisonment for one year
in the Penitentiary at Blackwell's Island. The Appellate Division
of the Supreme Court and the Court of Appeals affirmed the
convictions in lengthy and elaborate opinions.

There was but one ray of judicial enlightment and courage

in the whole litigation. Supreme Court Justice Charles F. Maclean, with a somewhat sarcastic opinion riddling the contention of the prosecution, granted the defendant a "certificate of reasonable doubt," which released him on bail pending the appeal.

"The only proof appearing on the return to support this judgemeht," the judge found, "is that the defendant purloined an article, written by another half a century ago, and published it as his own in a paper professedly of some circulation, but of which is shown the sale of but a single copy, that purchased by the policeman probably for the purpose of prosecution. . . . It is not shown that the defendant's expression of borrowed sentiments has worked injury to any individual by falsifying any fact, or to the public by disturbing or endangering the public peace." The judge sustained the defendant's contention that the article was protected by the constitutional safeguard of liberty of the press.

At the time of his conviction Most was fifty-five years old. He looked much older. The hardships of his unsteady and strenuous life and the years of prison had undermined his robust constitution. His last year on Blackwell's Island told heavily on his health and spirit. He came out of jail a broken man, sluggish, cynical, and indifferent. During the remaining four years of his life he went through the accustomed motions of the anarchist writer and propagandist, but he was no longer the former spirited and impetuous Johann Most.

In the course of the litigation and our frequent conferences in connection with it, the anarchist leader had developed a genuine fondness for me. We remained in friendly personal relations to the end of his days.

One of the direct results of the Most case was the enactment by the New York legislature of a drastic "criminal anarchy" statute. The law, passed in 1902, makes it a felony punishable by imprisonment up to ten years to advocate the forcible overthrow of government or the assassination of the executive head or other executive official of the government or to justify the assassination of such an official in this or any other country.

This was the precursor of the anti-anarchy and anti-syndicalism statutes which have since been incorporated in the laws of most states of the Union.

CHAPTER IX

A MURDER TRIAL WITH A SOCIAL BACKGROUND

THE year 1910 stands out as a landmark in the history of New York's cloak workers. Until then they were among the worst exploited workers in the country. About fifty thousand in number, they accounted for a large part of the badly congested lower East Side. Practically all were recent immigrants, prevalently Jews from Russia, Austria, and Roumania with a sprinkling of Italians and other nationalities. Their pay was miserable, their work hours were long, and their general conditions of work and life were almost intolerable.

Like most Jewish workers they were long-suffering, meek, and submissive. But every once in a while they would flare up in an outburst of despair and revolt, and go on strike. The strikes were spontaneous and without preparation or organization. Invariably they broke out on the eve of a busy work season, and in almost every instance they forced some wage increases. But no sooner did the season slacken down and workers become again more abundant than work, than the contractors evened up their scores with their employees by slashing wages mercilessly.

Busy season, strike, wage increase, slow season, wage cut, new season, new strike—that was the ever-recurring cycle in the hectic industry. Every strike was accompanied by an organization of the workers into a union; every "victory" was followed by a disbandment of the union, and every new strike led to reorganization.

The cloak workers were long the despair of professional and

amateur union organizers, including my own circle of young Socialist propagandists. They seemed hopelessly unorganizable on a permanent basis.

The change came in 1910.

In the summer of that year fifty thousand cloakmakers by common accord laid down their tools and united in a strike, which at once assumed an infinitely more serious character than the customary sporadic stoppages of the past.

It may be that the limit of their endurance had been reached or that the twenty-five years of their sporadic struggles had developed in them a larger self-reliance and greater power of resistance. At any rate this time they stuck. The strike lasted almost ten weeks without a break in the ranks of the workers. It was well organized and efficiently managed. As a fight against the notorious "sweat-shop" system it received wide and favorable publicity and enjoyed general popular support.

In the early stages of the duel some public-spirited citizens of high standing, including Louis D. Brandeis, now a Justice of the United States Supreme Court, and the late Louis Marshall, interested themselves in the controversy and made persistent efforts to bring about peace between the direct manufacturers, the most responsible group of employers, and the workers. The result of the strike and the peace parleys was paradoxical. The most backward and disorganized industry in America adopted a most advanced and enlightened code of labor relations in the form of a collective agreement, styled Perpetual Protocol of Peace.

The "Protocol" became famous in American labor history. Its provisions were analyzed and its workings studied and described by the departments of labor of the United States and of several states as well as by numerous students of labor problems, and its general scheme was adopted in whole or in part by other industries.

It was in fact a remarkable instrument and went far beyond the usual stipulations in collective labor agreements fixing wages, hours, and other working standards.

To eradicate the "sweat-shop" a Joint Board of Sanitary Control was set up, composed of representatives of employers, workers, and the public, with elaborate machinery for periodical inspections of the work places and the abatement of unsanitary conditions in them. Provisions were made against oppressive treatment of workers and their arbitrary discharge from employment. All grievances and complaints between employers and workers were to be adjusted on their merits by a voluntary industrial court established for that purpose. Strikes and lockouts were outlawed.

The agreement was not limited to a specified time, but was to run perpetually. Any changes or revisions of its terms necessitated by altered conditions were to be made within the framework of the instrument itself.

The substantial principles and institutions of the Protocol have ruled the cloak industry ever since, but the covenant of perpetual peace has proved largely illusory. In the years that followed the execution of the agreement radical changes occurred in the methods and structure of the industry, creating new problems and calling for new adjustments. Sometimes these adjustments were made in conference between the employers and workers, but on several occasions the parties found themselves deadlocked and forced into new strikes or lockouts. These struggles generally resulted in some modification of the Protocol, usually arrived at through the mediation of public authorities.

The first of these breaks occurred in 1915. The employers, after the operation of the agreement during an unbroken period of five years, found some of its provisions irksome and demanded radical changes. The workers, who had by this time built up a permanent and powerful organization under trained leadership, resolutely refused to accede to the demands. An open fight

seemed imminent, and both sides prepared for it. The controversy was largely conducted in the press, each side endeavoring
to secure public sympathy and support for its cause.

At this critical juncture, in the month of May, 1915, the grand
jury of New York County found an indictment of murder in the
first degree against eight members and leaders of the cloakmakers union.

I was retained by the union as chief defense counsel, and no
case I have ever handled caused me greater anxiety and concern.

Among the defendants was Morris Sigman, the general secre-
tary-treasurer of the International Ladies' Garment Workers'
Union, of which the cloak makers' union was part, and one of
the most trusted and popular leaders of the organization. Two
of the other defendants held prominent positions, while the rest
were somewhat inconspicuous members of the union.

The case was grave in the extreme. Upon its outcome depended not only the life or death of eight human beings, but the
whole existence of the union. A conviction would brand it as a
criminal organization and would inevitably lead to demoralization and dissolution.

The task of the defense was baffling and tantalizing. All
that could be learned from the meager language of the indictment was that the alleged murder was committed on August 1,
1910, and that the victim was named Herman Liebowitz.

The name was not unknown to the union men. It was connected with the only incident which marred the otherwise
orderly and peaceful strike of 1910. Liebowitz was one of a
group of workers who had been found employed as strike breakers in an out-of-town shop and had been persuaded to abandon
their jobs and to join the ranks of the strikers. They had come
to one of the union meeting halls for that purpose, and as they
left they found themselves in a mêlée with a crowd of strikers
on the sidewalk in front of the hall. A fight started; blows were
freely exchanged on both sides. Liebowitz was struck and fell

on the pavement. He was picked up with a fractured skull by a policeman and taken to the hospital, where he died the next morning. The police investigated the case and were unable to discover the assailant. Upon a coroner's inquest the jury returned a verdict of death from a fractured skull "caused in a manner unknown to the jury." The case was dropped and generally forgotten.

What had happened to revive it after a lapse of five years? What was the evidence upon which it was now sought to fasten the crime on the eight men? On these momentous questions so essential to a successful defense, we were left absolutely in the dark, except for a mere hint, which was conveyed by the names of two grand jury witnesses endorsed on the indictment. These two men were known to be connected with a notorious strike-breaking outfit.

It must be remembered that, even in the best days of the union and the associations of employers and the periods of most harmonious coöperation between them, there always were groups of unscrupulous employers and some undisciplined workers constitutionally incapable of submitting to ordered and decent relations. These "bootleg" elements in the industry were a thorn in the flesh of the organized employers and workers alike. Around 1915 these employers were served by an underworld gang, whose business it was to furnish cheap nonunion labor and to "protect" nonunion shops. To pursue their nefarious activities more effectively they operated under the guise of a labor union and adopted a name closely resembling that of the legitimate union, which they carried until stopped by a court injunction.

This then was presumably the source of the prosecution. But what was its theory and its version of the Liebowitz killing?

Associated with me in the defense were William M. K. Olcott, an able and prominent lawyer and former district attorney of New York County, and Abraham Levy and Henry W.

Unger, outstanding members of the criminal bar. Max S. Levine, later a judge of the Court of General Sessions, who was then a very young man, also helped in the defense. We were groping in the dark until we succeeded in securing a transcript of the grand jury minutes. Then the situation appeared more desperate and baffling than ever.

Of the fourteen witnesses who had testified before the grand jury, no less than eight claimed to have seen the murder with their own eyes. The substance of their story was that Liebowitz and several other strike breakers had been brought to one of the union headquarters in New York from Hunter in the Catskills, where they worked in a "scab shop." Called to account for their conduct, they excused themselves on the ground of extreme poverty and pleaded to be allowed to go, solemnly promising to stand by the strikers and the union ever thereafter. They were detained until midnight, when Morris Sigman, who presided, ordered all but members of the "picket committee" out of the hall. The committee which remained with the Liebowitz group become the eight defendants. A few minutes later the strike breakers left the meeting hall, closely followed by the committee. When they reached the sidewalk, Morris Sigman struck Liebowitz over the head with an iron pipe or other heavy instrument, and when he fell to the ground the other defendants struck and kicked the prostrate body until they made sure of their deadly job and then ran away in different directions. The story was told with elaborate and gruesome detail.

It was by no means free from suspicion on the face of it. Each of the eight alleged eye-witnesses had come to the meeting hall on a separate mission, and each had concealed himself in a separate hidden recess on the opposite side of the street from which he had a full and free view of the murder scene. All of them had kept silent about the crime for five years, and now suddenly appeared to testify without prearrangement among themselves. There were besides numerous minor discrepancies in the stories of the different witnesses.

On the other hand, most of these witnesses had been union men and some claimed to have held responsible offices in the strike of 1910. Their charges were plain, direct, and mutually corroborative—and there were eight of them. Against this formidable array of positive witnesses we had nothing but the naked denials of the defendants. On what line of defense could we rely to batter down the seemingly impregnable case of the prosecution? Time and again our legal board of strategy approached the question from every conceivable angle. There were no eye-witnesses to contradict the version of the witnesses for the prosecution. Most of these witnesses were so obscure and so barren of any record that they could not even be discredited on the basis of general character and reputation. The last resort in criminal defenses—the alibi, was also out of the question. How could any person be expected to remember where he was and what he did at a certain day and hour five years earlier, when nothing had transpired during all these years to focus his attention on the particular date?

In the meantime the trial was approaching. On motion of the district attorney the court had ordered a "struck" jury i.e., a special panel of talesmen carefully chosen from the "better elements" of the community. We were thus likely to have a jury of conservative business men. How could we expect to imbue persons of this caliber with sympathy and understanding for the type of men they were called upon to judge—men of an entirely different world from theirs—workers, trade unionists, and foreigners?

In different forms and variations the question occupied my mind day and night. It haunted me and became a veritable and tantalizing obsession. Then, almost on the eve of the trial, the answer came to me in an illuminating flash.

After all, what was it that made me so thoroughly convinced

of the innocence of my clients? I knew few of them personally and those not intimately. And yet it did not even occur to me to weigh the concrete and detailed charges of their accusers against their own dry and naked denial. I took it for granted that the story of the eight witnesses for the prosecution, in spite of its outward convincingness, was a web of lies, and that none of the defendants was in any way implicated in the killing of Liebowitz. Why? Because I felt that the theory of the prosecution was utterly incompatible with the whole background of the workers' struggle, the aims and spirit of their union and the character and method of their leaders. I knew the depth of suffering and degradation which finally drove the cloakmakers into open revolt. The strike of 1910 was not a wanton riot of a reckless and violent mob. It was an earnest struggle for elementary human rights and tolerable lives. It was a crusade that brought out what was best and noblest in a mass of fifty thousand oppressed and abused workers and united them all in a new spirit of faith, hope, and solidarity reminiscent of the great popular movements for liberation in all ages. I knew the type and psychology of their leaders. I had worked with them and lived with them. They bared their hearts and souls to me. They were not criminals, not murderers.

Their highest aim and ideal were to include all workers in their union. They welcomed every converted nonunion man or strike breaker with open arms. It was preposterous to think that they would assault and kill a sinner returning to the fold.

On the other hand, I knew the nefarious character of the organized forces behind the prosecution and their criminal practices. I had fought them in court. I was certain that they would not scruple to perjure their souls and to forswear the lives of eight men in their relentless warfare against the union.

My belief in the innocence of the accused men was not based on the particular facts in the case but on my intimate knowledge of the whole background and surroundings, and our best chance to win was to impart that knowledge to the court and the jury, to make them see the case as I saw it.

With this thought in mind I hastily discarded almost all lines of defense I had tentatively adopted and resolved that my part in the defense would mainly consist of a course of instruction in the labor problem with particular reference to the conditions of the workers in the cloak industry and the aims and methods of their organized struggles for betterment.

The trial opened on the 23rd day of September, 1915, and was concluded on the 8th of October.

The prosecution finished the presentation of its evidence. Under the skillful direction of Assistant District Attorney James A. Delahanty it had built up a prima facie case along the lines foreshadowed by the grand-jury minutes.

It was now our turn to outline the defense to the jury. Here was the crucial point. The district attorney had steadfastly maintained that this was an ordinary criminal prosecution and did not involve any issue of labor or trade unionism. If he should object to my dissertation along the line I intended to follow and the judge should sustain him, our whole strategy would fail and the main foundation of our planned defense would collapse. The first few sentences of my opening address would decide the all-important question. I proceeded cautiously, feeling my way as I went along.

"In his very able opening," I began, "Mr. Delahanty asserted that this case did not involve any issue between capital and labor. We cheerfully acquiesce in this statement in so far as the direct charge and the intentions and motives of the prosecuting attorney are concerned. But, gentlemen of the jury, the testimony already before you has clearly demonstrated that this case is essentially a labor union case as much as there ever was a labor union case tried in a criminal court.

"It is not contended by the prosecution that these defendants committed the crime sought to be laid at their door for personal motives of either gain or revenge. It is asserted that these defendants were instrumental in taking the life of Liebowitz as union men and strikers, as an incident of the general strike of cloakmakers of 1910, and the District Attorney does not even contend that it was an accident. It was, according to his version, a logical happening to be explained by the conditions and circumstances of that strike, and we therefore maintain that in order that you, gentlemen, may be able to judge of the guilt or innocence of these defendants, it is not enough to lay before you the dry facts of the occurrence of that fatal night of the 31st of July, 1910. You are entitled to know who these men at the bar are and what they represent; what was the nature and character of that common enterprise that united them in 1910, and as a result of which it is claimed this unfortunate tailor came to his death. You are entitled to know the nature and the character, not only of these defendants but of the organization which they represent. You are entitled to see the background of the occurrence, the general strike with all it meant and all it produced, and for this reason I propose to outline before you briefly and concisely, but as connectedly as I can, all the essential facts in this case that will shed any light upon the probable guilt or innocence of these defendants."*

I was not interrupted. The preliminary skirmish was won, and for the next three hours I had my first seminar with the jury on the social, economic, and psychological aspects of the labor movement.

I took them back to the wretched homes and shops of the cloak workers before 1910 to explain the reasons and causes of the general strike of that year. I summarized the principal demands of the strikers and pointed out what they meant to them in terms of food and shelter, of health and human dignity, of opportunity for rearing and educating their children.

I unfolded before them a complete picture of the strike itself

* I quote from the official stenographic transcript.

as seen from the inside, its organization, methods, spirit, and achievements, and only when this foundation of economic facts and human suffering and struggle was laid I proceeded to the facts of the Hunter shop and to the history, character, and practices of the strike-breaking agency whose owners were among the principal witnesses for the prosecution.

In every important trial, particularly in a criminal case, there is always a courtroom atmosphere of sympathy or hostility. It may be produced by a plea of counsel or the manner of a witness or some other incident of the trial. It may manifest itself in the tone of the judge or the facial expressions of the jury, or it may be just "in the air." It is indefinable, and yet an experienced lawyer immediately senses it and notices every change of its mood. After my opening address we had for the first time during the trial a distinct feeling of a friendly court atmosphere.

Then each of the defendants took the stand in his own behalf. Almost without exception they were clean-cut, straightforward, and intelligent, and made an excellent impression on the jury by their sincerity and earnestness. Each of them told of his part in the strike and furnished additional sidelights on the aims and methods of the union. The economic and social education of the jurors thus continued for another week.

Then came the summing up, the charge of the court, and the deliberation of the jury.

One of the defendants had been discharged before the trial for insufficiency of evidence against him before the grand jury. Two additional defendants were acquitted at the close of the case on motion of the district attorney. The case of the remaining five went to the jury.

The jury was out only about two hours, but these were the most anxious hours in the lives of the defendants, their counsel, their union leaders, and the thousands of cloakmakers who thronged the corridors and swarmed in black masses in the street below. As the clock ticked off minute by minute in the oppressive stillness of the waiting courtroom, it seemed to be marking the passing of ages.

Suddenly the courtroom again became all life, action and expectancy. The solemn-faced judge ascended the bench. The jury filed in and took their seats. The fateful question, "Gentlemen of the jury, have you agreed on a verdict? The tense and breathless few seconds while the foreman arose to enunciate clearly the ardently hoped for and all-redeeming "Not guilty," was followed by a frenzy of joy and emotion, of tears and hysterical laughter.

BOOK II

DURING THE WAR

FOREWORD

THE World War lasted only a little over four years. Our participation in it was limited to about eighteen months. Personally, I was in no way involved in the actual combat. Yet the war affected my course of life and modified my whole outlook more deeply than any other event.

In common with hosts of others I was dismayed by the sudden collapse of human reason and the ugly sight of the world denuded of its thin veneer of civilization. But added to this feeling and rendering it unbearably poignant was the realization of the failure of the Socialist International in the supreme hour of the crisis, the shattering of cherished illusions about the temper and power of the Socialist movement, and the desertion of so many of its trusted leaders.

Before the 1st day of August, 1914, the Socialist movement seemed thoroughly harmonious in character and aim throughout the world. The Socialists of all countries were united in common struggle against the capitalist system everywhere. They professed a closer community of interest with their fellow workers in other lands than with the ruling classes of their own countries. They were solemnly pledged against all capitalist wars.

Upon the outbreak of the war the Socialists in both hostile camps overwhelmingly rallied to their capitalistic governments, and for four years millions of men who had called one another comrades were engaged in the ghastly business of mutual slaughter.

What was the nature of the sinister virus that had infected the movement and changed it overnight?

In spite of the many years that have elapsed since the fateful August days of 1914, I feel that the time is not yet ripe for a dispassionate analysis of the astouuding phenomenon. This will be the task of historians of more distant and calmer days, the historians of post-war generations.

Here I shall merely jot down some random thoughts on the subject and recount a few significant episodes in which I happened to play a part during the bewildering developments of the tragic years.

CHAPTER I

THE SOCIALIST INTERNATIONAL

SOCIALISM is not inherently a pacifist creed. The philosophy of Karl Marx is one of struggle. It was largely influenced by the biological discoveries of his great contemporary, Charles Darwin, and the conception of the struggle for existence as a lever of progress. The founders of the modern Socialist movement appraised every war by the practical test of its probable effects on the condition of the working classes and the progress of democracy. They frankly supported the more promising side and did not reject war as war.

In the course of time, however, the Socialist stand on war gradually developed into one of general opposition. The altered attitude was not due to a change of heart as much as to what the Socialists conceived as a change of the character of modern wars.

The European wars for liberation or national unification had come to a close by the seventies of the last century synchronously with the emergence of large-scale industry and the consolidation of the national capitalist states.

Henceforward wars, as a rule, were capitalist fights for world markets, imperialistic struggles tending to increase the wealth and power of the possessing classes and to place the whole burden of suffering and loss of life upon the workers.

Modern wars, actual or threatened, furthermore inevitably lead to evergrowing armaments and corresponding enhancement of the military power of the ruling classes. They also tend to breed national passions and prejudices, to divert the attention of the workers from their class interests, and to break their bond of international solidarity.

These views found their most finished expression in the famous anti-war resolution adopted at the international Socialistic Congress held at Stuttgart in 1907.

The resolution included an appeal to the workers of all countries and their parliamentary representatives to use all means in their power to prevent war whenever and wherever it threatened to break out; to work for a speedy peace if war should be declared in spite of their efforts, "and to take advantage of the opportunities offered by the economic and political crises brought about by the war by arousing public sentiment to hasten the overthrow of the capitalist class rule."

Significantly the concluding sentence was added at the suggestion of Nicolai Lenin, who was a delegate to the Stuttgart Congress.

From that time the preservation of peace became a regular and important part of the Socialist propaganda.

In November, 1912, when the Balkan War threatened to precipitate a world conflict, the International Socialist Bureau hurriedly convoked a special international congress at Basel, which was attended by 555 delegates from practically all countries of Europe, and adopted a ringing resolution calling upon the working classes to oppose the imperialistic policies of their governments with all the power at their command. It was a solemn and impressive demonstration and was credited with having exerted a serious influence in localizing and eventually terminating the war.

From June 28, 1914, the fateful date of the assassination of Archduke Franz Ferdinand, up to the first days of August, the Socialists of all countries made frantic efforts to avert the war, and organized numerous peace demonstrations in the principal cities of Europe.

The Socialist Party of France met in national conference in the middle of July and pronounced itself in emphatic terms against war, going to the extent of favoring a general strike "simultaneously and internationally organized" as a supreme measure to halt the threatened outbreak. A more radical resolution urging general strikes in each country regardless of the action of the workers in other countries was offered by the old communard Edouard Vaillant and supported by the rabid anti-militarist Gustav Hervé. It was opposed by Jules Guèsdes, the leader of the Marxian wing of French Socialism, on the ground that the principle, if adopted, would tend to deliver the countries of the most advanced Socialist movements to the domination of the most backward countries.

Upon the outbreak of the war Edouard Vaillant and Gustave Hervé turned chauvinist patriots and enraged war enthusiasts, and Jules Guèsdes became a member of France's first war cabinet.

The last concerted move of international Socialism to stem the tide of war was attempted at an emergency session of the International Socialist Bureau, which was held in Brussels on July 27th and 28th. It was a sad and disheartening meeting. Brave words were spoken and aggressive resolutions were taken, but the black shadow of the World War already hung over the gathering. Even while its deliberations were in progress Austria declared war on Serbia. Of the advocates of the general strike only the indomitable Scotch enthusiast J. Keir Hardie stuck to the program as one capable of immediate and successful application, while Victor Adler, the sober-minded veteran leader of Austrian Social Democracy, admitted with a heavy heart that all expectation of international proletarian action against the war, once it had been declared, was a vain delusion. The meeting concluded with a gigantic peace demonstration, the outstanding feature of which was a passionate and moving condemnation of war by Jean Jaurès. It was to be the last speech of the world's most eloquent champion of peace. The next day, on his return to Paris, discouraged but not dismayed, he was assassinated by a war-crazed fanatic.

On the 1st of August the Socialist Party of Germany issued a stirring manifesto against the war, calling upon the workers to rally to Socialism "as the great bond between nations," and on the 2nd the Labor Party of Great Britain organized a powerful peace demonstration in London. On the 4th of August the war was on, and the Socialists of all belligerent countries actively participated in it, generally without protest, often with enthusiasm.

What accounts for the sudden *volte-face* of the European Socialists?

One of the weak spots of the Socialist anti-war position before 1914 was the distinction which it drew between wars of aggression and wars of defense. Its opposition was directed mainly against the former variety, while the leaders of the movement, including such a thoroughgoing internationalist as August Bebel, invariably proclaimed it to be the duty of the Socialists to rally to the defense of their country in case of attack.

That the distinction is wholly ephemeral in modern warfare was clearly proved on the outbreak of the war. Every belligerent nation claimed and probably believed that it was attacked, and that its war was purely defensive.

With respect to Belgium and France, the defensive character of the war seemed obvious, while the people of Germany and Austria were made to feel that their countries were in imminent danger of invasion by the "hordes of Russian barbarians." The skillfully stimulated fears of invasion degenerated into a hysterical panic and turned peace-loving peoples into howling, war-mad mobs.

On the 1st of August, Herman Müller, a prominent Socialist

leader and subsequently Chancellor of the German republic, conferred with the parliamentary group of the French Socialists in Paris and informed his comrades that the only question before the Social Democratic members of the Reichstag was whether they would abstain from voting war credits or vote against them. Three days later Hugo Haase, as chairman of the party, cast the vote of German Social Democracy in favor of the war credits asked by the government. "To prevent the triumph of Russian despotism," he announced, "we now make good what we always promised. In the hour of danger we rally to the defense of Germany."

It is rather idle to speculate about what the Socialists would have done in 1914 if they had not been committed to the theoretical distinction between wars of aggression and wars of defense. The chances are that they would have followed the same general course. In any event, the nationalistic fears and passions engendered by the World War would probably have proved stronger than the reasoned ideal of working internationalism. Great social and political events have a provoking way of ignoring abstract declarations of principle. Still, the way of the transgressors in all Socialist camps might have been made a little more difficult in the absence of an accepted sanction of "defensive" wars, and their peace efforts might have come earlier and been pursued more vigorously.

Since the war international Social Democracy has practically abandoned the distinction between wars of aggression and wars of defense and has developed a marked tendency in the direction of absolute pacifism.

The customary statement that "the Socialists of Europe supported the war" is furthermore too absolute and sweeping. As a matter of fact it is entirely true only with respect to the Socialists of Belgium and France.

While the Social Democratic Party in the German Reichstag

cast its vote as a unit in favor of the war credits, it appeared subsequently that the decision of the parliamentary group was by no means unanimous. Fourteen members had voted in caucus against supporting the war, but submitted to the majority as a matter of party discipline. It is interesting to note in this connection that Hugo Haase, who read the official party declaration of loyalty in the Reichstag, was one of the most vigorous dissenters.

In England a considerable section of Socialists led by J. Keir Hardie, J. Ramsay MacDonald, and Philip Snowden, remained true to their pacifist creed and consistently opposed the war.

In Russia only a portion of the right wing of Social Democracy, the "Mensheviki," led by George Plekhanoff, the foremost Russian Marxist, supported the war. The fourteen Socialist deputies of the Duma voted unanimously against war credits, with a strong statement of condemnation of the "imperialistic war."

The Socialists of Italy opposed the entry of their country into the war on either side and remained consistent opponents of the war after their hesitating and haggling government had executed its cold-blooded *volte-face* and joined the forces of the Allies against its erstwhile treaty associates. There was only one notable instance of betrayal in their ranks. The editor-in-chief of the *Avanti* and titular head of the Party, while the country was still neutral, published an article in the Party paper advocating war participation on the side of the Allies. He was immediately removed from his office and expelled from the party—and later wreaked savage vengeance on his former comrades. His name was Benito Mussolini.

As the war continued and the intoxication of the conflict wore off, the Socialists gradually sobered up. The number of war opponents in their ranks grew, and their efforts to bring about peace and to reëstablish the broken bond of international Socialist solidarity increased.

In France a minority group of anti-chauvinist Socialists, under the leadership of Jean Longuet and Paul Faure, was constituted by the middle of 1915 and steadily gained strength. In the early part of 1917 the "minority group" of peace advocates had become the majority in the Socialist Party.

A number of Socialist deputies in the French parliament voted against new war credits and Socialist participation in the government ceased.

During the same time an organized anti-war faction was springing up among the Socialists of Germany. Karl Liebknecht and Rosa Luxemburg inaugurated an underground agitation for a general strike to stop the war, while an increasing number of Socialist Reichstag members favored refusal of war credits as a measure of forcing the government into peace negotiations. In December, 1915, nineteen Socialist deputies, including Hugo Haase and the veteran Eduard Bernstein, openly voted against further war credits. The antagonism between the war Socialists and anti-war Socialists became so sharp that there was an open rupture. The anti-war Socialists left the party and founded the Independent Socialist Party, which grew steadily in numbers and in influence among the German workers.

Simultaneously with these developments, efforts were being made to organize international action in favor of peace among Socialists of all countries, neutral and belligerent. Under the existing war conditions the task proved well-nigh impossible of performance. Most of these attempts failed, including one initiated by the Socialists of the United States, who sought to convoke an international Socialist peace congress in Washington, D.C.

It was not until September, 1915, that the first semblance of a general international conference was realized, the romantic and now historic Zimmerwald Congress. The initiative in calling the conference was taken by the Socialists of Italy and Switzerland. Its organization and preparations were kept secret. The delegates, thirty-one in number, were instructed to report at the Socialist headquarters in Bern, and from there were quietly conveyed to the little village of Zimmerwald in Switzerland, where the proceedings were conducted without publicity in a small room in the village hotel. The participants had come from ten different countries, including Germany, France, Italy, and Russia. They denounced the war as imperialistic in origin and character, urged an immediate democratic peace and appointed a permanent committee charged with the task of reuniting the Socialist parties of the world on the basis of its platform.

The conference proved to be the starting point of a concerted Socialist anti-war movement. Not less than thirty-three Socialist parties or organized groups from twenty different countries, neutral and belligerent, including the Socialist Party of the United States, endorsed the Zimmerwald program and pledged their adherence to the movement.

In April, 1916, a second and larger conference of the same character was held in Kienthal, likewise a little village in the vicinity of Bern.

But the decisive change in the Socialist war attitude was brought about by the Russian revolution of March, 1917. That revolution was a world event, which for the time being overshadowed even the war. Russian absolutism, for generations the main bulwark of European reaction, had suddenly been overthrown and was replaced by a liberal democratic régime, supported and largely maintained by the working classes under Socialist leadership. The Russian revolution was to a great extent a revolt against the war. The powerful Council of Workers and Soldiers issued a stirring appeal to the world for an immediate peace "without annexations or indemnities and with the right of all peoples to freely dispose of themselves." It created an entirely new situation for the Socialists in both belligerent camps. Those of the Central Powers could no longer justify their support of the war by the specter of a triumphant Russian despotism. Those of the Allied countries had no excuse for rejecting the peace program of their Russian comrades. To the Socialists of the whole world, peace had become an urgent necessity not only for its own sake, but also for the preservation of democracy and for the success of the rapidly growing Socialist and labor movement of Russia.

It was under these circumstances that the official machinery of the dormant Socialist International was set in motion for the first time since the outbreak of the war, to convoke a world congress of Socialism for peace. The immediate initiative came from the Socialists of Holland. With the formal approval of what remained of the International Bureau, the governing body of the Socialist International, a committee, representing the Socialist parties of Holland and the Scandinavian countries, was constituted and issued a call for a general Socialist conference to be held in Stockholm on the 15th day of May, 1917. The order of business was stated to be the "examination of the international situation," and invitations were issued to all affiliated parties in the countries at war as well as in the neutral countries. Later the organization committee was reinforced by representatives of the Socialist parties in Russia.

The movement was enthusiastically acclaimed by the Socialists all over the world. Practically every party affiliated with the International accepted the invitation and elected delegates to the Stockholm conference. But the conference was never held. It was frustrated by the action of the United States government.

I was designated by the Socialist Party of America as a delegate to the Stockholm conference together with Victor L. Berger and Algernon Lee, and immediately applied for a passport. I considered the application a mere formality since American citizens were freely permitted to travel abroad during the war on any legitimate business, but my application was promptly denied by Secretary of State Lansing, who attempted to justify his action in a lengthy public statement.

Mr. Lansing characterized the proposed Stockholm conference as "a cleverly directed German war move." The charge was absurd, since the plan originated in neutral countries and the Socialists of the Central Powers would constitute a decided minority in any general international Socialist congress. Moreover, the generally accepted Socialist peace program—"the evacuation of all occupied foreign territory and peace without indemnities or annexations and with the right of the peoples to freely dispose of themselves" was by no means one favored by Germany in May, 1917. It was on the contrary in full accord with the American war aims as formulated by President Wilson just twenty-four hours before Mr. Lansing's announcement. The Stockholm conference could be described with more seeming reason as an Allied peace move than as a German war move.

The legal justification for the action of the state department was even more curious than its diplomatic motives.

It appears that a way back in the days of George Washington—to be exact, in 1799—one Logan, a leader of the Society of Friends and a prominent Pennsylvania politician, had made a tour of France on a self-constituted mission to reconcile the governments of the two nations, whose diplomatic relations had just been severed.

To prevent the recurrence of unauthorized meddling in the foreign policies of the country, Congress enacted a law making it a crime punishable by a fine of $5,000 and imprisonment for not less than six months for any American citizen to negotiate with a foreign government "in relation to any dispute or controversies with the United States" without permission or authority of the government. The law, popularly known as the Logan Act, passively encumbered the statute books for 118 years, when it was for the first time invoked by the state department in our case.

Mr. Lansing took pains to emphasize that his action was not "a reflection upon the sincerity of the Socialists of this country," but law is law.

I was deeply disappointed by the refusal of passports and went to Washington in an effort to persuade the department to lift the ban. I argued that the Socialist parties of Europe were not governments and had no disputes or controversies with the United States, and that there seemed to be no reason why American Socialists should not urge upon the workers of the world the adoption of a peace program which the American President publicly advocated. My plea was in vain. Politely and firmly I was told that the decision would stand.

The governments of France and Italy followed the policy of our state department even without the sanction of a Logan Act.

The English government had consented to issue passports to the delegates of the Labor Party, but subsequently withdrew its consent under pressure of the "Allied and Associated" Powers. The reversal of policy towards the Stockholm conference created a lively controversy in British politics and led to the resignation of Arthur Henderson from the concentrated war cabinet of Lloyd George.

An international Socialist peace conference without participation of the parties in the Allied countries was, of course, unthinkable, but the "Stockholm idea" was not abandoned. The organization committee constituted itself into a permanent body with the object of ascertaining and collating the views of the Socialist parties of all countries on a peace program and on ways and means of reëstablishing the Socialist International.

To this end a questionnaire was prepared and submitted to all affiliated parties. Elaborate written replies were received from twenty-three parties in sixteen countries, including all principal countries at war, and a large number of oral reports were made to the committee by such delegations as managed to get to Stockholm.

Stockholm became the Mecca of the war-weary Socialists. Its proceedings were widely reported, though often distorted, by the press of the whole world. As an instrument of peace propaganda it was infinitely more effective than one regular international Socialist conference ever could have been. Its significance for the Socialist movement lay in the fact that it marked the abatement of war enthusiasm on both sides of the firing lines, demonstrated general agreement on the most essential points of the peace program and laid the foundation for the resumption of international Socialist coöperation.

CHAPTER II

THE AMERICAN SOCIALISTS

UNTIL our entry into the war the Socialists of the United States were practically a unit in their condemnation of the European conflict.

Separated from the battle fields by the vast expanse of the Atlantic Ocean and unaffected by the immediate objects of the quarrels between the belligerent powers, they could see nothing in the war except a savage carnage, a collapse of the international Socialist movement, and a danger to human civilization.

Throughout the period of American neutrality their untiring efforts were centered on three main objectives—to reëstablish harmonious coöperation between the Socialists of the different countries, to urge a speedy and lasting peace, and to keep the United States out of the war.

As early as September, 1914, the Socialist Party of the United States invited the Socialists of all countries to send delegates to an international conference to be held in Washington, D.C., "for the discussion of ways and means to most speedily and effectively stop the war." The invitation was transmitted by cable to the Socialist parties of France, Belgium, England, Germany, Austria, Italy, Holland, Sweden, and Denmark, as well as to the Bureau of the Socialist International.

In view of the precarious financial conditions in Europe the Party offered to pay the traveling expenses of all delegates. It was figured that the cost would be in the neighborhood of $200,000, and the American Socialists were confident that they

159

could raise the money for the extraordinary undertaking by voluntary contributions; but the generous gesture remained without practical results. The Socialists of the belligerent countries had neither the facilities nor the desire to meet for a general peace confab one month after the outbreak of the war.

All subsequent efforts made by other Socialist parties to reunite the International during the war were actively supported by the American Socialists.

In January, 1917, the party once more attempted to take the initiative in convoking a full international congress, this time at The Hague, to set in motion "a concerted working-class movement for an immediate, just and lasting peace." The proposed conference was set for June 3. America was itself deep in the war before the date arrived.

The Socialist Party of the United States may justly claim the credit of the first formulation of a comprehensive program of what later came to be known as a "democratic peace."

In May, 1915, the National Committee of the Party adopted a manifesto, which I had prepared at its request, and which contained an analysis of the historical, political, and economic causes that precipitated the war, and a statement of the main reasons for Socialist opposition to war and militarism.

The peace program embodied in the manifesto included the following terms:

(1) No indemnities.

(2) No transfer of territories except upon the consent and by the vote of their people.

(3) All countries under foreign rule to be given political independence if demanded by their inhabitants.

(4) An international parliament with legislative and administrative powers over international affairs and with permanent committees, in place of present secret diplomacy.

(5) Universal disarmament as speedily as possible.

(6) Political and industrial democracy.

The Socialist Party of the United States thus anticipated by two years, the terse slogan of the Russian Council of Workers and Soldiers, "no annexations or contributions and the right of peoples to dispose of themselves," and anticipated by three years some of the Fourteen Points of President Wilson.

As a method of enforcing its peace program the Socialist Party proposed that "the President of the United States convoke a congress of neutral nations, which shall offer mediation to the belligerents and remain in permanent session until the termination of the war."

A resolution to that effect was offered in the House of Representatives by Meyer London, its lone Socialist member, and the party appointed a committee to urge the plan upon the President. The committee was composed of Meyer London, James H. Maurer of Reading, Pennsylvania, a veteran in the Socialist and trade-union movement, and myself. Our interview with Woodrow Wilson proved exceedingly interesting.

The President received us in the White House at the appointed hour, among many other delegations who had come to see him on various missions. He looked preoccupied and tired, and at first seemed inclined to give us a short and perfunctory hearing; but as we proceeded with our argument he became interested and animated and our interview developed into a serious and confidential conversation. Mr. Wilson, after some general discussion of the international situation and the terms of our peace program, informed us that he had had a similar plan under consideration, but that he hesitated to put it to the test because he felt uncertain about its reception by the other neutral nations.

"The fact is," he asserted, "that the United States is the only important country that may be said to be neutral and disinterested. Practically all other neutral countries are in one way or another tied up with some belligerent power and dependent on it."

He hinted at the possibility of a direct offer of mediation by the government of the United States and assured us that he would continue to study the question with deep and serious interest.

Throughout the interview I acted as spokesman for our committee; but as we got up, ready to take our leave, James Maurer, looking at the President with steady and appraising eyes, delivered himself with slow and pondering tones of the following sentiment: "Your promises sound good, Mr. President, but the trouble with you is that you are surrounded by capitalist and militarist interests who want the war to continue; and I fear you will succumb to their influence."

The Pennsylvania-Dutch bluntness of my diplomatic colleague evoked an amused smile on the pale and intellectual face of Woodrow Wilson.

"If the truth be known," he said, "I am more often accused of being influenced by radical and pacifist elements than by the capitalist or militarist interests."

This ended our interview. I have often thought of it, wondering whether subsequent events did not bear out the apprehension of James Maurer rather than the reassurance of Woodrow Wilson.

The third objective of the Socialist Party, to keep the country out of the war, at first did not meet serious resistance. On the contrary it seemed fully in accord with the policy of the government and the temper of the nation. The President had enjoined the people of the United States to remain neutral "in thought as well as in action." Our statesmen, newspapers, and churches joined in a chorus of condemnation of the war and abhorrence at its atrocities. Pacifism was the vogue, and the Socialist anti-war propaganda generally met with favorable response.

But as the war went on the "neutrality of thought" was gradually abandoned in certain quarters, and voices began to be heard, speculating on the possibility of American participation. It is undoubtedly true that the change of sentiment was largely induced by American business interests, which became more and more entangled in the fortunes of the Allied arms, but it cannot be denied that many Americans were moved by sincere sympathy for the Allies, especially in view of the truthless methods of German warfare.

The unrestricted use of submarine boats by Germany made the task of American pacifists extremely difficult. The cold-blooded and atrocious destruction of American lives on the *Lusitania* furnished the first pretext for an open and aggressive war propaganda by militarist interests and the jingo press.

The Socialist Party immediately issued a solemn warning to the people of the United States against the dangerous agitation. "No disaster, however appalling, no crime, however revolting, justifies the slaughter of nations and the devastation of countries," it proclaimed. "The destruction of the *Lusitania* and the killing of hundreds of non-combatants, men, women and children, on board the steamer, brings more closely home to us the fiendish savagery of warfare and should inspire us with stronger determination than ever to maintain peace and civilization at any cost."

The U-boat controversy slumbered for more than a year, during which time a Presidential election took place, and Woodrow Wilson was triumphantly reëlected, largely on the strength of the reminder that "he has kept us out of the war."

Then the controversy was revived and led to the severance of our diplomatic relations with Germany, a certain prelude to declaration of war.

The National Executive Committee of the Socialist Party on my motion issued a proclamation of protest, which read in part as follows:

"Europe is a dread house of mourning in which the disconsolate sobs of the widows and orphans at home mingle with the agonized groans of the wounded and dying on the battlefield.

"In this savage carnival of wholesale and indiscriminate murder, there was but one powerful member of the family of nations that preserved an attitude of comparative sanity—the United States of America. Removed by the vast stretch of the Atlantic Ocean from the scene of the inhuman conflict, safe in our economic self-sufficiency, and proud of our advanced and democratic institutions, we watched the self-destruction of our European brothers with bleeding hearts, eagerly waiting for the opportunity to bring them back to reason and peace, to life and happiness.

"And suddenly with little notice or warning, without the sanction or consent of the people and without consultation with the people's chosen representatives in Congress, we are practically ordered to join in the mad dance of death and destruction and to swell the ghastly river of blood in Europe with the blood of thousands of American workers."

.   .   .   .

"The policy of unrestricted and indiscriminate submarine warfare recently announced by the German Government is most ruthless and inhuman, but so is war as a whole and so are all methods applied by both sides.

"WAR IS MURDER!

"War is the climax of utter lawlessness and it is idle to prate about lawful or lawless methods of warfare.

"The German submarine warfare does not threaten our national integrity or independence, not even our national dignity and honor. It was not aimed primarily at the United States and would not affect the American people. It would strike only those parasitic classes that have been making huge profits by manufacturing instruments of death or taking away our food and selling it at exorbitant prices to the fighting armies of Europe.

"The workers of the United States have no reason and no desire to shed their blood for the protection and furtherance of the unholy profits of their masters and will not permit a lying and venal press to stampede them into taking up arms to murder their brothers in Europe.

"The six million men whose corpses are now rotting upon the battlefields of Europe were mostly workingmen. If the United States is drawn into war it will be the American workers whose lives will be sacrificed—an inglorious, senseless sacrifice on the altar of capitalist greed."

From that point on events moved with vertiginous and frightful rapidity.

The President called an extra session of Congress for April 16th for the purpose of declaring war on Germany. The Socialist Party called a special "emergency" convention for April 14th, to protest against the contemplated declaration.

Subsequently the date of the extra session was advanced to April 2nd, and the Socialist Party hurriedly changed its convention date to April 7th.

War was declared on April 6th, and the emergency convention of the Party opened in St. Louis the next day. It was a tense and nervous gathering of about two hundred delegates from all parts of the country. The sole business of the convention was to take a stand on the war just declared, and never did I witness a more solemn or dramatic proceeding.

Algernon Lee of New York, Charles E. Ruthenberg of Cleveland, and I were elected a subcommittee to prepare a proclamation and war program. Secluded in a small hotel room, we worked on the draft for many hours. We worked on it earnestly and tensely, carefully weighing every phrase and every word, but determined to state our position without circumlocution or equivocation, to leave nothing unsaid.

We put our whole soul into the proclamation, the agonized Socialist soul crying out in anguish against the savagery of war, against the needless sacrifice of American lives in the quarrels of clashing capitalist interests in Europe and against the atmosphere of passion, hatred, and terror which the war was sure to breed.

Our draft was adopted by the overwhelming majority of the convention delegates.

It was a powerful document bristling with strong statements. The preamble, after a searching analysis of the causes and effect of modern wars, rendered judgment against the war just declared in the following emphatic language:

"We brand the declaration of war by our government as a crime of our capitalist class against the people of the United States and against the nations of the world.

"In all modern history there has been no war more unjustifiable than the war in which we are about to engage."

The practical course of action recommended included:

"1. Continuous, active and public opposition to all capitalistic wars, through demonstrations, mass petitions and all other honorable and effective means within our power.

"2. Unyielding opposition to all proposed legislation for military or industrial conscription.

"3. Vigorous resistance to all reactionary measures, such as censorship of the press and mails, restriction of the rights of free speech, assemblage and organization, or compulsory arbitration and limitation of the right to strike."

How many times in the next two or three years did I have occasion to read familiar passages from the St. Louis proclamation in accusing and inciting newspaper editorials and in the reports of the numerous legislative committees set up to investigate "radical and seditious activities"; how many times did it fall to my lot to hear them dramatically declaimed in courtrooms by prosecuting attorneys!

It is estimated that during the war about two thousand persons were convicted under the Espionage Law and sentenced to terms of imprisonment aggregating twenty-five thousand years. In many if not most of these convictions the St. Louis proclamation played a large and fatal part.

As I read over the document after a lapse of sixteen years and in the calmer atmosphere of comparative peace and sobriety, I can find in its preamble nothing but a reiteration of the oft-expressed and well-known Socialist position on war, and in its program nothing that offended against the law. But it must be admitted that the tone of the proclamation was extraordinarily aggressive, defiant, and provocative. Had it been written in normal circumstances, it would undoubtedly have been couched in more moderate and less irritating language; but it was not written under normal circumstances. The authors of the instrument and the delegates to the convention were in a mood of tense exaltation. For three years they had witnessed the frightful ravages of the war and had carried on a relentless campaign against all movements to draw the United States into it; for three years they had felt mortified over the failure of their European comrades, and had vowed that they would remain true to international Socialism and world peace under all circumstances. And now the test had come. It had come with such stunning suddenness that they had no time for calm deliberation. Their poignant disappointment and their indignation sought expression in strong utterances.

It must also be borne in mind that at the time of the adoption of the St. Louis resolution the political and intellectual atmosphere of the country was still free from the stifling terrorism which a morbid war psychology created in later days. American citizens were accustomed to speaking their thoughts freely and unreservedly on all subjects, including war.

The doctrine that in time of war all criticism and opposition must cease was never accepted or even seriously urged before the days of the "liberal" administration of Woodrow Wilson. The War of 1812 was freely criticized in the press and at public meetings, and the Mexican War was condemned in unmeasured terms by such statesmen as Abraham Lincoln, Daniel Webster, Henry Clay, and Theodore Parker.

The St. Louis proclamation of the Socialist Party is mild in tone compared with the statement of Charles Sumner, who publicly characterized the Mexican War, while it was still on, in this language: "The Mexican War is an enormity born of slavery. . . . Base in object, atrocious in beginning, immoral in all its influences, vainly prodigal of treasure and life; it is a war of infamy, which must blot the pages of our history."

The reason why the accepted American doctrine of tolerance during war was superseded by a policy of narrow and rigid intolerance during our last war may be found in the peculiar circumstances of our entry into the war.

In practically all previous wars with foreign nations, the major political parties were divided in their support, treating the war as a political issue. As a rule the Republican Party was the war party, and the Democratic Party, the party of peace. Until the election of 1916 the Democratic Party maintained its traditional position in favor of peace, while the Republican Party inclined toward participation in the war. The Presidential campaign of that year was largely conducted on this issue. If Mr. Hughes had been elected instead of Mr. Wilson, as he almost was, the probable result would have been that the Republican Party would have drawn us into the war, while the Democratic Party would have remained in the opposition and continued to condemn the policy of "hurling us headlong into the maelstrom of the war across the seas," as did Martin H. Glynn in his eloquent keynote speech at the National Democratic Convention of 1916. But as it happened it was a Democratic administration that led us into this war. The Democratic Party thus changed from a peace party to a war party, leaving the Republicans no choice except to go it one better as an ultra-war party. The issue between the two old parties was no longer one of peace or war, but one of war or more war. This rivalry in jingoism and "superpatriotism" inevitably bred the atmosphere of hysteria and terror which obsessed America in the World War.

The only party that still remained a peace party in American politics was the Socialist Party, and that not in its entirety. A number of prominent party leaders, among them some who had been ultrapacifist during the period of our neutrality, became ardent supporters of the war and turned their backs on the Socialist movement. Those who remained loyal to the party and its anti-war stand bore the whole brunt of official chicanery and persecution which sprang up during the latter period of the war and continued long after the armistice. Socialist newspapers were refused second-class mailing rights or wholly excluded from the mails; Socialist meetings were suppressed, and Socialist speakers and writers were indicted and convicted by the score under the Draconic provisions of the Espionage Law.

The air was infested with spying, denunciations, and false accusations. No person suspected of radical or pacifist opinions was safe. The spirit of heresy hunting and witch burning had come back to America in the year of our Lord 1918.

CHAPTER III

THE ODYSSEY OF THE PEACE COUNCIL

WAR was declared and the Conscription Act was adopted. It was futile to cry out against the accomplished facts. The pacifist elements of America turned from a negative policy of protest against war to constructive proposals for an early peace. The movement was sponsored by men and women of different social and political faiths, Socialists, trade unionists, liberals, and conscientious objectors on religious grounds. It sprang up so spontaneously that it would be difficult to trace its exact origin and beginnings.

Several informal conferences were held here and there, and peace programs were discussed. Among the most active promoters of the movement at that time was Judah L. Magnes, a rabbi of an unusually fine type. Young, enthusiastic, eloquent, and of rare personal charm, he was rapidly becoming the idol of the wealthy Jews of New York and had before him a most promising career. But this Jewish rabbi was one of the very few divines who took the spirit and teachings of Christ seriously. He abhorred the brutality and inhumanity of war on the battle fields and the spirit of despotism and intolerance at home. He was sincere and courageous, and he threw himself into the fight headlong and in utter disregard of the admonitions of his shocked parishioners and patrons.

I came to know him well in those days of storm and stress, and my respect and affection for him grew with the acquaintance.

From our frequent desultory talks sprang a vague plan to organize the forces of peace and democracy on a permanent basis. A preliminary committee of volunteers was set up, and its first act was to call a public conference. The call was issued to a number of friendly organizations and individuals, and the conference was held on the 31st of May in the Garden Theatre in New York.

It was a memorable meeting. Open under the title "The First American Conference for Democracy and Terms of Peace," it was attended by representatives of a large number of organized bodies and a host of well-known Socialists and pacifists. Speeches were made and resolutions adopted demanding the repeal of the Conscription Law and pledging support to conscientious objectors. Enthusiasm ran high, and applause was vociferous in spite of the fact that the Department of Justice had given formal warning that the meeting would be watched, and that "obstructionists" would be arrested.

"All Secret Service men are invited to come to the platform so that they may see and hear better," Dr. Magnes blandly announced in opening the meeting. But the Department of Justice agents preferred to maintain their modest incognito.

The conference was meant to be mainly in the nature of a public demonstration, but its character and objects were unexpectedly changed under the inspiration of a young woman, Rebecca Shelly, who attended the meeting as the representative of an organization known as the Emergency Peace Federation. She was little known in radical or pacifist circles and somehow disappeared from the scene after the war, but in the formation and activities of the People's Council she played an important part. She was, in a way, the Maid of Orléans of the movement.

Rising towards the end of the deliberations, she addressed the audience in impassioned tones, declaring that Congress had ceased to represent the will of the people, and that the time had come to organize the citizens into a sort of informal government on the model of the Russian Council of Workers and Soldiers.

"The functions of the council," Miss Shelly argued, "would be to work for the repeal of the Conscription Law, to combat all violations of the constitutional rights of citizens, to urge an early and democratic peace on the terms announced by the Russian government, and to let the American people know that there is in existence a definitely constituted body through which the democratic forces of the country can express themselves. She proposed that the Council remain in permanent session, meeting for a month at a time in different cities and, in times of special crises, at Washington.

The suggestions of the young enthusiast met with instantaneous and whole-hearted approval. I was elected on a committee to draft a plan of permanent organization together with Dr. Magnes, Amos Pinchot, A. C. Townley, Emily Greene Balch, and Mary Ware Dennett.

Our plan was to create a nation-wide body at a constituent convention to be called for that purpose at an early date. In the meantime we set up a preliminary organization to take care of the preparatory work.

An office was opened at 2 West Thirteenth Street in New York, and a permanent name was adopted—"The People's Council for Democracy and Peace." Branch organizations were established in several parts of the country, and public demonstrations were held in New York, Philadelphia, Chicago, San Francisco, and Los Angeles.

No less than 284 organizations were represented at a conference which took place in New York towards the end of June. Of these 93 were trade unions, while the rest were local Socialist groups, peace organizations, and fraternal societies.

The list of individual members and supporters of the Council grew to formidable proportions. Its active leadership included, besides those already mentioned, ex-Senators John D. Works and R. F. Pettigrew, David Starr Jordan (president emeritus of Leland Stanford University), Fola La Follette (daughter of old "fighting Bob"), Bishop Paul Jones, Eugene V. Debs, Victor L. Berger, James H. Maurer, Scott Nearing, Algernon Lee, Norman Thomas, Job Harriman, George E. Roewer, Jacob Panken, Seymour Stedman, James Oneal, Max Eastman, Benjamin Schlesinger (general president of the International Ladies' Garment Workers' Union), Joseph Schlossberg (general secretary of the Amalgamated Clothing Workers' Union), Professor Harry W. L. Dana of Columbia University (a grandson of Henry Wadsworth Longfellow), Gilbert E. Roe, Mrs. Herbert Parsons, Florence Kelley, John Haynes Holmes, Roger Baldwin, Clara Packard, Louis Lochner, and many other men and women prominent in Socialist, radical, liberal, and pacifist circles.

The date of the constituent convention, which was to see the birth of the Council as a national body, was set as September 1st. The city of Minneapolis, Minnesota, was chosen as the place of the convention.

The choice was made on several considerations. The people of Minnesota were reputed to be generally friendly to the aims of the Council; the labor movement of Minneapolis was well organized and progressive and, above all, the mayor of the city, Thomas Van Lear, was a Socialist and a member of the Council.

The convention was staged on a grandiose scale. About two thousand delegates were expected, and accommodation was to be provided for no fewer than fifty thousand visitors. It was reported that farmers were preparing to come by automobile "from a radius of one hundred miles."

The call for the convention had gone out and was met with enthusiastic response; but as the date drew near, difficulties arose and multiplied.

The first sign of trouble appeared when the owners of the Minneapolis auditorium, which had been hired for the convention, suddenly canceled the contract. There was no other hall of sufficient size in the city, but the officers quickly solved their problem by hiring a tract of thirty-five acres of vacant land in the outskirts of Minneapolis and pitching a huge tent on it.

But here Governor Burnquist of Minnesota stepped in. He vetoed the convention in emphatic terms. "If anti-American meetings cannot be stopped by local officials," he declared in a threatening public statement, "every resource at our command will be used to punish the offenders and to prevent such meetings from being held. If by means of this action on our part bloodshed and loss of life result, the responsibility thereof will rest on those who are back of, and support by their presence, these un-American demonstrations."

The proposed meeting was a local matter and did not come within the scope of the governor's functions or competence. Mayor Van Lear made a bold fight against the unwarranted interference. "I assume," he declared in a public statement, "that constitutional democracy is still the form of government in the United States, and that the people may, with all propriety, peaceably discuss subjects of vital importance to themselves.

"By the oath of office taken when I became mayor, I am bound to defend the constitution of the state of Minnesota and of the United States.

"As chief executive of this city I shall undertake to see that the law is in every respect complied with in connection with the meeting of the People's Council. I shall not tolerate either breach of the law by participants in the Council or violations of the constitution by non-participants."

Those were brave words, but back of them unfortunately there was little power. The Minnesota legislature had just passed an act empowering the governor to remove any public officer when in his judgment such removal was required in the interest of public safety. The law was understood to be aimed primarily against the Socialist administration of Minneapolis, and it seemed certain that Mr. Burnquist would not hesitate to summarily remove Mayor Van Lear, if the attempt were made to hold the convention in Minneapolis with his sanction. There was nothing left for the Council but to look around for another meeting place.

At this juncture Lynn J. Frazier, then governor of North Dakota, stepped into the breach, inviting the convention to meet in his state.

"People's Council of America for Democracy and Peace will be guaranteed their constitutional rights in North Dakota," he wired to the organizers. "We are loyal and patriotic and believe in freedom of speech for all people."

The message spread cheer in the ranks of the Council, but on closer examination it proved to be of little practical help. The only city in the state large enough to furnish hotel and other necessary accommodations for the contemplated convention was Fargo. Fargo was the financial center of the state, and its administration was reactionary and bitterly opposed to Governor Frazier and the Non-Partisan League, which had elected him.

It was clear that an attempt to meet at Fargo would lead to a clash between the local authorities and the governor and possibly to grave disturbances. Again the Council was compelled to decline an invitation in order to save a friendly public officer from embarrassment.

Only two days remained before the opening date of the convention. There was no time to be lost. After a hurried conference it was determined to transfer the convention to the town of Hudson in the state of Wisconsin. Hudson was near Minneapolis, and the Wisconsin authorities were supposed to be friendly to the aims of the Council.

An arrangement committee was immediately dispatched to Hudson. It arrived on the 30th of August and left the same day escorted by a mob of "patriotic" citizens, who made it plain to them that the convention would not be tolerated in Hudson. It appeared that Governor Philipp of Wisconsin, who was understood to have consented to a meeting of the Council in his state, had wired to the local authorities of Hudson denying that he had granted such permission and calling on them to prevent the holding of the conference in their town.

Immediately on learning these facts, Daniel W. Hoan, the Socialist mayor of Milwaukee, came gallantly to the rescue of the much perplexed Council and invited it to meet in his city.

"If the principle of the Bill of Rights and the Constitution of the United States, which guarantee the liberty of speech and the right of the people to peaceably assemble and to consult for the common good, has been suspended in the state of Minnesota," he wired to the secretary of the Council, "I desire to inform you that both are living realities in the city of Milwaukee and the state of Wisconsin. I can assure you that should your organization desire to meet in this city, it will be welcome."

Another serious conflict between city and state authorities was thus looming in the tortuous path of the People's Council Convention.

In the meantime delegates were on their way. A large group of representatives from the East had chartered a special train from New York—westbound, that is as near as they came to knowing their place of destination. They were kept informed by wire of the kaleidoscopic changes of the situation, and finally made up their minds to stop in Chicago and try their luck.

Here a situation similar to that of Minneapolis and Milwaukee confronted them. William Hale Thompson, the mayor of the city, had adopted a liberal policy of toleration during the war and was almost certain to permit the Council to hold its convention. Governor Lowden of Illinois on the other hand was an enraged war "patriot" and was equally certain to prevent the convention if he could.

The delegates decided to take the chance. The West Side auditorium was hurriedly hired and the convention was promptly opened at ten o'clock in the morning of September 1st, as scheduled. It barely had an opportunity to effect a temporary organization when it was dispersed by the police.

It appeared that Mayor Thompson happened to be out of the city on that day and the governor, going over his head, had directed the chief of police to suppress the meeting.

Dr. Magnes and I had been detained in New York to direct the movements of the perambulating delegates. We took a later train and arrived in Chicago on the morning of September 2nd.

It was no easy job to get in touch with the dispersed delegates, but finally we managed to locate a group of them in a factory building in the outskirts of the city. The factory belonged to a sympathizer who had placed it at the disposal of the Council for the day, which happened to be a Sunday.

There in a large deserted room amidst machines and packing cases we found a few dozen delegates in secret deliberation with the approved air of regular conspirators. We took charge of the meeting, and having learned that Mayor Thompson had returned to the city we went to confer with him.

The mayor was readily located. He listened impassively to our protests and representations, and when we were through he calmly remarked: "You can hold your meeting as far as I am concerned and the police will not interfere with it, but the governor will probably send state troops to suppress it."

We learned that there were no state troops in Chicago and that the only military force at the disposal of the governor was some battalions of colored troops in Springfield, which had not yet been mustered into national service. If they entrained immediately, they could not reach Chicago before the evening. We had thus a leeway of several hours and decided to make the most of it.

Word was passed to the delegates that the convention would reassemble in the afternoon and promptly at two o'clock the session opened with an attendance of about four hundred participants.

As the meeting opened, we were informed that the Springfield troops had been ordered out against us, and throughout the afternoon we were kept advised of their progress. It was a race between the movement of the troops and the proceedings of our convention. We had to work fast. For the first time in my experience I witnessed a meeting of radicals ready to cut out discussion and eager to settle down to practical work. The main business of the convention was to adopt a permanent constitution as a basis of future activities. A committee on constitution was accordingly chosen with myself as chairman, and while the delegates were entertained with speeches from the floor our committee worked feverishly in an adjoining room. We terminated our labors at about six o'clock and immediately reported back to the convention. As I read the draft of the proposed constitution paragraph by paragraph, other delegates would move adoption "without debate," and the motions would be followed by a unanimous chorus of Ayes. By seven o'clock we had adopted a constitution and adjourned.

It was high time. The Springfield contingent of troops was within less than an hour from Chicago. We had to adjourn for the day anyhow, as the hall had been hired for the night for a wedding. The wedding was in full progress when the troops arrived and surrounded the hall, spreading alarm and consternation among the guileless wedding guests.

The convention had adjourned without finishing its work. It was contemplated among other things to draft an address to the

American people and a statement of the views and aims of the Council. These tasks were delegated to an executive committee of fifteen members hurriedly elected before adjournment. The problem now was to find a place of hiding for the committee, safe from the intrusion of the press and the state troopers.

We decided on a place where, we thought, we should be least likely to be looked for, one of Chicago's most fashionable hotels. I engaged a suite of rooms in an assumed name. "Your best and largest suite," I commanded, "for I expect a number of friends." The friends were my co-members on the executive committee of the Council. They called promptly and stayed up all night. It was a night of animated and continuous discussion, which amply made up for the repressed flow of oratory in the convention. Between speeches we found time to draft and to type our manifestoes.

Bright and early next morning, when our work was done and we were congratulating ourselves on our clever ruse to evade publicity, a horde of newspaper reporters invaded our secret quarters asking for news about our conspiratory deliberations, which we cheerfully furnished.

The People's Council of America for Democracy and Peace continued in existence until the end of the war. Several large public meetings were held under its auspices in different parts of the country, but its experience in connection with the first constituent convention had convincingly demonstrated the impossibility of organizing an extensive peace propaganda during the war.

CHAPTER IV

THE MAYORALTY CAMPAIGN OF NEW YORK

THE year 1917 was a political "off year," but local elections were to be held in several large cities, including New York, Chicago, Cleveland, and Buffalo.

With the war censorship rapidly tightening, it soon became apparent that the political campaigns would offer the best chance for a comparatively free discussion of war issues, and the Socialist Party determined to take full advantage of the opportunity.

In New York, where the Socialists named a full city ticket, the campaign was destined to become one of the most dramatic and spectacular political battles ever waged in an American municipality. The inherent importance of the election and the unusual conditions under which it was fought combined to make it the focus of interest of the whole country.

It was a four-cornered contest between the reform forces in power and the regular organizations of the Republican, Democratic, and Socialist parties.

The incumbent of the mayoralty chair was John Purroy Mitchel, an independent Democrat, who had been elected four years earlier on a "Fusion" ticket supported by the Republican Party and a group of nonpartisan municipal reformers. He was swept into office by an impressive plurality on one of the sporadic waves of civic awakening with which New York breaks the monotony of Tammany rule once in a long while. Young, energetic, and capable, John Purroy Mitchel had given the city an ideal business administration—clean, economical, impersonal, and cold. He was the idol of the business men and professional reformers and had the warm support of the most powerful metropolitan newspapers, including the *Times, Tribune, Herald,* and *Sun.*

It was the general expectation that Mr. Mitchel would be renominated by the Republican Party, which had been the backbone of his organized political support in 1913, and he was formally designated by the organization as the official choice of the party, but the primary election completely upset the plans of the Republican leaders.

Under the election laws of New York, candidates for city office are named at official party primaries. The party as such, designates its choice for every office, but rival nominations may also be made by groups of enrolled voters. As a rule, the primaries are mere formalities and the party designee carries the election.

In this case, one William F. Bennett, a lawyer and former state senator, had himself nominated in opposition to John Purroy Mitchel in the primaries. His claim to the support of the voters rested largely on the fact that he was a regular Republican, while Mayor Mitchel was a Democrat. Mr. Bennett's candidacy was not taken seriously, and little effort was made by the Mitchel forces to combat it; but when the vote was counted it was found that he had run a very close second to Mitchel, thus furnishing the first sensational surprise in a campaign which was to be replete with unexpected turns and surprises.

Nor did it end there. Immediately upon the official announcement of the result, Mr. Bennett raised the cry of fraud and demanded a recount of the vote. Mr. Mitchel chivalrously joined in the demand. The ballots were recounted and found to give a clear majority to Bennett over Mitchel.

William F. Bennett thus became the official candidate of the

Republican Party against the wishes and without the support of the party machine. Mr. Mitchel remained in the race as an "independent."

The Democratic Party nominated one John F. Hylan, a judge of a local court in Brooklyn and a man of vaguely radical political leanings. Judge Hylan was a rather colorless figure, without prominence in his own party and practically unknown to the body of New York citizens. His nomination was forced upon the Democratic political machine by the all-powerful influence of William Randolph Hearst.

I was nominated by the Socialist Party and accepted the nomination with no illusions about my chances of election.

In the preceding election of 1913 the party's candidate for mayor was Charles Edward Russell, a popular writer and eloquent speaker, who conducted an energetic campaign. He received a little over 32,000 votes, which was somewhat less than five per cent of the total. Mr. Russell had broken with the Socialist Party on the war issue and was actively supporting Mayor Mitchel for reëlection. Associated with him were a number of former Socialist leaders, mostly of the "intelligentsia," who had worked with him in his last campaign.

I expected a "good vote" measured by the standard of past Socialist performances, but did not anticipate anything much more strenuous and sensational than the usual propaganda campaign of my party. On this point my opponents' estimates were in full accord with mine, and we proved equally mistaken.

Almost from the outset it became apparent that the Socialist campaign had taken fire. It was conducted on the usual Socialist platform of municipal reform, which had acquired a particularly sharp edge because of the soaring cost of living; but during the campaign the social and economic planks were soon overshadowed by the issue uppermost in the minds of the people— the all-absorbing issue of war and peace.

In my speech of acceptance I defined the bearing of our campaign on the pending war problems in this language:

"We are for peace. We are unalterably opposed to the killing of our manhood and the draining of our resources in the bewildering pursuit of an incomprehensible 'democracy,' a pursuit of democracy which has the support of the men and the classes who habitually rob and despoil the people of America; a pursuit of democracy which begins by suppressing the freedom of speech, press, and public assemblage and by stifling legitimate political criticism. Not warfare and terrorism, but Socialism and social justice will make the world safe for democracy. . . .

"During the last three years all movements for social progress and human betterment have been halted by a mad frenzy of ruin and destruction.

"It was the capitalist system of industrial and commercial rivalry, the system of exploitation, hatred, and intrigue, the capitalist system with its Kaisers on the thrones, in the factories and the countinghouses of all lands that brought on the war."

Picturing the war-weariness of the workers in the Allied countries and the triumph of political democracy in Russia, I continued:

"The workers and Socialists of Germany are also beginning to show signs of revolt against their Kaiser and their Junkers, their war lords, and their money lords. They begin to realize that they have been deceived and betrayed and led to wanton slaughter. They demand peace and the abandonment of all plans of world domination and conquest. The triumph of German democracy is only a question of a short time. The murderous Hohenzollerns and Hapsburgs are doomed to share the fate of the bloodthirsty Romanoffs.

"In the historic process of world regeneration the Socialists of America must and will play their part. For, contrary to the protestations of the self-styled patriots in our public press and platforms, the people of the United States, like the people of Europe, want peace. Of all of the political parties the Socialist Party alone has the courage to voice its desire, openly, vigorously, aye, defiantly.

"And therein lies the unusual significance of our present campaign. The municipal election in this city will be the only great political contest in the United States since our entry into the war. It will offer the first real opportunity to express the sentiments of the people on war and peace. The verdict of the citizens of New York will be eagerly awaited by the people of the country, aye, we may say without exaggeration, by the whole world. The verdict will be expressed in the number of votes cast for the Socialist ticket. Every vote will weigh heavily in the balance, for it will be a vote not only for the workers and the people, for right and liberty, but also an emphatic vote for democracy and peace."

The ratification meeting at which the speech was delivered was a revelation to the Socialists and their opponents alike. It was held in the old Madison Square Garden, the largest public hall in the city, with a capacity audience of about twelve thousand, while countless thousands were turned away. The enthusiasm and fervor of the men and women in the hall were indescribable. Every allusion to peace was greeted with thunderous applause and loud shouts of approval. The demonstration was reminiscent of a powerful religious revival meeting rather than a political campaign rally.

The Socialists were not alone in advancing the war issue to the foreground of the municipal campaign. Mayor Mitchel and his campaign managers were quick to perceive its inevitability and took a clear and definite stand on it.

Mr. Mitchel was for war to the end. He supported the war policies of the government unreservedly and aggressively. From first to last he made "Americanism" one of the principal issues of his campaign and proclaimed himself the only true patriot in the mayoralty contest. "Patriotism" and "Americanism" to him were synonymous with uncritical acceptance of all that emanated from Washington in connection with the conduct of the war. All criticism of the administrative war methods or peace program was rank treason.

In justice to Mr. Mitchel it should be said that he was straight and uncompromising in his views, and that he remained true to his principles throughout the campaign. The line of difference between him and myself was clearly drawn.

A similar attitude of political candor could by no means be claimed for Judge Hylan, the Democratic candidate. Mr. Hylan was Hearst's man, and William Randolph Hearst was generally charged with pro-Germanism, Anglophobia, and lukewarm support of the war. Besides, the leaders of the Democratic political machine had serious doubts about the popularity of the war among the voters of New York, and preferred to remain silent on the subject. John F. Hylan was an ideal candidate for a silent campaign. Unimpeded by a gift of political oratory, and mildly interested in the discussion of concrete administrative problems, he was satisfied to rely on the customary unspectacular but efficient campaign methods of his organization.

He made few speeches, and these were always read from carefully revised and censored manuscript. He confined himself entirely to criticism of Mayor Mitchel's administration and vague tirades against the predatory interests. He accused the Mayor of "using the American flag to hide the wrongs of his administration," but was careful to avoid any mention of his own stand on the war, in spite of the fact that Mr. Mitchel and I repeatedly challenged him to state his position.

Towards the end of the campaign, when the newspapers had worked up the issues of "Americanism" and "patriotism" to the point of frenzy and all political camps were paralyzed with fear of the Socialist inroads, the Democratic Party hastily prepared a campaign document, which represented the first attempt at a statement of Mr. Hylan's position.

The proposed Tammany broadside paid little attention to Mayor Mitchel, dismissing him with a quotation from a speech of Supreme Court Justice Cropsey: "The man who uses Patriotism as a shield is a coward at heart." Its main attack was directed against my candidacy.

"Defeat Hillquit for Mayor," it admonished in big type, "because:

"He opposes the war plans of his country.

"He speaks of peace when there is no peace.

"He seeks support from those who are not in sympathy with the nation's policies in the time of the nation's crisis.

"His idealistic schemes would increase instead of diminish the present unbearable burden of taxation.

"Every practicable scheme of betterment in which the Socialists believe is already incorporated in the Democratic platform.

"He believes in municipal ownership and operation of public utilities, but it is not Hillquit who can accomplish it, but Judge Hylan, who will be elected. Why should even a Socialist vote for a man who has no chance of election instead of another who will be in a position to carry into effect the sensible and practical part of the Socialist program."

And then, by way of a parting shot, this profound observation:

"He will not be able to make the lazy and inefficient contribute their equal share to work or to government.

"He cannot convince the people that every man ought to share equally in the benefits of government without regard to his contribution to it."

A printer's proof of the literary gem was sent to me by a sympathizing "insider," but the document itself never saw the light of day. After the impulsive move in the hour of alarm, wiser counsel prevailed in the Wigwam, and the remarkable campaign pronunciamento was quietly suppressed.

In the uncertain state of the public mind neither the qualified acceptance of the Socialist program nor the unqualified approval of the war seemed to be the part of wisdom.

It was not until the votes were counted and Hylan's election was assured that he saw fit to proclaim his "thorough Americanism and loyal support of the government in the war." Safety First was ever the political motto of the Tammany braves.

As to Mr. Bennett, he practically made no campaign. He had neither organization nor program behind him and was compelled to rely on the irreducible Republican vote.

The active campaign fight was largely confined to the Socialists and the fusion forces.

This situation led me in one of my campaign speeches to remark somewhat facetiously that I was the only perfect candidate running for mayor. "The others are all defective," I argued. "Mr. Bennett is a candidate with a party but without a platform; Mr. Mitchel is a candidate with a platform but without a party; Judge Hylan has both a party and a platform, but he is speechless, whereas I have a party and a platform and a good deal to say."

On another occasion when I spoke in a theater at the close of a play, I likened our campaign to the show on the stage.

"We have the traditional hero in Mayor Mitchel," I observed. "If you do not believe me look at the posters in the streets. We have outraged virtue, played by the gentleman who was almost robbed of his nomination at the outset of the campaign, and we have the actor without a speaking part in the person of the Honorable John F. Hylan. As to myself, I am the villain in the play, the man who will run away with the City Hall, if elected, the Socialist, pacifist, and ally of the Kaiser."

But it was not all fun.

As the campaign waxed warmer it became more strenuous. During the closing weeks I addressed several public meetings every night, and day by day the meetings grew in attendance and in fervidness. Twenty-four hours' notice would bring forth a gathering that crowded the hall and jammed the surrounding streets in any part of the city.

One evening I was to speak at three meetings in the lower East Side. No street demonstration was planned, but a gigantic parade was formed spontaneously. The whole East Side seemed to be on its feet, and for three hours countless thousands of men and women surged and swarmed through miles of street before and behind the car in which I made my laborious progress from one hall to another. They sang and shouted and cheered, and their numbers swelled incessantly. It was a touching scene never to be forgotten.

These demonstrations of strength caused wild alarm in the political opposition camps, an alarm which degenerated into a veritable panic when several extensive "straw votes" taken by newspapers, particularly the *New York Herald,* indicated a large and growing trend in my favor.

Charles F. Murphy, the astute Tammany chieftain, announced that a careful canvass by his organization indicated that I would run second to Hylan. "The fight is between Hylan and Hillquit," he asserted. The Fusion forces, not to be outdone, proclaimed that the fight was "between Mitchel and Hillquit." The newspapers were aroused and began training their batteries against my candidacy. Their opposition was solid, aggressive, and abusive, and gradually the whole press of the country joined in the fight, voicing the alarm of the well-intentioned citizenry in lurid accounts of the campaign and in fulminating editorials.

As the campaign drew nearer to the close and the issues were more sharply defined, the attacks became venomous and reckless.

In the enthusiasm of one of my campaign meetings I declared

that "a Socialist victory in the New York City election will be a clear mandate to our government to open immediate negotiations for a general peace."

I was careful to explain that "we do not stand for a separate peace, which would save our skins and leave the unfortunate nations of Europe to their own destinies. We want a general, negotiated, and permanent peace, which would bring relief and blessing to the people of all countries involved in the insane and disastrous war."

But the "mandate" was seized upon by the hostile newspapers and violently denounced as an expression of high treason. A patriotic New York lawyer immediately wired to President Wilson demanding my summary arrest, and my "mandate" ever thereafter furnished an inexhaustible source of caustic campaign argument against me.

At another meeting a professional anti-Socialist heckler interrupted my speech with the significant question: "Mr. Hillquit, are you an American and do you stand behind the President?"

Amidst the tumult caused by the interruption, I answered calmly:

"I am an American, if by that term you mean a citizen of the United States who seeks the greatest welfare of his country and his fellow citizens.

"I stand behind the President when I honestly believe that he is right, and only then. I stand behind the people all the time."

I added that I happened to stand fully behind the President in his earlier declaration: "A victory in arms would mean terms of peace imposed upon the vanquished. It would lead to rancor and striving for vengeance. It would not be a peace on firm foundation but one founded on quicksand and would lead to more war."

As I re-read the statement now, it appears to me as a rather inoffensive declaration of political attitude in a democracy, but it was rank heresy in the days of war hysteria, when "standing behind the President" with a total abdication of individual judgment was the supreme test of loyalty and patriotism.

"Hillquit Gives the President Only Divided Loyalty" was the damning line in heavy type with which the *New York Times* headed its report of the meeting; and my "divided loyalty" became another aggravated count in the political indictment against me.

But the heaviest storm against me was precipitated by a rather fortuitous incident.

One afternoon an enterprising newspaper reporter telephoned me at my office to inquire whether I had bought any Liberty bonds. He informed me that he had made similar inquiries of my opponents, all of whom had answered in the affirmative.

I was opposed to the flotation of the Liberty bonds for several reasons. I believed that the cost of the war should be borne by the wealthy, and particularly by those who were amassing colossal fortunes in war industries, rather than by government loans calculated to burden the people for generations to come. I was repelled by the methods of moral terrorism employed in the sale of the bonds, and, holding the views on the war that I did, I felt that I could not in good conscience give it voluntary support.

My first impulse was to make a full statement of my attitude to the inquisitive reporter, but on second thought it occurred to me that a long theoretical dissertation might give the impression of equivocation and evasion. I confined my statement to the last and most important ground of my opposition and answered the question tersely and directly.

"No, I have not bought any Liberty bonds," I said. "I am not going to do anything to advance the war, if I can help. I would subscribe to the limit of my ability to any fund or efforts to the advancement of peace."

Answering a further question of my persistent interviewer, I added:

"I consider that the best way to support the soldiers and help the civilians is for the government to initiate an immediate movement for peace. The notion that this war must be fought to a finish is not in the interests of our soldiers, ourselves, our allies or of mankind at large."

The published statement provoked a howl of indignation and a torrent of invective. The rest of the campaign was directed against me in the spirit of a holy, patriotic crusade against a traitorous infidel and in a tone of red-hot rage.

To the newspapers of New York and all over the country I was no longer a mere Socialist preaching a subversive social doctrine. I was the "enemy within the gates," the "agent of the Kaiser," the "traitor to his country," who should not be allowed to go at large, let alone run for important political office. Their critical opposition and mild ridicule had given way to abuse, hatred, and fear.

At the breakfast table every morning I was greeted by screaming headlines on indignant accounts in the papers of my doings and sayings and by condemnatory and inciting editorials. In the afternoon the evening papers brought me similar heartening messages and greetings. Lurid, full-page cartoons often carried the outraged editorial feeling to points far beyond the limitations of written language.

Nor were the attacks confined to the newspapers.

The New York Chamber of Commerce adopted a sizzling' resolution in which it stigmatized Senator La Follette and myself as the most notable examples of persons allowed to spread "seditious and unpatriotic sentiments," deplored that "many avenues of publicity are still permitted to disloyal persons," and urged upon the departments of justice in nation, state, and city a more vigorous prosecution of those "who abuse the privilege of citizenship."

The Business Men's League of New York issued a confidential circular to members of the business community warning them that its private investigations showed that "the candidacy of Morris Hillquit, the Socialist nominee for Mayor, is not a joke but a dangerous menace to New York City."

The circular concluded:

"As a business man you are confronted with this condition: The next Mayor of New York will either be Hylan, a Democrat, or Hillquit, a Socialist.

"You must be guided accordingly."

The Lawyers' Club, tactfully omitting the mention of any names, issued a general appeal to the voters to make the strongest opposition to any candidate for mayor "who is unwilling to support the Liberty Bond Loan," and numerous other patriotic bodies adopted similar condemnatory resolutions.

The issue of "patriotism," now rendered acute, brought many formidable protagonists into the camp of Mayor Mitchel and as many opponents to me.

Among the most zealous of these were the so-called pro-war Socialists. Many of the men who only a few months ago had been my warm political friends, and whom I had called "comrades," now led in the most violent and unscrupulous personal attacks against me. They were sent out by the Fusion forces to do battle for their "bourgeois" candidate, individually and collectively, in public meetings and in the press, and always and everywhere they assailed me with apostatic glee and fervor. Only war can inspire such a spirit of passion and hate. To me their activities were among the saddest and most shameful features of the campaign.

But the biggest gun in the heavy Fusion artillery was Theodore Roosevelt. He had espoused the cause of Mayor Mitchel largely because of his "patriotic" war stand and had thrown himself into the campaign with his characteristic vigor and emphasis. I was the favorite object of his smashing attacks.

He rose to the height of Rooseveltian eloquence and invective in a speech at the Madison Square Garden held a few days before the election.

"Morris Hillquit is pandering to treasonable and cowardly Americanism," he declared, "to the pacifists, the pro-Germans, and the man who wishes Uncle Sam to negotiate an inconclusive peace," and reaching the climax of his impassioned oration, with fists clenched and famous jaw projected, he fairly yelled: "Yellow calls to yellow."

Yellow? I am thinking back to the hectic days of the campaign, the open or covert incitements to violence emanating from the press, the pulpit, and war-frenzied "leading citizens," the threatening letters that came to me in almost every mail, the rows of sullen home-guard soldiers often surrounding my meetings, the Department of Justice shadowing me at every step and having stenographers to take down every word of my campaign speeches; I am thinking of the heavy atmosphere of hate and terrorism in which I constantly moved. It took infinitely greater physical and moral courage in those days to defend an unpopular minority position than to howl with the infuriated mob.

And all the time Washington was watching the New York campaign with intense interest. "For the first time in history," the newspapers reported, "mayoralty elections in different cities are demanding the attention of the government. There is particularly a growing uneasiness about New York, where Hillquit may possibly win."

In view of the uncertainty of the outcome, the administration in Washington wisely withheld formal support from any candidate in the New York contest, but the unofficial utterances of some of its spokesmen left no doubt as to where it stood. Probably the most outspoken of these was the Assistant Treasurer of the United States, who inadvertently bore the Teutonic name of Martin Vogel. In a public statement violently attacking one of my campaign speeches Mr. Vogel demanded that I be interned or "externed."

Camp Upton, a military training camp at Yaphank, Long Island, contained many thousands of New York boys who were entitled to vote in the city election and Major General J. Franklin Bell, in command of the camp, had announced that he would permit representatives of all parties to address the soldiers. The Democratic and Fusion forces maintained regular headquarters in the camp.

But when application was made in my behalf for permission to speak to the soldiers, the General denied it, holding that the city platform of the Socialist Party was "subversive of military discipline," because of its plank demanding the repeal of the Conscription Law and its general opposition to war.

The arbitrary discrimination brought forth a chivalrous protest from Mayor Mitchel, who urged the General to rescind the order, pointing out the impropriety of withholding from me the right to address the soldiers after that right had been freely granted to other candidates.

The incident was given wide publicity in the press and induced me to enter a public protest in the form of an open letter to General Bell, which read in part:

New York, Oct. 26th, 1917.

MAJOR-GENERAL J. FRANKLIN BELL,
Camp Upton,
Yaphank, L.I., N.Y.

SIR:

Mayor Mitchel's letter to you requesting you in substance to reconsider your decision barring me from addressing the soldiers at Camp Upton and your reply to the Mayor's request, have been given such wide publicity by the New York press and have been so freely used as campaign material in behalf of one of my rivals in the pending mayoralty contest, that it becomes necessary for me to address you on the subject in order to state my stand to you and to the public.

To begin with I have no criticism to make of your order prohibiting public discussion of a nature "subversive of military discipline" at the camp. I fully appreciate that any expression of opposition to war and any criticism of the government's war policies would be out of place in a military camp, and in applying for permission to address the soldiers I had intended to confine my discourse strictly to the political and economic issues directly involved in the municipal campaign. Explicit assurances to that effect were given to you by my representatives, but you chose to disregard them without even making an effort to ascertain my attitude or intentions by direct communication with me.

The result of the extraordinary proceeding is that while all my rivals for office are permitted to urge their claims to the votes of the boys at Camp Upton by direct appeal to them and personal meeting with them, this right is withheld from me and the political party I have the honor to represent in this campaign. You are thus giving a distinctly partisan political advantage to some candidates, whom you have chosen to single out for your approval, and you are putting at a practical disadvantage a candidate who has been unfortunate enough to incur your personal displeasure. The stand taken by you is, besides, grossly unfair to the soldiers at camp. In voting on candidates for public office the drafted men at Camp Upton will not perform a military duty but exercise a civil right. They will vote not as soldiers but as citizens. As such they are entitled to all the facilities afforded to their civilian fellow-citizens for acquiring first-hand knowledge of the programs, issues and aims of all contending political parties and of the views and personalities of the candidates. By your order you have arbitrarily curtailed a vital and fundamental civic right of the citizen soldiers at Camp Upton.

. . . .

The military tutelage of the soldiers in the sphere of their civil rights and privileges and the political discrimination among rival candidates may be technically justified on the plea of military necessity, but it cannot fail to make it clear to all thinking men that militarism is fatally subversive of true democracy.

Respectfully yours,

MORRIS HILLQUIT.

General Bell was a fine type of the professional soldier, straightforward, conscientious, and courteous, but his answer to my letter throws a glaring light upon the singular limitations of the one-track military mind and its complete disassociation from civic interests and principles of democracy. Here is the letter:

Headquarters, 77th Division
Camp Upton, N.Y., Oct. 29, 1917.

MY DEAR MR. HILLQUIT:

Your letter of last Friday, October 26th, has just been received by me this morning.

I am not in the slightest degree responsible for the publicity given by the New York Press to my letter in reply to the one received from the Mayor. I recognize, and have always been aware of, the difficulties involved in a consistent adherence to the policy outlined in regulations issued by me for the government of political meetings in this camp. Of course, I am not infallible, nor do I possess more than average wisdom or ability, but I have made conscientious efforts to interpret my duty correctly and to adhere to what I believed was necessary in order to discharge it.

You are in error in believing that explicit assurances were given me by your representatives to the effect that you would confine your discourse strictly to the political and economic issues directly involved in the municipal campaign.

Had I had any idea that my making an effort to ascertain your attitude or intentions by direct communication with you would have been considered appropriate and have been welcomed by you, I might have made it.

I have chosen to single out no candidate for my approval. I have absolutely no political bias and have never voted in my life. I wish it might be possible for you to believe that I have not experienced the slightest personal feeling or displeasure toward you. I have absolutely never read a single speech or a single word published in the papers as having been uttered by you. This was not because I might not have been enlightened thereby, but because I take no interest in local political discussions and have not time to read them. Mr. Schwartz has kindly sent me your small work entitled: "Socialism

Summed Up," but I have not yet had time to read it. Everything I have ever been told about you, even by those who disagree with your political views, has been favorable to you as an individual member of society. There has never existed, therefore, the slightest basis for displeasure on my part toward you. I can hardly think it should be difficult for men of intelligence, like yourself, to believe that men in my position can have many righteous motives for their acts, entirely uninfluenced by personal feeling or displeasure, this notwithstanding their views and judgment may appeal to you as fallible.

Your letter makes reference to the status of soldiers as citizens, and to the fact that in voting they will be exercising "a civil right, not a military duty." As the law provides that they shall have the privilege of voting in military camps, I did not consider myself privileged to prohibit political meetings of every kind.

I fully recognized the existence of the "elusive line" referred to in your letter and never expected to be able to discharge my duty in such manner as to be satisfactory to every one. That was no reason why I should not endeavor to do what I conceived to be my duty.

Assuring you of my highest personal esteem, believe me,

Cordially and sincerely yours,

J. F. BELL
Major General, U.S.A., Commanding.

Camp Upton was an important strategic point in the campaign for New York's mayoralty. There were some sixty thousand soldiers in it, and most of them came from the city and were entitled to vote.

Deprived of the opportunity to speak to the soldiers, I addressed an open letter to them, which was circulated in the camp in thousands of copies and was extensively reproduced in the newspapers.

The letter appealed to the soldiers as workers and stressed their material interests during and after the war, but I did not evade the issue of peace.

"The citizens of New York," I asserted, "can at this time strike no more telling blow against the Kaiser's government, can in no way do more to rouse all the people of Europe to vigorous action in favor of a universal, durable, democratic peace than by sending out the word that the second largest city of the world has declared for Socialism and for the destruction of the root causes of war."

It was currently reported that the sentiment in Camp Upton was overwhelmingly Socialistic. On November 4th the *New York Tribune* made the alarming prediction that "fifty to sixty per cent. of the men at Camp Upton will vote for Morris Hillquit on election day."

Mayor Mitchel's gallant intercession with General Bell in my behalf was quite in keeping with the general tone of personal decency we had adopted toward each other in marked contrast to the mud-slinging methods which characterized the fight between Mr. Mitchel and the candidates on the Democratic and Republican tickets. "The Socialist candidate is at least a gentleman," conceded the Fusion press bureau, while I always made it a point to admit Mr. Mitchel's personal qualities and to confine the discussion to our wide differences in principle.

But my courteous opponent did not always practise the policy of broad-minded tolerance which he so eloquently preached to General Bell.

After a public meeting had been held in the City Hall Park to ratify the Mayor's candidacy for reëlection, I addressed to him a note reading:

My dear Mayor:

Allow me to congratulate you upon the precedent you have set in permitting the City Hall steps and park to be used for the purpose of a public meeting in support of your candidacy for reëlection.

I feel confident that in doing so you had no desire to take advantage of your official position for personal political purposes, and that you are ready to accord the same privilege to your opponents. I, for one, should like to have an opportunity to state my position in this campaign to the voters of New York from the steps of their City Hall, and, incidentally, to reply to your criticism of my candidacy.

I hope the candidates of the Democratic and Republican parties will welcome a similar opportunity to present their claims to the electorate, so as to aid the citizens in making an honest and intelligent choice.

I respectfully request the permission to hold a public meeting on the steps of the City Hall and in the City Hall park on Saturday, October 6, at noon.

Very sincerely yours,
MORRIS HILLQUIT.

His Honor's reply indicated a certain embarrassment about the request. It read:

CITY OF NEW YORK
OFFICE OF THE MAYOR

October 3, 1917

MY DEAR MR. HILLQUIT:

The City Hall is and has been my official residence for the past four years. Several days ago I was advised that a group of citizens would call upon me there and present certain demands that I become a candidate for reëlection to the office of Mayor. Because of the limited space inside City Hall, it was necessary that I meet these citizens on the steps of the building, where I made answer to their demands. If you desire to receive a number of citizens who may call upon you at your official or business residence, and it is necessary for the police to make special traffic arrangements, I shall be very happy to ask the Commissioner to accommodate you in every way in his power.

You are in error in assuming that I have set a precedent in permitting City Hall steps and park to be used for political purposes. It would be most inadvisable to create any such precedent.

For the Mayor to receive any and all who come to see him at his office is one thing. For political organizations to make of the steps of City Hall a hustings is quite another.

Therefore, in spite of my high personal regard for you, I am compelled to decline your request for permission to hold a public meeting in the City Hall Park on Saturday, October 6th, at twelve o'clock noon.

Very truly yours,
JOHN PURROY MITCHEL, *Mayor.*

The answer was, of course, not satisfactory. I replied to Mr. Mitchel: "The City Hall is not the Mayor's official 'residence,' but his place of business for administering the affairs of the city, and it seems to me that the candidacy of the present incumbent for reëlection is no more a concern of the city than the candidacy of the nominee of the Socialist Party."

Consistently with this stand I publicly announced that I would be in the City Hall Park on October 6th, at noon, and invited all my friends to meet me there. I expected an imposing reunion of friends, but as I recall it, it rained heavily on the appointed day and the meeting was called off. Many a promising revolution has thus been spoiled by rain.

As the attacks upon me multiplied, my support grew in proportion. To all outward appearances the Socialist campaign in New York had grown to the size of a popular uprising. Meetings were held by the hundreds in all parts of the city, in halls and on street corners, and every day they grew in size and enthusiasm. In the working-class districts the other parties seemed to have no chance at all. In the few meetings arranged by them the speakers addressed empty benches or had to submit to severe heckling from the audience. The regular campaign committee of the Socialist Party was supplemented by a number of auxiliary volunteer bodies from the ranks of trade unions and other groups of citizens. Thousands of dollars, mostly in very small amounts, poured into the meager war chest of the party from sympathizers all over the country.

The climax of enthusiasm and fervor was reached at the closing meeting in Madison Square Garden, held on the 4th of November, two days before the election. Long before the hour of the opening the vast hall was crowded to the last seat with thousands standing in the aisles, while many more thousands were unable to gain admission.

The *New York Tribune* characterized the meeting as a "demonstration bordering on hysteria."

"Fourteen thousand persons," the newspaper reported, cheered for sixteen minutes after Hillquit stepped forward to speak. They stood on their chairs and cheered. They ripped campaign placards from the walls and tossed them into the air and flung their hats to the speakers' platform, stamped their feet and yelled, shrieked and whistled.

With Mr. Hillquit, Dudley Field Malone, Amos Pinchot, and Frank Sieverman in turn raised their hands to implore quiet. The crowds broke out again and again with "Hillquit our next Mayor."

It was a memorable demonstration, warm, spontaneous, and big. It was a thunderous mass answer to the weeks of misrepresentation, abuse, bullying, and incitements. It almost unnerved me by the depth of sentiment. In my final campaign speech at this stirring meeting I seized the opportunity to square accounts with my opponents.

"The outstanding feature of this campaign," I said, among other things, "has been the clear line of cleavage which it has drawn among the opposing camps. We know just where the different classes of the people of New York now stand.

"With us are aligned the forces of labor, men and women of toil, the workers of muscle and brain, the workers in the factories and mills, in the countinghouses, in the offices, in the schools, the great mass of the men and women who carry the burdens of this world and are excluded from its joys and pleasures, the great mass of disinherited, the humble, the poor, the large mass of the people of this city.

"Aligned with us also are the men and women of all other classes who have an idealistic vision, a passion for fair play, for democracy, and for social justice.

"Aligned with us are the best, the noblest, the most progressive elements in the city of New York, and arrayed against us are all the powers of oppression, the preachers of reaction, and the dark elements that make for lawlessness and suppression.

"It is to the credit of the Socialists in this campaign that they have forced off the mask of hyprocrisy from the hideous faces of these base elements and have shown them up to their fellow men in all their brutal nakedness.

"The great philanthropic and humanitarian body known as the Chamber of Commerce has honored us by singling out your candidate for a special censure; they say my candidacy is a menace to the American people, their American people. The Business Men's League has likewise thought it necessary to caution their fellow men, the men of their class, of the dangerous menace of the candidacy of the Socialist standard bearer.

"And arrayed against us also is that valiant and fire-eating band of patriots who veil their anarchism and lawlessness under the mask of patriotism and Americanism: Colonel Theodore Roosevelt, the hero, who calls for the formation of vigilantes to suppress hostile criticism and views, just a thinly veiled disguise, which is in substance an appeal to mob law and to lynching; Mr. Elihu Root, who publicly advocates shooting of dissenting editors, and, finally, the Christian Reverend ex-Ambassador van Dyke, who only a few days ago suggested that the most expeditious manner of disposing of the election issues was by hanging the Socialist candidate for Mayor.

"These men are openly inciting to crime and to murder, and in these days of crisis, of hysteria, their appeals may lead to actual bloodshed. If a plain, ordinary anarchist would be guilty of very much milder incitement, he would be behind the prison bars, but these anarchists of distinction, position, and wealth can preach murder with impunity."

An episode that had been gleefully reported in the newspapers of that morning had stirred me so deeply that I recounted it to my audience at the closing meeting. It was so characteristic of the pseudo-patriotic mob spirit engendered by the war propaganda and now happily forgotten that I think it worth while reproducing my comment on it at this time:

"The other day some of these 'patriots' held an 'anti-disloyalty' meeting at Carnegie Hall. I take the account of what happened there, among others, from one of our morning papers, not the Socialist paper, not the *Call,* but a good respectable capitalist paper supporting Mayor Mitchel. Listen—it is interesting:

" 'A man who hailed United States Senator La Follette as our "next President" was ejected from the Anti-Disloyalty meeting of the American Defense Society in Carnegie Hall last night. Before a well-aimed kick from the size eleven foot of a sturdy and irate pro-American assisted him from the steps to the sidewalk, where he fell sprawling, the disturber had encountered a varied experience. The man was first dragged from his aisle seat in the sixth row and booted toward the door by half a dozen men in evening dress. A woman in evening attire reached over from an aisle seat and slapped his face. This was the signal for everybody—men and women—within striking distance to take a punch at the stranger. When he attempted to cover his face his arms were pinioned behind him.'

"The crime of this man was that he, as an American citizen, had voiced his preference for the next president of this republic, and his preference did not meet with the approval of the evening-dress ruffians. And our newspapers, your newspapers, have the shamelessness of approving it with laudatory comment. Oh, if I were only Mayor of New York at this time! If I were in command of the police force of this city, these evening-dress cowardly loafers would be arrested for assault and battery.

"It is this kind of mob spirit, it is this lawlessness, it is this hell of anarchism against which this city is now rising in revolt. It is this mob spirit, this lawlessness which we, the Socialists, are determined to combat and to crush until it exists no longer. And these men, who by their conduct disgrace the fair fame of the American republic, who trample underfoot everything that is best and noblest in American democracy, they have the hardihood to come before you as the only Simon-pure Americans in this election contest. Americans! If Americanism stands for America of the oppressors and despoilers and privileged classes and lawlessness, then indeed they are fit representatives of that kind of Americanism. If Americanism stands for the oppressed, for the despoiled, for fairness, for liberty, for democracy; if Americanism stands for the America of the masses, the America of the people, the America of the Americans, then we and we alone represent America here."

About one week before the election, the feeling gained that I would carry the city. Consternation spread in the camps of my opponents and the New York Stock Exchange experienced a sinking spell avowedly caused by the menace of my candidacy.

It was probably one of those indefinable psychic campaign sentiments that are sometimes borne in the air with or without foundation in reason or fact. Possibly also that particular period marked my high point on the political barometer, always a highly sensitive instrument, and if the vote had been cast at that psychological moment, the result might have been substantially different from what it turned out to be after the cooling influence of another week of delay.

An amusing and heretofore unrecorded incident that took place at about that time may at least partly account for the turn of my practical political fortunes.

One afternoon several gentlemen announced their visit at my office. By their names I identified them at once as prominent leaders of the numerous "German-American" colony of the city. They did not leave me long in the dark about the object of their visit, and informed me frankly that the body of organized German citizens of New York were hesitating in their choice between Judge Hylan and myself, and that they had been designated a committee to interview both of us on our respective attitudes towards citizens of German birth or extraction and particularly on the question of continuing the German language in the curriculum of the public schools.

The opposition press and parties had, of course, consistently characterized me as pro-German, and in the course of the campaign I had addressed two meetings in German. I had spoken to similar audiences in German before the war, and I continued the practice during the campaign in a spirit of challenge. "German is the language not only of the Kaiser but also of Karl Liebknecht," I explained, "and it contains words of love as well as words of hate." My callers strongly hinted that their personal preferences were with me rather than Mr. Hylan because I was more familiar with the "German culture" than my Democratic opponent.

My reply was brief and utterly unsatisfactory. "Gentlemen, I do not want the 'German' vote," I said in substance. "I am running as a Socialist and nothing else. My opposition to war is purely a Socialist attitude, and as it happens my personal sympathies and inclinations are largely on the side of the Allies." This, by the way, was the mental or psychological attitude of most of the "pro-German" Socialist opponents of the war.

After an embarrassing pause, the interview was terminated, and the "German vote" turned its metaphorical back on me forever. Judge Hylan's campaign managers probably never knew what a good turn I had unwittingly done them.

Finally, the election day arrived. The newspapers had reserved the last hour for a concerted and smashing blow. The morning and evening papers of November 5, 1917, vied with each other in scare headlines over articles warning against the danger of my election and summarizing my sins of omission and commission.

Up to the hour when the vote was fully counted and the result announced, the city seethed with passion and excitement probably unparalleled in its political history.

The election results belied all forecasts and deceived all expectations. Judge Hylan, the silent, non-committal candidate of Tammany Hall, was elected by a vote slightly exceeding the combined vote of Mayor Mitchel and myself. His vote was announced as 313,956 against 155,497 credited to Mayor Mitchel and 145,332 conceded to me. The Republican candidate trailed in the rear with 56,438 votes.

The Socialist watchers at numerous polling places charged that the election returns had been slightly doctored in favor of Mayor Mitchel in order to accord him the academic honor of second place, which rightfully belonged to me, but whether the charges were true or not, it was a neck-to-neck race between us. In view of the fact that Mr. Mitchel had the tremendous advantages of incumbency in office, the vast facilities of the city administration and the support of practically the whole of the powerful press of New York, his defeat was highly significant of the true war sentiment of the people of America's metropolis.

As to myself, I succeeded in increasing the Socialist vote almost fivefold, and carried twelve assembly districts out of the city's sixty-two, while Mayor Mitchel led in only eight. Over twenty-two per cent of the voters had expressed their preference for my candidacy.

My unprecedently large vote was by no means a mere personal triumph. It was a legitimate victory of the Socialist Party. While I was necessarily kept in the front line of the battle as the head of the party ticket and had to stand the brunt of the fight, the whole of the organized Socialist movement of New York was mobilized for active campaign work and all did yeoman service. All those who could speak spent their days addressing public meetings, thousands of street meetings in all corners of the city. All those who could write filled the columns of the few Socialist newspapers printed in several languages and wrote campaign leaflets or appeals. All others distributed campaign literature, organized meetings, and did the hundred and one other humble chores which go to make up an active and spirited campaign. And all of it was volunteer work, work of love, without recognition and without pay.

When the statements of election expenses were filed, it appeared that Mayor Mitchel's campaign had cost his supporters about $1,300,000. The Socialist Party obtained the same result in number of votes with a total expenditure of about $50,000. Every Fusion vote cost twenty-six times as much as a Socialist vote.

And the campaign was conducted mainly along Socialist lines.

On one occasion I thus summarized the special points in the Socialist program:

"There are four main issues in this campaign, two direct and two indirect. Stated in their order they may be formulated as follows: (1) the policy and character of the city government; (2) the high cost of food; (3) the preservation of civil liberties; (4) the effect of the campaign on the movement for peace."

While the last point turned out to be the most sensational and spectacular, we never neglected the social and economic issues and never failed to stress the fundamentals of the Socialist philosophy and program. The Socialist appeal was invariably made in behalf of all candidates on the party ticket, and the phenomenal Socialist vote of 1917 was practically a straight party vote. With all the special prominence given to the contest for the mayoralty, I led the Socialist ticket by only 20,000 to 25,000 votes, and the big vote came heavily from the working-class districts, the logical and most legitimate recruiting grounds of a Socialist movement.

Nor was the election devoid of practical Socialist victories. The large vote swept into office ten Socialist members of the State Assembly, seven members of the Board of Aldermen and a justice of a local civil court.

Less spectacular Socialist campaigns were crowned by equally successful results in other local elections. In Chicago the Socialist Party, confronted by a fusion of all other political forces, polled almost a third of the total vote, and phenomenal increases of the Socialist vote were recorded in Cleveland and Buffalo. The war-time election of 1917 signalized the high-water mark of the Socialist political strength in the United States.

Among the practical achievements of the New York election there was besides a very important by-product. It has, I believe, never been fully appreciated to what extent this Socialist campaign helped the women of the country to secure the right to vote.

In 1917 there was submitted to the voters of the state of New York a proposed constitutional amendment extending the franchise to women. In the city of New York, containing about one-half of the state's voting population, the amendment was to be voted on in the same election in which the mayor was to be chosen. Two years earlier a similar amendment was heavily defeated by the voters of the state and in the earlier stages of the 1917 campaign the prospects of carrying it did not look any too bright. I happened to know that the leaders of the movement were rather pessimistic about the outlook and were preparing to curtail their campaign activities.

The aroused public interest that marked the mayoralty campaign from the outset, seemed to me to offer a splendid opportunity to serve the cause of woman suffrage.

On the 10th of October I addressed an open letter to all of my opponents in the mayoralty contest, calling their attention to the pending amendment and urging them to give it public support as a nonpartisan measure of fairness and justice.

"If each of us," I urged upon my rivals, "will make an appeal, an earnest appeal, to his supporters to vote for woman suffrage, the measure will carry and we will be instrumental in righting the age-old wrong. Knowing the great importance of the direct and indirect issues involved in the city campaign, I assert that the issue of woman suffrage overshadows them all as a permanent measure of social justice and progress."

Without malice aforethought I put my opponents in a rather embarrassing position. None of them really wanted to take a definite stand on a collateral issue on which the sentiment of the voters was divided, but, on the other hand, they felt that to ignore my challenge might mean giving me an advantage with a large body of woman suffrage sympathizers. They hesitated and the Socialists kept on stressing the issue. In our meetings and in our campaign literature we urged the support of the woman suffrage amendment as ardently as the support of our candidates, and the other parties could not long remain silent on the issue.

The first to come out in the open was Mayor Mitchel. "Although I expect to vote for the amendment and hope it will be adopted," he wrote to me, "I do not consider the question one of the issues of the campaign. I feel that the wise course is to confine our discussions strictly to the issues."

I countered by asserting that the issue of woman suffrage is more closely related to the issues of the campaign than for instance the question of patriotism injected by Mr. Mitchel and reminded the Mayor that I called upon my opponents not to "discuss" but to advocate the measure.

"It seems to me," I concluded, "that we can rise above our immediate partisan interests to help a good nonpartisan cause. I am sorry my opponents do not see their way clear to accept the suggestion."

They finally did see their way. One week after my challenge Mr. Bennett, in a letter addressed to me and given to the press, avowed himself a whole-hearted supporter of the amendment; and shortly thereafter it was announced from the Democratic campaign headquarters that Judge Hylan also favored the measure.

Thus all candidates in the mayoralty race stood publicly committed to woman suffrage; and the leaders of the movement were quick to take advantage of the unexpected turn in favor of their cause. Anxious to clinch and emphasize New York's political unanimity for woman suffrage they organized a public demonstration, inviting all rival mayoralty candidates as the chief speakers. The meeting was held in the Brooklyn Academy of Music. Of the four invited candidates only two, Mayor Mitchel and I, appeared in person. Mr. Mitchell had lost his voice campaigning. His speech was read for him, while he stood on the platform enacting an eloquent pantomime in accompaniment to the reading. I had preserved or recovered my voice for the occasion, and proclaimed my faith in loud tone and unmistakable terms. The remaining two candidates sent written statements of their endorsement of woman suffrage, which were read at the meeting. From that night on the adoption of the amendment was practically assured. New York became the twelfth state in the Union to give the women the right to vote. The suffrage amendment enfranchised two million women in the state and practically compelled the adoption of the Federal constitutional amendment granting the vote to all women citizens of the country.

The New York amendment was carried by a majority of about 100,000 votes, practically all of which had been piled up in the city. The increase of the Socialist vote was about 110,000 and as a rule every Socialist voter supported the suffrage amendment. In Ohio, where a similar amendment was submitted to the voters at the same time and where there was no such powerful Socialist campaign to back it, it was defeated at the polls.

"The suffrage victory in New York is a Socialist victory," asserted the opponents of the cause. The middle-class leadership of the suffrage movement mildly denied the charge. The Socialists did not care to claim the credit. They were satisfied with the conviction that they had materially helped in the triumph of a good and progressive cause.

CHAPTER V

UNDER THE REIGN OF THE ESPIONAGE LAW

THE political campaigns of 1917 offered the last opportunity for a comparatively free discussion of war issues. Thereafter the government laid a heavy hand on all criticism of its war policies and expressions of pacifist sentiment.

In June, 1917, Congress passed the so-called Espionage Act—a war measure with Draconic penalties for military offenses, such as causing insubordination in the armed forces or obstructing the recruiting service.

The Act also conferred on the Post Office Department broad powers to exclude from the mails all matter violating the provisions of the Espionage Law or advocating treason, insurrection, or forcible resistance to the law.

The law was obviously intended to prevent actual interference with the war operations of the government, and there was nothing on the face of it to curtail the right of general discussion or criticism of war policies or peace aims.

It was not until a year later, in June, 1918, that the Act was drastically amended to include such non-military offenses as "profane, scurrilous and abusive language" about the government and Constitution of the United States, "or saying or doing anything" to obstruct the sale of government bonds or the making of loans by the United States.

But long before the amendment the government began to use the Espionage Law for the ruthless and indiscriminate suppression of criticism and opposition. Scores of newspapers and magazines were either totally excluded from the mails or deprived of the privilege of lower postage rates usually accorded to such publications, sometimes because of their dissent from the war policy of the government and sometimes also because their social, economic, or political views failed to meet the approval of the Post Office authorities.

It was the custom of the Department to call upon the offending publications to show cause why they should not be barred from the mails and to grant them a hearing before swinging the ax, but that was in most cases a mere formality. The Post Office just would not be shown, and its powers were complete and arbitrary.

Since most of the Socialist periodicals fell under the ban of the Department, I had frequent occasions to appear in such hearings on their behalf.

In those days the destinies of the Post Office Department were presided over by Albert S. Burleson, a Wilson appointee and an urbane politician from Texas, who was strong on patriotism but rather vague in his conceptions of social and economic philosophy.

The first case which brought me into contact with him was that of the *American Socialist,* the official weekly of the Socialist Party. The Department had declared three successive issues of the paper unmailable, and we were there to "show cause" why they should not remain unmailable, and why the "second class" mailing privilege should not be withdrawn from the publication.

Mr. Burleson conducted the hearing in person, although it was his general custom to refer such matters to the Third Assistant Postmaster General.

The issues of the paper under fire seemed to me particularly inoffensive, and I tried to impress upon Mr. Burleson that it was up to him to show cause why they should be barred from the mails rather than to us to prove the negative of the proposition.

Mr. Burleson had copies of the *American Socialist* before him with the incriminating matter marked in heavy red-pencil lines. A smile played on his lips as he indicated the first *corpus delicti*. "Here is, for instance, your own article, Mr. Hillquitt," he observed.

I knew the article, of course. It was a reprint of a preface I had written for a booklet entitled *American Socialists and the War*. It contained a summary of the familiar Socialist theory of the causes of modern wars with a brief review of the stand the Socialist Party had taken on all principal phases and developments of the World War before and after our entry in it. The booklet was circulating without molestation.

"What is wrong about this article?" I queried. "It is no more than a restatement of an economic theory and historical doctrine which Socialists all over the world have been consistently expressing at all times before and during the war."

"It may be," was the reply, "but the article nevertheless conveys the impression that the war is not fought for the high idealistic purposes which the President has announced, but for sordid business advantages. It tends to impair the spirit of enthusiasm for the war."

Almost immediately after the Armistice, President Wilson flatly declared that the causes of the war had been economic; but it was treason to state the obvious fact while the war was in progress. I realized the futility of any further attempt to argue the point and turned to the other two proscribed issues, inquiring wherein they had offended.

Mr. Burleson pointed out several articles in the nature of exposés of some particularly revolting instances of war profiteering. It almost took my breath away.

"You do not mean, Mr. Burleson, that profiteering is helpful to the conduct of the war and should be immune from criticism while it is going on?" I asked.

"It is an indirect attack on the war," was his reply in substance, and there the matter rested.

"But," I objected, "if Socialist newspapers are not to discuss the causes or problems of the war or any economic or political abuses in its conduct, what can they write about during the war?"

The predicament of the Socialist editor did not seem to embarrass Mr. Burleson in the least. "You can write all about the poor people," was his ready advice.

The restricted field of discussion thus assigned by the Post Office proved rather inadequate. While the poor remained with us and their woes were grievous and many, the monotonous subject of their poverty was not of sufficient interest to the Socialist Party or to the "poor people" themselves to warrant the continuation of the *American Socialist*. The paper suspended publication.

The suppression of the *American Socialist* was the prelude to all Socialist papers. Mailing privileges were withdrawn in rapid succession from the *Milwaukee Leader,* the Jewish *Daily Forward* (a Socialist and trade-union paper with a circulation of two hundred thousand copies in all parts of the country), and from several Socialist daily newspapers printed in German, Russian, and Hungarian.

In the early part of October and in the midst of the mayoralty campaign, the *New York Call* was ordered to show cause why its mailing privileges should not be withdrawn. The *Call* was the only Socialist daily newspaper printed in English in the city. It was highly aggressive and effective in support of the Socialist ticket, and the Post Office attack on the paper was generally interpreted as a blow aimed at the Socialist campaign.

Indignation ran high in the ranks of our supporters. On the eve of my departure for Washington to argue in behalf of the *Call,* a protest meeting was held in Madison Square Garden. It was a remarkable demonstration. The meeting was called on short notice, but long before the opening hour the immense hall was filled to capacity by an eager throng of men and women. Every expression of protest from the numerous speakers, against the arbitrary rule of the Post Office Department, was applauded to the echo.

While the meeting was going on in the hall, a street demonstration was spontaneously organized by masses of people who had failed to gain admission to the hall. "The waiting crowd after Madison Square Garden was filled to capacity," the *New York Tribune* reported the next morning, "extended two persons abreast, for twelve blocks in a serpentine line up and down and through the cross streets from Twenty-fourth to Thirtieth Street. It was estimated that eight thousand persons stood outside. They echoed the cheering that came from within the building."

When the meeting was over, the dispersing audience was joined by the crowds outside, and together they formed an impromptu parade marching up Fifth Avenue and shouting their protests against the contemplated strangling of their paper.

Three Post Office inspectors were detailed to attend the meeting and to hear the speeches. They heard and saw plenty and duly reported to their chief, but the vox populi did not go any farther with Mr. Burleson than my legal arguments. The *Call* lost its second-class mailing privileges.

One of the most interesting and amusing cases I was called upon to defend before the Post Office authorities was that of *Pearson's Magazine.*

Pearson's at one time a prosperous and widely read monthly magazine, was gradually losing its popularity, when in 1916 it

fell into the capable hands of Frank Harris, an unusually picturesque figure in the world of letters. Born in Ireland in 1855,
he ran away from school and came to the United States at the
age of fourteen. In New York, Chicago, and various midwestern towns he followed successively the occupations of boot-
black, hotel porter, cowboy, gambling-house "bouncer," and
butcher. He wound up the first period of his variegated American career by taking a course in the University of Kansas, and
returned to Europe after six years to study in Heidelberg, Göt-
tingen, and Berlin. He then embarked on a colorful and adven-
turous journalistic career. After a literary apprenticeship as a
war correspondent in the Russian-Turkish War of 1877, he associated himself with the *Evening News* of London and soon
rose to the position of managing editor of the paper. In a characteristic literary somersault he left the most sensational and
yellow newspaper of London to assume the editorship of England's most sedate and respectable journal, the *Fortnightly Review*, a position which he filled for eight years.

The next journalistic venture of Frank Harris was to purchase
the *Saturday Review*, which he sold four years later to embark
on the publication, one after another of several unsuccessful
magazines.

Contributors to the various periodicals owned or edited by Mr.
Harris were among the most illustrious of England's men of
letters, including G. Bernard Shaw, Oscar Wilde, H. G. Wells,
Rudyard Kipling, and Thomas Hardy, and some of these became his intimate personal friends.

Frank Harris was a prolific writer as well as a busy editor.
His first work of fiction, *Elder Conklin and Other Stories*, appeared in 1894. Fourteen years later his best-known novel, *The
Bomb*, was published. It was a powerful piece of realistic writing based on the Chicago Haymarket tragedy and attracted general attention. But the author's best achievements lay in the

field of literary essay and biography, such as *That Man Shakespeare, The Women of Shakespeare, Contemporary Portraits,* and *Oscar Wilde.*

Disheartened by failure in his later years in England, Mr. Harris came again to America in 1915 and settled in New York, where I was privileged to make his acquaintance.

Frank Harris' physical appearance was utterly incongruous with his mental make-up, his career and achievements. Slight of figure, nervous in movements, sharp-featured and flashily dressed, he looked like a "ringmaster in a circus," to borrow an apt description of Art Young's, rather than a student and writer.

Pearson's Magazine, under the editorship of Frank Harris, underwent a sudden and radical change in character and type. From a conventional and impersonal journal of popular fiction, it turned into an intensely personal organ of expression of its versatile editor. Literary essays, biographical sketches, and short stories alternated on its pages with discussion of social problems and expression of radical political opinion. Mr. Harris was on the whole opposed to the war, but his opposition was somewhat inconsistent and temperamental and not without a tinge of pro-Germanism and Anglophobia. He made no secret of his sentiments, and expressed them freely in his magazine.

The first foreboding of trouble with the Post Office Department came in the shape of a news story printed in the *New York Times* under the title "Watch on Pearson's."

"The attention of the Federal authorities," the newspaper reported, "was called to the January [1918] issue of Pearson's Magazine, which contains many articles sympathetic to Germany, laudatory references to Trotzky and Lenin, the Russian Bolshevist leaders, adverse comment on the peace attitude of President Wilson and uncomplimentary references to Premier Lloyd George of England." The paper then proceeded to print copious excerpts from articles in *Pearson's Magazine* in support of the charges.

Frank Harris' reaction to the *Times* story was characteristic. He reprinted the article in the next issue of his magazine with his own comment, ample and unrestrained. He had demanded a retraction from the editor of the *Times,* Mr. Harris informed his readers, but this was declined with the curt statement that "the article conveys the attitude of the United States Government towards Pearson's."

Mr. Harris questioned the truthfulness of the statement. "As no other paper, so far as I know, had the communication," he argued, "this implies that the *Times* was chosen to speak for the government.

"On reflection I could not believe this, for there are in the libel misstatements of facts, false inferences and ambiguous, bad English. Because of the English I am inclined to attribute the article wholly to the New York Times. Mr. Ochs, the owner, knows German, I believe, better than English. The purpose of the libel is manifestly to injure Pearson's Magazine.

"Accordingly the directors of the magazine have instructed our solicitor to take immediate proceedings against the Times."

I was the aforementioned solicitor thus instructed.

But there was not much to solicit about a libel suit, for the ink on Mr. Harris' article denying the authenticity of the *Times* story was hardly dry, when *Pearson's Magazine* was cited by the Post Office to show cause why its second-class mailing privileges should not be revoked. The order was based on the articles pointed out in the *Times* story, and as if to add insult to injury Mr. Harris' reply and disclaimer was made the basis of an additional charge. And so we found ourselves journeying to Washington to defend *Pearson's* before the high tribunal of the Post Office—Mr. Harris as the publisher and editor of the magazine, and I as its "solicitor."

Frank Harris was a great *causeur,* and in the first five hours of our train travel he entertained me with recitals of some of his amusing adventures and encounters and with exposition of his social and political views. He was a determined opponent of the Eighteenth Amendment in theory and practice and carried with him an abundant supply of whisky, to which he helped himself from time to time. I never saw a man drink whisky so freely, naturally, and copiously. He drank it like water, and the continuous libations seemed to have no effect beyond making him a little more emphatic in utterance and determined in purpose. He recognized that his case involved the fundamental issue of the freedom of the press and proposed to stand by it and to have some very plain talk with the Postmaster General. As he warmed up to the subject he rehearsed some of the anticipated dialogue and did not mince words in his part of it. It became quite apparent that I had an unruly client on my hands, and I felt it necessary to impress upon him the wisdom of toning down his language without compromising on the principle.

The hearing took place the following morning. One glance at my client satisfied me that he had not passed the night in undisturbed and thirsty slumber. I took the argument wholly into my hands, trying to save him from an undiplomatic outbreak. But my strategy was not entirely successful. "Why not come down to the crux of the question?" suggested the Assistant Postmaster General in charge of the proceeding, and turning to Mr. Harris he inquired point-blank: "Are you in favor of the war as conducted by our government and the Allied Powers?"

The question was sudden, and the answer was startling. "Passionately, sir, passionately," announced Frank Harris with his customary emphasis.

I do not know to this time whether the inquisitor or I was more embarrassed by the unexpected declaration of faith. The bottom had been knocked out from the charges—and from the defense. The only person in the room who seemed to be entirely pleased with the situation was Frank Harris. On our return trip he repeatedly referred with great satisfaction to the way he had nonplussed the Assistant Postmaster General. "He asked me a catch question," he said, "but I met it. 'Passionately,' I said, 'passionately.'" And he dwelt lovingly upon the expressive word.

The mailing privileges of the magazine were not withdrawn, but the Post Office held up the issue under attack for three weeks before releasing it. A similar procedure was followed with respect to six later issues of *Pearson's* within that year, and while Mr. Harris eventually obtained a clean bill of health in each instance, the circulation of the magazine was thoroughly disorganized and disrupted and the magazine itself was well-nigh ruined.

This was one of the subtle ways of the Post Office Department in dealing with opposition publications during the war.

And while the Post Office thus exercised its plenary powers under the Espionage Act against the recalcitrant press, the United States courts were busily operating under the criminal sections of the law. Federal district attorneys in the different parts of the country vied with one another in their zeal to detect and prosecute actual or fancied infractions of the law. Federal grand juries handed down indiscriminate indictments on flimsy evidence; trial juries convicted almost as a matter of course, and judges imposed harsh and drastic sentences.

To the everlasting credit of the American judiciary, be it recorded that there were some judges in those abnormal times who maintained perfect judicial fairness, unaffected by the prevailing mental epidemic of witch-burning. But they were, alas, too few and too far between.

By the spring of 1918 it was reported that about one thousand indictments had been found and more than two hundred convictions obtained under the Espionage Law.

Many, if not most, of the victims were Socialists, and I was enlisted in the defense of a number of them.

CHAPTER VI

THE MASSES TRIAL

THE first case I was called upon to defend under the Espionage Law was that of *The Masses*.

The defendants named in the indictment were Masses Publishing Company as publisher, Max Eastman, editor-in-chief; Floyd Dell, managing editor; Merrill Rogers, business manager, and John Reed, Arthur Young, Henry J. Glintenkamp, and Josephine Bell, contributors.

They were charged with conspiracy to "obstruct the recruiting and enlistment service of the United States" by publishing seditious articles, poems, and cartoons. The penalty for the alleged offense under the Espionage Law was imprisonment up to twenty years and a fine up to $10,000.

The Masses was a magazine of unique type. Founded in 1910 as an organ of the coöperative movement, it was taken over some two or three years later by a group of young writers and artists with radical political leanings, to be used as an outlet for their free and untrammeled expression. Most members of the group wrote or drew for conventional newspapers and magazines and were chafing under the restraint imposed by their despotic editors. They took their revenge in the columns of *The Masses*.

At the masthead of its cover page the magazine carried the following statement of its objects and policy:

"Searching for true causes."

"Against rigidity and dogma."

"Printing what is too naked or true for a money-making press."

"To do as it pleases—conciliate nobody, not even its readers."

Here are a few passages from Art Young's delightful account of the history of the magazine:*

". . . We decided to keep on publishing the magazine without funds—something nobody but artists would think of doing. When the question of an editor arose, I said we might try to get Max Eastman . . . to act as editor. I had met Max at the Jack London dinner and knew he was interested in *The Masses*. I had talked with him about the possibility of developing *The Masses* into something that would measure up to the quality of *Simplicissimus, Jugend,* Steinlen's *Gil Blas, Assiette au Beurre,* and other publications that were being watched by the alert young artists of the world. . . . John Sloan or Louis Untermeyer, I have forgotten which, wrote a letter addressed to Max which we all signed. The letter was as follows: 'You are elected Editor of *The Masses,* no pay.'

. . . .

"It is true we did not have many readers at that time, hence, 'nothing to lose,' but we were determined to enjoy our playground as long as our pent-up opinions and artistic emotions would supply the power.

"Our circulation varied as the years went on, always small compared to regular magazines—from fifteen thousand to twenty-five thousand—but at one time up to forty thousand.

"No money was paid for contributions, but most of us held stock in The Masses Publishing Company just for fun.

. . . .

"Once a month, sometimes twice, these gatherings of the artists and writers continued throughout the magazine's existence . . . to draw up the curtain on the personnel of a typical *Masses* meeting as I saw it would show something as follows:

"Near a table piled with manuscripts and drawings would be seen

* From *On My Way,* by Art Young. Copyrighted 1928 by Liveright Publishing Corp.

Max Eastman, a picturesque, slow-moving, tall boy with a careless head of hair and a passion for truth, polemics, tennis and swimming. He was fond of colorful surroundings, and had a genius for 'seeing' the feeling in a manuscript or drawing and detecting the artificial or imitative. He relished the artists' unfinished spontaneous sketches, yet to be organized into completeness. There was Max, his languorous frame draped over a comfortable chair, not always looking happy—for he was more responsible than the rest of us for the high-jinks that the contributors were indulging in, and the raising of funds to pay the fiddler. Near by was Floyd Dell, frail, nervous, taking short puffs at a cigarette, hacking, blinking and smiling, giving a funny little toss of his nicely modeled head in conversation. In those days he wore white pants, an orange-colored tie and a Byronic collar. Besides writing essays, stories and book reviews he would dash off a play between puffs for the Provincetown Theatre.

. . . .

"John Sloan was there, dressed in black, holding a drawing off and squinting at it critically. Sloan was a man of universal vision and understanding. We elected him art editor whenever we thought it time to have another election."

Among the galaxy of famous authors and artists who contributed to the magazine more or less regularly were, besides those mentioned, Inez Haynes Gillmore, Mary Heaton Vorse, Lincoln Steffens, Eugene Wood, Sherwood Anderson, Carl Sandburg, James Oppenheim, Ernest Poole, Leroy Scott, John Reed, George Bellows, Stuart Davis, Arthur B. Davies, Maurice Sterne, W. J. Glackens, Boardman Robinson, A. Walkowitz, and Maurice Becker.

Max Eastman at the time of the trial was thirty-four years old. He had been associate professor of philosophy at Columbia University and quit the post in 1910 to devote himself to literature. He already had several noteworthy books to his credit, including one on the Appreciation of Poetry. His engaging personality, indulgent manner, and keen mind made him the cementing force of the individualistic and temperamental contributors that made up the shifting and ill-defined staff of *The Masses*. He was generally considered as the "ring leader" of the indicted group.

Floyd Dell, who was then thirty-one, had not yet attained the success as a novelist and playwright that was to come to him later, but in the narrower circle of his friends his talents and critical acumen were highly appreciated.

John Reed was a noted war correspondent and a writer of unusually virile and trenchant style. His account of the Bolshevist revolution,* which he described as an eye-witness, is a masterpiece of vivid and fascinating narrative. He bade fair to become a literary star of first magnitude, equal to if not exceeding the power of Jack London, but his promising career was cut short by typhus, which he contracted in Russia in the service of the Soviet government at the age of thirty-three years.

Young, who presumably was baptized Arthur and was thus designated in the indictment, was never known to anybody by any other name than "Art." His cartoons are superb in artistic execution and in the exquisite ironical portrayal of social types. Art Young may be justly called the American Daumier.

He was the oldest of the group, fifty-two years of age, stocky, bald, and jovial. He had the talent of a genius and the soul of a child. He is loved by everybody who has had the privilege of being admitted to his intimacy, and Art does not make admission difficult. There was something inexpressibly humorous in haling Art Young before the bar of justice as a political conspirator.

The specific publications upon which the indictment was based were:

A short article by Max Eastman entitled "A Question," which expressed admiration for the moral courage of those who resisted

* *Ten Days That Shook the World* (New York: Boni and Liveright, 1919).

conscription on conscientious grounds and protested against the tone of ridicule and contempt generally adopted against them by the press;

A collection of letters written by conscientious objectors in English prisons and accompanied by an introduction from the pen of Floyd Dell commending their example to their comrades of the United States;

A poem in blank verse by Josephine Bell, entitled "A Tribute," and dedicated to the famous anarchist Emma Goldman and Alexander Berkman, who had just been convicted under the Espionage Law (about this poem we shall have more to say a little later);

An "article" by John Reed, which consisted wholly of quotations from a statement of the medical director of the National Mental Hygiene Committee, published in the *New York Tribune* (the gist of the doctor's observations was "that the frequency of mental disease among the soldiers has been an unexpected and staggering factor of the present war"), with only a headline supplied by the "author"—"Knit a Strait-Jacket for Your Soldier Boy";

A cartoon by Henry J. Glintenkamp representing "Death" taking the measurements of a drafted soldier for his coffin (inspired by a press notice to the effect that the Department of War had ordered an enormous quantity of coffins);

And, finally, a cartoon by Art Young entitled "Having Their Fling." This represented a mad war dance of the principal institutions of the country, the press, business, government, and the pulpit, symbolized by characteristic figures and postures of the editor, capitalist, politician, and clergyman. "All for Democracy," shouts the thin smooth-shaven editor. "All for Honor," proclaims the corpulent capitalist under a shower of coins and dollar bills. "All for World Peace," asserts the sleek shirt-sleeved politician. "All for Jesus," intones the man in clerical garb with his hands joined in prayer and his eyes piously gazing upward. In the background is an orchestra playing dance tunes on war implements, gleefully led by his Satanic Majesty.

The indictment was found in November, 1917, and the case was reached for trial in the United States District Court in April, 1918. It was one of the first important cases to be tried under the Espionage Law, and for that reason and because of the prominence of the defendants it attracted widespread attention. Throughout the eight days of the trial the courtroom was thronged with distinguished and other visitors, and the newspapers gave generous accounts of the proceedings.

In the course of the trial the number of defendants shrank to five. John Reed was in Russia. He came back as soon as he could arrange for passage when he learned that he was wanted, but too late for trial. Glintenkamp had departed to parts unknown and the indictment against Josephine Bell was dismissed at the close of the prosecution's case.

Art Young thus describes the latter incident:

". . . Mr. Hillquit was sure that there was no line in the poem that could be construed as illegal, so he appealed to the Judge to quash the indictment against Josephine Bell. Mr. Hillquit handed the poem to the Judge to read. His Honor adjusted his glasses, read it slowly, then handed it back to Mr. Hillquit, saying: 'Do you call that a poem?'

"Mr. Hillquit replied, 'Your Honor, it is so called in the indictment.'

"The Judge said, 'Indictment quashed.'"

The story gained considerable currency in this amusing form, but in justice to the court and the poetess I am impelled to confess that it represents a somewhat colored artistic interpretation of a prosaic legal procedure. As I recall it the indictment against Miss Bell was dismissed for legal insufficiency rather than for lack of artistic merit in her poem. I leave it to the discerning reader to judge whether it deserved to be dismissed on both grounds. Here is the poem:

> *Emma Goldman and Alexander Berkman*
> *Are in prison tonight*
> *Although the night is trembling beautiful*
> *And the sound of water climbs down the rock*
> *And the breath of night air moves through*
> *the multitudes and multitudes of leaves*
> *That love to waste themselves for the sake*
> *of the summer.*
> *Emma Goldman and Alexander Berkman*
> *Are in prison tonight*
> *But they have made themselves elemental forces*
> *Like the water that climbs down the rocks;*
> *Like the wind in the leaves;*
> *Like the gentle night that holds us;*
> *They are working on our destinies;*
> *They are forging the loves of the nations;*
>
> .   .   .   .
>
> *Tonight they are in prison*

By irony of fate three of the four individual defendants had radically changed their views on the war between the date of the publication of the offensive articles and cartoons and the trial.

Max Eastman had been won over to the support of the war when the onerous terms of the Brest-Litovsk "Peace Treaty" seemed to endanger the Russian revolution, and when President Wilson in his answer to the Pope on February 11th, practically endorsed the Soviet peace program.

Floyd Dell had undergone a similar mental evolution and had even come to accept conscription as "probably the most successful way of prosecuting a war." He registered for the draft, waived his original conscientious objections, and at the time of the trial expected to be called to service any day.

Merrill Rogers had also veered around to the support of the war.

The Masses itself no longer existed. It had ceased publication largely on account of difficulties with the Post Office Department, and had been succeeded by a new magazine baptized *The Liberator,* which adjusted itself to the conditions of war and censorship with better grace than its rebellious predecessor.

Thus the principal objects of the prosecution's attack had been largely eliminated. What remained was the issue of the freedom of the press in war times and, of course, that twenty years' penalty.

In justice to the former *Masses* editors it must be stated that they disdained to take advantage of their altered war attitude and were determined to fight the case on the principle involved.

Associated with me in the defense was Dudley Field Malone, who was anything but a pacifist or Socialist, and whose interest in the case was largely confined to the free-press issue.

We realized at the outset that our task would be exceedingly difficult, but not until the opening of the trial could we appreciate the whole depth of prejudice and the impenetrable atmosphere of hostility that confronted our clients.

The first test came in the selection of the jury. The panel consisted of several hundred citizens, most of them middle-aged or elderly business men, active or retired, of hopelessly conventional middle-class psychology, mentally paralyzed by the war. The men from among whom the defendants were to choose twelve of their "peers" to sit in judgment over their thoughts, aims, and conduct belonged to a species of humanity entirely different from theirs, intellectually, morally, almost physically.

"Are you prejudiced against pacifism and pacifists?" was one of the first questions I addressed to each talesman as he took his seat in the jury box, and invariably the answer would come promptly and emphatically, "Yes." They were prejudiced against pacifists and Socialists, against writers and artists, against anything that tended to disturb the dead level of drab conformity and uniformity, and they gloried in their prejudices.

The most promising statement of mental attitude I was able to extract from some of the prospective jurors was that, while they were prejudiced against the defendants, they thought their prejudices might be overcome by proof and argument, thus starting with the assumption of the defendants' guilt and casting the burden on them to prove their innocence.

When I asked Judge Augustus N. Hand, who presided at the trial, to excuse talesmen of that frame of mind, the Judge, who was eminently fair in all his rulings and in his charge to the jury, dryly remarked: "You cannot get a jury anywhere in the United States not prejudiced against pacifism." The observation was undoubtedly true, but it did not add much to the happiness and comfort of the defendants.

At last twelve men as "good and true" as could be found in the adverse circumstances were selected, and the trial proper started.

It proceeded in an atmosphere of unrelieved tenseness reminiscent of a court-martial rather than an ordinary criminal trial before civil authorities. As the prosecuting attorney read the incriminating articles to the jury in accusing and impressive tones, supplementing them by other pacifist and heretical utterances of the men before the bar, and as each of the jurors gravely examined the offending cartoons submitted for their inspection, a solemn and concentrated silence reigned in the courtroom which boded the defendants no good.

The windows of the courtroom overlooked the City Hall Park in which booths were erected for the sale of Liberty bonds and loud and lively canvassing was carried on uninterruptedly. Every now and then a band in the park would strike up a patriotic tune, whose familiar strains would penetrate into the courtroom. Then the proceedings would be spontaneously suspended, and everybody, including the judge and the jury, would rise and remain standing until the last note would gradually die away, and the jurors would resume their seats glowering at the defendants with an expression of grim determination to do their full patirotic duty by them.

At last the case for the prosecution was in and the defendants had the floor.

In our opening addresses Mr. Malone and I made valiant efforts to divorce the jurors from their admitted prejudices against the defendants and their views on war. In different language and from different approaches each of us entered upon an elaborate discussion of the constitutional rights of American citizens to think as they are moved to, and to freely express their thoughts so long as such expression does not run counter to a definite law which prohibits it. How trite and commonplace these elementary principles seem in normal times, and how bold and defiant they sounded on April 18, 1918, in the war-laden atmosphere of the courtroom!

I tried to explain to the jurors the mental processes of the men they were called upon to judge, the purity of their motives in opposing our entry in the war and the system of conscription. I argued that true patriotism, the concern for one's country and its people is at least as consistent with a desire to protect them from mass slaughter as with honest war enthusiasm, and I concluded:

"These then were our honest views. Were we wrong? Were we right about it? Gentlemen, you are not called upon to pass on this question. History will be our Jury. No human being today can assume to render final judgment on the great problems which the world catastrophe has put before us. You are called upon to pass on only one thing: Are these men criminals? Did they conspire to injure their country? Did they conspire with the Imperial German Government in this war?"

Then each of the defendants took the stand to explain his attitude and to deny the mythical conspiracy.

The witness stand was turned into a lecture platform, and for four days Max Eastman, Floyd Dell, and Art Young were given an opportunity to instruct the judge, the jury, and the numerous spectators in their views on war, conscription, conscientious objections, peace programs, Socialism, Russia, international relations, and other academic topics not usually associated with the daily preoccupation of criminal conspirators.

To Max Eastman, as the star witness for the defense and the master mind of the "conspiracy" fell the largest part of the explaining. Cool and self-possessed in manner, clear and frank in statement, he seemed to impress the jurors or at least some of them.

Floyd Dell also made an excellent witness, while Art Young had a rather uncomfortable time of it on the stand. He was asked to explain the intent and meaning of his cartoon "Having Their Fling"; but Art can say infinitely more with one stroke of the pencil than with a hundred words. The cartoon, besides, was perfectly obvious and stood in no need of explanation. The best the hard-pressed cartoonist could say by way of explanation was that he tried to picture the world as war-crazy. "But why represent the devil as conducting the orchestra?" insisted Earl Barnes, the energetic but rather fair-minded prosecuting attorney. For a moment Art seemed stumped by the question, then he answered somewhat impatiently: "Well, since, in the definition of General Sherman, war is Hell, it seemed to me appropriate that the devil should lead the band."

On the whole the proceeding bored Art Young and one afternoon when the air in the courtroom was close and the prosecutor was introducing a particularly damaging piece of evidence, he fell asleep. My attention to the blissful state of my client was called by the rhythmical sounds of his gentle snoring.

I shook him cautiously, whispering: "Wake up, Art. You are on trial for your life!" He did, looked bewilderedly around him, and mechanically reached for a sheet of paper on which he rapidly sketched a most amusing cartoon of the incident.

It took the jury forty-eight hours to make up their minds that they could not agree on a verdict. Our strenuous defense, our arguments and pleas, had won over two jurors, who at least were willing to give the defendants the benefit of a doubt. The remaining ten jurors voted solidly for conviction.

Characteristic of the temper of the time was the fact that the righteous majority jurors informed the authorities of the proceedings in the jury room, charging that they were thwarted in their determination to convict by two "recalcitrant" jurors "who consistently displayed Socialist and pacifist tendencies." The newspapers unblushingly reported the scandalous incident, with the assurance that "a Federal inquiry is practically certain to result."

The case was retried several months later. Another disagreement of the jury followed, and the government dropped the prosecution.

CHAPTER VII

EUGENE V. DEBS, VICTOR L. BERGER, AND SCOTT NEARING

PROSECUTIONS under the Espionage Law became a veritable epidemic in the Socialist movement. Personally, I escaped unscathed to the deep chagrin of some of my patriotic contemporaries. One of New York's aggressive newspapers made it a habit to refer to me invariably as the "unindicted Mr. Hillquit," and other press suggestions in the nature of "memento mori" were not lacking. I was myself rather puzzled by my unindicted state, and it was not until a few years later that I happened to learn the secret of my immunity. It appears that the government seriously considered taking proceedings against me, but that on taking counsel with certain influential advisers it decided against the move, fearing that it might antagonize a considerable body of people in New York. My large vote in the mayoralty election had the effect of quashing the contemplated indictment before its birth.

As to reasons for an indictment, hardly any were required in those balmy days. I saw persons indicted, convicted, and sentenced to long prison terms on grounds much flimsier than those furnished by some of my frank public utterances, and I was the avowed author of the greater part of the proscribed St. Louis War Proclamation of the Socialist Party.

But if I was free from personal prosecution I was exceedingly busy with the defense of many of my less fortunate comrades. Those were strenuous times for Socialist lawyers, and especially for me. Almost every day brought new indictments under the Espionage Law in all parts of the country, and I undertook the defense in a number of these cases. Among the most important and noteworthy of these were the cases against Eugene V. Debs, Victor L. Berger, and Scott Nearing.

Mr. Debs was indicted for a speech he made at a convention of the Socialist Party of Ohio at Canton on June 16, 1918. It was a characteristic Debs speech and was made under circumstances illustrative of the nobility of mind of the great Socialist humanitarian.

By the summer of 1918 a large section of the Socialist movement was beginning to feel a certain change of heart on the question of supporting the war. The harsh terms of the Brest-Litovsk Treaty forced by a triumphant German militarism upon the revolutionary government of Russia and threatening to crush the "first Socialist republic in the world," together with President Wilson's announcement of generous and progressive peace terms and their haughty rejection by the government of the Kaiser, had combined to arouse a sentiment of greater friendliness to the cause of the Allies and stronger hostility to the Central Powers in radical anti-war circles, and the sentiment was shared by a number of Socialists. A proposal was made for a special party convention to consider the advisability of modifying the strict anti-war attitude of the St. Louis Proclamation. It was rejected by the National Executive Committee of the party solely on the ground that a free exchange of opinion was impossible under the conditions then prevailing, and that those still adhering to the party's uncompromising anti-war stand would be placed in serious jeopardy if they attempted to express their views.

Eugene V. Debs was among those who favored a restatement of the Socialist position on the war. He had frankly and publicly expressed his views on the subject. He had come to abhor Prussion militarism as the greatest menace to the peace and progress of the world, and at the time of his Canton speech his sympathies were largely on the side of the Allies in this war.

But shortly before the date of his speech outrageous sentences had been imposed against some of his comrades convicted for alleged anti-war activities.

In Canton, where the convention was held, three of the most active Socialist leaders in Ohio, Charles E. Ruthenberg, Alfred Wagenknecht, and Charles Baker, were serving one-year sentences in the workhouse for alleged infractions of the Conscription Act.

Kate Richards O'Hare, a popular Socialist propagandist of St. Louis, was sentenced to imprisonment for five years on testimony which was palpably false and absurd.

Rose Pastor Stokes was convicted for a speech delivered in South Dakota in the course of which she asserted that "the government could not serve both the profiteers and the employees of profiteers." She was sentenced to ten years in prison. The conviction was subsequently reversed on appeal, but at the date of Debs's Canton speech it still stood.

In Chicago a wholesale trial of 112 members of the Industrial Workers of the World (I.W.W.) was in progress before Judge Kenesaw M. Landis. Their strikes and other normal trade-union activities were made the basis of a charge of conspiracy to obstruct the war. It was a naked and brutal class prosecution conducted to the accompaniment of unleashed capitalist fury in and out of the courtroom.

Gene Debs was stirred to flaming indignation. His fine sense of justice and fair play was outraged. His comrades were being persecuted. He would not place himself in a position of safety as he well could if he had limited himself to a frank statement of his war views.

As it was, his speech was mainly devoted to the propaganda of

Socialism. He made but few references to war in general and none at all to the particular war then going on.

But he was emphatic in declaring his sympathy for and solidarity with his convicted comrades.

"I am proud of them," he said, referring to Ruthenberg, Wagenknecht, and Baker. "They are there for us, and we are here for them."

And about Rose Pastor Stokes:

"What has she said? Nothing more than I have said here this afternoon. If she should be sent to the penitentiary for ten years, so ought I."

He ardently denounced the I.W.W. trial and declared that "the I.W.W. in its career has never committed as much violence against the ruling class as the ruling class has committed against the people."

It was not an anti-war speech that Gene Debs made in Canton. It was mainly a protest against the brutal prosecution of opposition opinion. He felt unhappy at large while his comrades were in jail and challenged the government to deal with him as it had dealt with other Socialists.

The challenge was speedily accepted.

On the 20th day of June, 1918, four days after the Canton speech, a Federal grand jury empaneled in Cleveland returned an indictment against Eugene V. Debs, charging him with violation of the Espionage Law on ten counts.

The "Berger case" presented different features which made it not less interesting than the Debs case.

Victor L. Berger was indicted jointly with Adolph Germer, J. Louis Engdahl, William F. Kruse, and Irwin St. John Tucker of conspiracy to violate the Espionage Law. The indictment was found by a Federal grand jury in Chicago.

Adolph Germer was the national secretary of the Socialist Party; J. Louis Engdahl was the editor of the party's official

organ, the *American Socialist;* William F. Kruse was the director of the Young People's Socialist League; Irwin St. John
Tucker had no official position in the party, and Victor L. Berger
was one of seven members who constituted its National Executive Committee.

The charges against Adolph Germer were that he had printed
and distributed copies of the St. Louis "Proclamation and War
Program" and three anti-war pamphlets written by Irwin St.
John Tucker and entitled "Down with War," "The Price We
Pay," and "Why You Should Fight."

J. Louis Engdahl was charged with publishing in the *American
Socialist* certain articles, poems, and cartoons of a character construed to be in opposition to war.

William F. Kruse was accused of having written letters to two
members of the Young People's Socialist League offering to
advise them on claims of exemption from the draft and approving the position of conscientious objectors.

The offense of Irwin St. John Tucker was predicated on the
authorship of the pamphlets already mentioned, while Victor L.
Berger was charged with responsibility for five articles printed in
his paper, the *Milwaukee Leader,* at different times.

It was quite obvious that the five defendants were charged
with separate and independent offenses. Mr. Berger was in sole
control of the *Milwaukee Leader,* and none of the other defendants had any part in the paper; none of William F. Kruse's
co-defendants had any connection with his incriminating private
letters; Mr. Tucker was in no way concerned with the management of the party affairs or of the *Milwaukee Leader;* Engdahl's activities were confined to editing the *American Socialist,*
and Germer's functions were purely administrative and did not
extend beyond the direct routine work of the party.

Yet, under the indictment, each of the five defendants was
made responsible for all the acts and utterances of the other four.

Victor Berger could be convicted for the youthful indiscretions of William Kruse, although he knew nothing about them. William Kruse could be punished for the outspoken articles of Victor Berger, although he was not consulted about them and perhaps never read them. Both could be held accountable for the pamphlets of Irwin St. John Tucker, although they might never have met the author, and J. Louis Engdahl could be convicted for offenses committed by Berger, Kruse, and Tucker or any of them, although there might have been nothing objectionable in the *American Socialist* for which alone he was responsible.

The absurd and revolting result was achieved by resort to the legal fiction of conspiracy, which stultifies the Anglo-Saxon law and which has been so often abused by the courts in labor cases. It was the favorite form of prosecution under the Espionage Law.

The theory of conspiracy moves in a fantastic, vicious circle. A number of individuals unconnected in the offense charged or with each other are tried together. Everything said or done by any of them is admissible against everybody else on the ground that they are responsible for one another as fellow conspirators, and the alleged conspiracy is established by combining the individual acts and statements of the different defendants.

The Nearing case was also based on the theory of conspiracy.

Scott Nearing, a former college professor and recent convert to Socialism, had written a pamphlet under the title "The Great Madness," and the American Socialist Society, which operates the Rand School of Social Science, had published it.

It was a booklet on war and the causes of war written from the orthodox Socialist viewpoint. The author and publisher were jointly indicted on the charge of a conspiracy to obstruct the war.

The Debs case was to come on for trial some time in September, 1918, and the Berger case a little later. In both cases I was associated with Seymour Stedman, a Socialist lawyer of prominence, experience, and ability. The Nearing case I handled alone.

I felt tired. The strenuous work of the mayoralty campaign in the preceding year, followed by an uninterrupted series of preparations, trials, and appeals in espionage cases, in addition to incessant activities in Socialist and peace movements and my regular professional work, had begun to tell on my health. I lost weight and developed other disquieting symptoms and decided to take a rest before plunging into the trials ahead of me.

I chose for my contemplated vacation the village of Saranac Lake in the Adirondack Mountains, where I had spent several summer vacations in the past, and settled down for what I thought would be a "solid rest" of two weeks.

Incidentally I decided to consult a physician.

Dr. Hugh Kinghorn, who was practising in Saranac Lake and specialized in tubercular diseases, which was the principal industry of the village, was an old friend of my family, and to him I applied. He was a Scotch Canadian, and was known for the soundness of his judgment and thoroughness of his methods. He examined me carefully and then inquired: "How long do you intend to remain in Saranac Lake?" To my airy answer, "Oh, I can stay two full weeks if necessary," he remarked slowly and gravely: "No, Mr. Hillquit, it is not a question of two weeks or two months. You will be fortunate if you can resume work in two years."

I gasped. Two years, when every day counted; two years of inaction when the world was aflame with convulsive activity. My whole mind was absorbed by my pending espionage cases, the cases of my friends and comrades for which I had assumed prime responsibility. No prison sentence could have struck me such a heavy blow as did the sentence of this friendly, mild-mannered, and sympathetic physician. My mind was quickly made up.

"Doctor, I cannot do it. I must go back to work regardless of consequences," I announced.

My emphatic determination did not impress Dr. Kinghorn. He quietly remarked: "You cannot go back to work. If you attempted to, you would probably not last through your first trial. The disease (pulmonary tuberculosis) has got a strong grip on you. You must go to bed and remain in bed for at least six months before you can hope for any sign of improvement."

There I was, torn out of life and activity without warning and consigned to the impotent and useless existence of an invalid for years, perhaps forever.

I was despondent and in black despair, but soon I was to learn how readily the human mind can adjust itself to all situations.

Within a day or two my wife had joined me in Saranac Lake and taken full charge. For two years she remained practically my sole contact with outside life, always at my bedside, watching me, cheering me up, and gradually nursing me back to health. And after the first shock was over, I soon developed a realistic sense of proportions and values in life. The world was moving along its tortuous and irrational course without me, as well or badly as it had been doing with my active and ardent participation.

The Socialist movement followed its inevitable development determined by the peculiar social and political conditions of the times. The defense of my espionage cases passed into the capable hands of Seymour Stedman, and their outcome was predetermined by the fixed state of the judicial and public mind.

From my sick bed in Saranac Lake I followed the developments of these cases with intense interest through newspapers and private communications.

Eugene V. Debs went to trial in the early part of September, 1918. He was found guilty and at the age of sixty-two years was sentenced by Judge D. C. Westenhaver, a "progressive," to serve ten years in the penitentiary.

It was an extraordinary trial. The defendant's conduct throughout it was reminiscent of the meek martyrdom of an early saint rather than the defiant demeanor of a dangerous revolutionary agitator of the twentieth century.*

The main charge against him was based on his Canton speech, but the prosecution also called as a witness against the aged Socialist leader a newspaper reporter, who had interviewed him before the speech.

The witness testified that he had interviewed Mr. Debs before the meeting and asked him whether the newspapers had correctly quoted him as repudiating the St. Louis anti-war proclamation. Mr. Debs, according to this witness, had answered: "In the light of the Russian situation I think we should have put forth a restatement of the aims of the Socialist Party, but I approved of the St. Louis proclamation at the time it was adopted in form and substance." He denied that he had ever repudiated the document.

The witness was not aggressive or malicious and seemed rather reluctant to incriminate the accused. When he concluded, Eugene Debs leaned over to him and said softly:

"All you said about me is true. I don't want you to ever feel that you have done me an injury by testifying against me. You had to do it, and you did it like a gentleman."

The only other witness for the prosecution was a stenographer who had taken the Canton speech by direction of the Department of Justice. He was young and inexperienced and frankly admitted that he was unable to take the speech verbatim and

* A detailed and moving account of the trial is contained in David Karsner's *Debs* (New York: Boni and Liveright, 1919).

that his notes were only in the nature of summaries of Debs's statements as he understood them. But Debs declared that the notes were substantially correct, and would not permit questioning their accuracy. He offered no testimony to deny, correct, or explain any of the statements attributed to him. He waived the customary summation of counsel at the close of the case and limited his defense to a speech to the jury. And what a speech it was! There was no denial, apology, or plea for mercy in it. It was a scathing indictment of the capitalist system and of the government prosecutions under the Espionage Law. The culminating point of his eloquent speech was his reference to the war. "I have been accused of having obstructed the war. I admit it," he calmly remarked. "Gentlemen, I abhor war. I would oppose the war if I stood alone. When I think of a cold, glittering steel bayonet being plunged into the white quivering flesh of a human being, I recoil with horror. I have often wondered if I could take the life of my fellow man, even to save my own."

Debs's speech in his defense was infinitely more provocative than the Canton speech for which he was tried. It sealed his fate.

During the deliberations of the jury Eugene Debs found time to write me one of his characteristically affectionate letters expressing sympathy with my condition and reassuring me about his own fate. He was perfectly at peace with himself.

The deliberations of the jury were comparatively short. After six hours they returned a verdict of "Guilty as charged in the indictment."

An appeal was taken to the United States Supreme Court which affirmed the conviction. The decision was unanimous, and the opinion was written—of all men—by Justice Holmes.

I always had a great admiration for the intellectual integrity and moral courage of Oliver Wendell Holmes. I have read and re-read his opinion in an effort to discover a justification for his conclusions even from a formalistic legal viewpoint. In vain. The opinion is mediocre in style and superficial in substance. It evades the fundamental issues and does not rise above the dignity of the police court philosophy. It is to my mind the poorest performance of Justice Holmes in his long and otherwise brilliant career on the bench.

The case of Berger, Germer, Engdahl, Kruse, and Tucker was tried before the redoubtable Judge Kenesaw Mountain Landis, who has since transferred his autocratic activities from the bench to the more congenial field of baseball. It was a bitterly fought and protracted contest, which ended in the conviction of all defendants. They were each sentenced to the maximum penalty of twenty years' imprisonment. Pending their appeal they were released on bail and the merciful judge fixed the amount of the bond at the sum of one hundred thousand dollars for each defendant. It is characteristic of the spirit which prevailed in the Socialist movement at the time that the enormous security was raised within twenty-four hours.

The defendants had objected to Judge Landis as their trial judge and·filed an affidavit of prejudice under the federal practice, charging that the judge had on a previous occasion delivered himself of a violent diatribe from the bench against all German-American citizens, saying that "their hearts reek with disloyalty." Victor L. Berger was a native of Austria; Germer was born in Germany, and Kruse was of German parentage. The judge disregarded the objection, but the conviction was subsequently reversed by the Circuit Court of Appeals on that very ground. The case was never retried.

The trial of the Nearing case resulted in one of the amusing paradoxes so prolific in our jury system. The charge was one of conspiracy, and the only two defendants and possible conspirators were Scott Nearing, the author of the pamphlet under attack, and the American Socialist Society, which had published it. The jury brought in a verdict of acquittal as to Mr. Nearing and one of conviction against the Society. The jurors had compassion for Scott Nearing, a person in the flesh, whom they saw and heard, but they had little sympathy with an impersonal corporation, a mere abstraction without physical existence.

The peculiar verdict left the American Socialist Society convicted of conspiracy with itself.

A motion to set it aside was denied by the presiding judge, who saw no inconsistency in the verdict. The American Socialist Society was sentenced to pay a fine of $3,000. The fine was paid by a sort of public subscription. The Society called on its friends to contribute one dollar each, and the sidewalk in front of the entrance to its office was immediately lined with rows of eager contributors. The Rand School is reported to have made a handsome profit on the transaction.

With the declaration of peace, prosecutions under the Espionage Law ceased, and the patriotic zeal which it had aroused found an outlet in the new sport of "Red baiting."

CHAPTER VIII

A LYNCHING OF THE CONSTITUTION

Lous Waldman has written a book of absorbing interest entitled *Albany: The Crisis in Government,* on the expulsion of the Socialist members of the New York Assembly in 1920.

As I scan its pages again, it brings back to me a flood of memories, memories of busy days and heated controversies, of humor and shame and of the darkest days in the political history of the country.

Five Socialist candidates had been returned to the Assembly by working-class districts of the city of New York. They were August Claessens, Louis Waldman, Charles Solomon, Samuel Orr, and Samuel A. De Witt.

At the, opening session of the Assembly on January 7, 1920, they were sworn in as members and participated in the election of a speaker and other officers.

Thaddeus C. Sweet, an up-state Republican and former speaker of the Assembly, was reëlected to that office and almost immediately staged the most dramatic scene ever enacted in any American legislative body.

Without notice or warning of the impending proceeding he turned to the sergeant-at-arms, and in slow and measured tones announced:

"The chair directs the sergeant-at-arms to produce before the Bar of the House Samuel A. De Witt, Samuel Orr, Louis Waldman, Charles Solomon, and August Claessens."

When the five Socialists, bewildered by the mystifying sum-

246

mons, were conducted in front of the speaker's rostrum, he addressed to them an obviously prepared speech in the manner of a judge imposing sentence upon a convicted criminal.

"You, whom I have summoned before the Bar of this House," he began, "are seeking seats in this body—you who have been elected on a platform that is absolutely inimical to the best interests of the State of New York and of the United States."

The amazing opening statement was followed by an enumeration of specific charges against the Socialist Party to the effect that it was not a regular political party but a "membership organization admitting within its ranks aliens and minors"; that Socialist elected officials were bound by the instructions of the party's executive committee; that the party was disloyal during the war, and that it was in sympathy with the Communist International and its program of violence and civil war.

Having publicly expressed his conviction that it was "quite evident" that the accused Assemblymen were guilty, he generously assured them that they would later be given an opportunity "to prove their right" to seats in the House.

The extraordinary statement of the speaker was immediately followed by a formal resolution offered by the Republican majority leader in substance reciting the charges of the speaker as findings of fact and proposing that the Socialist Assemblymen be denied their seats pending an investigation of their qualifications by the Committee on Judiciary to be thereafter appointed by the speaker.

No sooner was the resolution read by the clerk than it was put to a roll-call vote without debate. Of the one hundred and forty-five Republican and Democratic Assemblymen only two, William S. Evans and J. Fairfax McLoughlin, be it recorded to their everlasting credit, had the decency and courage to vote "No." All others as their names were called joined in the monotonous chorus of "Aye."

Thus the thing was done. Five members of an American legislative body duly elected by the citizens of their districts, were denied seats on the ground that the platform and constitution of their party did not meet with the approval of their fellow members belonging to other political parties. They were convicted first and given a trial afterwards with the burden of proving innocence placed upon them. Their judges, thirteen in number, were appointed by their accuser, and with one single exception consisted of men who, by voting in favor of the resolution, had publicly expressed their conviction that their Socialist colleagues were not fit for membership in the House.

For years Socialists had been represented in the Legislature of New York by delegations of varying strength. Their right to membership had never been questioned.

The New York State Constitution jealously guards the rights of elected public officials. Prescribing the usual qualifications of citizenship and age and the form of oath of office, it adds the emphatic injunction, "and no other oath, declaration or test shall be required as a qualification for any office or public trust."

Under this constitutional provision the Assembly had repeatedly and consistently held that it had no power to remove a member except for personal disqualification under the constitution or for misconduct.

How then could such a political monstrosity be perpetrated by a public official in such important and responsible position as the speaker of a legislative assembly and be condoned by an almost unanimous vote of the whole body?

For answer one must go back to the morbid psychology of hysteria and intolerance which still infested the country in that period.

Our active participation in the World War had been comparatively brief and did not afford enough time to our people to dissipate the fear, hate, aggressive nationalism, and high-handed lawlessness that are inevitable by-products of war. In other countries they were born and largely died out during the war itself. With us they sprang up during the war and became most virulent after the Armistice.

The Communist revolutions in Russia and Hungary and the general conditions of political and economic unrest in many countries of Europe added an element of panic to the prevailing hysteria in conservative and propertied circles of America.

The movement which began with wholesale prosecutions and monstrous sentences in flimsy "sedition" cases, was followed by lawless raids on headquarters of dissident organizations, seizures of their books and papers, and illegal deportation of "radicals."

The Overman Committee of the United States Senate and the Lusk Committee of the New York Legislature were busy securing "evidence" from all corners of the world to build up a fantastic theory of a mysterious, powerful, and dangerous movement in the United States to overthrow our government and to hoist the red flag of Communist revolution on the national Capitol.

Red baiting and heresy hunting became the fashion. Brutal force in dealing with everybody and everything suspected of radicalism met with general public favor. America had reverted to the practice of witch burning. Many third-rate politicians won fame and recognition in the disgraceful crusade, and many more envied them their laurels.

Thaddeus C. Sweet, who was a wealthy manufacturer with a limited intellectual horizon, had gubernatorial aspirations, and he undoubtedly expected that his drastic move in the Assembly would make him a popular hero. The 140 members of the Assembly who voted on his command were, with few exceptions, political nonentities and cowards.

Even in normal times it is sad to contemplate the cultural inferiority and lack of independence of the average American legislator. In other countries some of the most ambitious and able persons in public life strive for seats in parliament. To the practical American politician legislative office has little attraction because of its meager emoluments and limited patronage. There have, of course, always been men of ability and integrity in the legislative bodies of the United States, particularly in Congress, but they are the exception rather than the rule.

During the war and the period immediately after the war the legislative branch of our government had been largely reduced to the function of a rubber stamp of the executive department. And the prevalent caliber of the New York Assembly was particularly low at that period.

But the psychology of Mr. Sweet and his camp followers in the Assembly proved somewhat too simple and their strategy too raw. If they expected loud praise and commendation from the press for their "patriotic" move, they must have been badly disappointed.

The morning papers of January 8th seemed stunned and bewildered by what had happened in Albany, and none gave editorial expression of approval or disapproval except the New York *World*—which characterized Mr. Sweet's proceeding as "Bolshevism masquerading in the livery of Americanism"—and, of course, the New York *Call,* a Socialist newspaper. But within twenty-four hours the criminal folly of the proceeding was realized by a chastised and sobered public opinion. A shout of emphatic condemnation and indignant protest went up from the whole New York press. The *Evening Journal* characterized the suspension of the Socialists as "the most serious assault upon the liberties of the American people that has been made since a British king and parliament forced our fathers to protect their freedom with arms in their hands." The *Evening Post* denounced it as "a sinister threat against the fundamentals of democracy and representative government," and the Brooklyn

Standard Union decried it as "utterly wrong in principle and lamentable as a matter of policy." A similar critical stand was taken by other newspapers of New York, and by most of the press in the country. Even the hidebound conservative Republican *Tribune* characterized the act of the Assembly as "official lawlessness."

An avalanche of protests came to Mr. Sweet from persons of high standing in all walks of public life, here and abroad. The Association of the Bar of the City of New York, on motion of Charles E. Hughes, adopted a resolution severely condemning the suspension of the Socialist Assemblymen and appointed a special committee "to take such action as may in their judgment be necessary to safeguard and protect the principles of representative government." The committee consisted of Mr. Hughes, Morgan J. O'Brien, Joseph H. Proskauer, Louis Marshall, and Ogden L. Mills.

Realizing that they had made a bad break, a group of the more intelligent Assemblymen, headed by the Democratic floor leader, moved to rescind the suspension of their Socialist colleagues. Thirty-three members voted in favor of the motion, seventy-one against it, while forty-one preferred to dodge the issue by absenting themselves from the House while the vote was taken.

News of the astounding events reached me at Saranac Lake, where I was beginning to recover from my protracted illness.

A day or two later I was visited by a representative of the Socialist Party who had come to consult me about the situation and to inquire whether I felt well enough to take charge of the defense. I did.

The "trial" was opened in the Assembly Chamber at Albany on January 20, 1920, in an air of tense expectation.

The large hall was filled to the last inch of space with members of both houses of the Legislature, public officials, and a throng of private citizens who had been privileged to secure admission.

Special arrangements had been made to accommodate a horde of newspaper men from all parts of the country.

The Judiciary Committee, in charge of the proceedings, was headed by Louis M. Martin, as chairman.

Mr. Martin looked exceedingly unhappy and uncomfortable in his rôle. He was a good lawyer and probably had a certain private sense of justice. He must have known that the case was prejudged and that the "trial" was a farce, and must have suffered keenly in putting over some of the "rough stuff" of the proceeding. But private morality has no place in the political game as practised by the old parties. Mr. Martin knew exactly what was expected of him and was constrained to play his part.

He was subsequently made a Justice of the Supreme Court. A few years later business brought me to Watertown, where Mr. Justice Martin happened to be presiding. Through another judge he extended to me an invitation to have dinner with him. I did not accept.

To assist it in its investigations the Committee had retained a galaxy of eminent counsel, including John B. Stanchfield, Martin W. Littleton, Martin Conboy, former Supreme Court Justice Arthur E. Sutherland, former State Senator Elon R. Brown, besides the Attorney General of the State and members of his regular staff. These gentlemen introduced a new element in the complicated juridical relations of the case by assuming the dual rôle of advisers to our "unbiased" judges and prosecuting attorneys charged with the duty of establishing the guilt of the accused.

I had for my associates in the defense Seymour Stedman of Chicago, former candidate for Vice-President of the United States on the Socialist ticket, the late Gilbert E. Roe, a progressive Republican and former law partner of the elder Senator La Follette, Walter Nelles, S. John Block, and William Karlin, prominent Socialist lawyers.

We had carefully studied and prepared the case in all its phases. We had no illusions about its outcome. We knew that the cards were stacked against us, and that no amount of argument and persuasion would prevail against the dictates of the Republican machine.

But we felt that we were defending the fundamental principles of representative democracy for all time to come; that we were speaking to the whole people of the country and that perhaps never again should we have a similar opportunity to answer the criticisms and absurd accusations against Socialism as fully and before an audience as numerous and attentive.

We had nothing to lose and everything to gain from the "trial," and we engaged in it with vim and enthusiasm.

After the appearances of counsel on both sides had been noted, Mr. Hughes announced his presence in behalf of the Bar Association and offered his services and those of his colleagues on the committee "to make such suggestions and representations to the Committee as in our judgment may be deemed important in order that the proceeding may be heard and determined in accordance with sound constitutional practice."

Mr. Martin, however, had his own notions about sound constitutional practice and coldly turned down the offer of the distinguished jurist.

The field was now open to counsel for the accused assemblymen to launch an attack against the whole proceeding and the methods of the Committee.

Our first move was to challenge the right of the Committee to sit in the case.

"We hold," I said addressing the chairman and members of the Committee, "in the first place that you were appointed and selected by our accuser, and in the second place, that you have publicly and solemnly expressed your conviction of the guilt of the men who are before you now."

The challenge was duly overruled, and I followed it up by a motion to dismiss the proceeding on the ground that it was "without warrant in the Constitution or in the statutes of the State of New York and totally illegal and void." This was, of course, our heaviest legal battery, and I tried to make the most of it. I argued the motion exhaustively and earnestly, quoting the Constitution and citing numerous precedents in proceedings of both houses of Congress and the New York Assembly itself. I dwelt upon the dangerous character of the precedent about to be established and warned against its political consequences for all time to come.

My impassioned argument only served to bring forth an amazing instruction by Mr. Stanchfield, to the Committee.

"The Assembly of the State of New York has the power, unqualified power, to expel any member with or without reason, with or without cause," he declared. "You are the judges of the case. You may determine what in your judgment renders a man fit to sit in the Assembly, and nobody can question your conduct or your act."

This brutal doctrine of naked power and arbitrary judgment was adopted by the Committee, and determined its attitude throughout the proceeding.

My unsuccessful motion was followed by an argument by Mr. Stedman in the nature of what may be technically called a demurrer. In short, he contended that if all the charges against the Socialist Assemblymen were proven to be true they would still not afford legal ground for removing the Assemblymen from office. His argument was a masterpiece of keen analysis and logical reasoning, but it had no more effect on the Committee than the subsequent application of Mr. Block for a bill of particulars, so that the accused might at least be apprised of the specific acts charged against them. All motions and requests in behalf of the defendants met with blank and dry denials.

The second day of the "trial" was enlivened by a sensational speech by Martin W. Littleton. Ostensibly it was an answer to Mr. Stedman. In fact it was a specious plea in justification of Mr. Sweet and the Assembly. It was a masterpiece of brilliant oratory of the Fourth of July type, interspersed with copious quotations from the inspired text of the Declaration of Independence and invoking the memory of the fathers of the country, their struggles, and their political creed.

It was a great oration and held the large audience spellbound. As I sat there watching the effects of a magnificent gift enlisted in the service of a base cause and listening to the perversion of America's best revolutionary traditions and spirit to the support of the most flagrant and reactionary act of political oppression, I could not ward off a deep feeling of mingled sadness and indignation.

Although Seymour Stedman was slated to and subsequently did reply to Mr. Littleton, I could not resist the impulse to come back at him on one of his most telling points.

Rising somewhat out of order, I voiced my indignation in these words:

"Mr. Chairman, Mr. Littleton quoted me as having said yesterday that what is treason to-day, may become the law of the land to-morrow. He added very eloquently and effectively: 'It will become the law of the land if the traitors be allowed to write the law,' with the inference that it is the duty of this Committee of the Assembly to see to it that those whom you regard as traitors shall not be given a part in the writing of the law of this State; and it was this statement of all statements which provoked applause in this House, to the everlasting shame of those who participated in the demonstration, for years and years to come. For I maintain, Mr. Chairman and gentlemen, that there was no more reactionary, no more un-American statement ever made in a representative Assembly than this statement made by Mr. Littleton.

"There was a time when a few Americans—one I believe

named Patrick Henry, one Thomas Jefferson, and a few more—uttered the doctrine that this country should be independent from the constituted sovereignty of England. It was treason, Mr. Littleton, in those days. It was treason in the sight of all Tory statesmen and politicians, and, Mr. Littleton, if the people had proceeded then as you want this Committee to proceed now, if these men had not been allowed to have a voice in the legislative assemblies or in the councils of the nation, this glorious country, whose flag you so frequently wave, would now be an insignificant colony of England.

"There was a time when a certain William Lloyd Garrison proclaimed a doctrine which was absolutely revolutionary in those days—which aimed at depriving a substantial class of property, of sacred property in slaves. It was treason, and they were called traitors. There were very eloquent attorneys for the vested interests in those days also. If those who were then characterized as traitors had not been allowed a voice in our government and our institutions; if they had not been allowed to voice their 'traitorous' policies and philosophies, chattel slavery would still disgrace this country.

"Now, we have a right to hold our opinions about the welfare of this nation, no matter how anybody else, no matter how our opponents, consider our views.

"Just as those patriots preached in other times political independence and emancipation of slavery, so we are teaching to-day economic independence, emancipation of the working class and of the whole community. It sounds treacherous and traitorous to you. But it is our good right to hold those doctrines, and you are not our judges any more than we are yours.

"What we want you to do is to say whether or not you claim the right to dictate our political conscience. Remember, gentlemen, at all times, 'The Star Spangled Banner' is a beautiful and inspiring hymn, but it is not a legal argument in a case of such grave, tremendous, and vital importance as the one presented to you."

Almost immediately after the conclusion of his eloquent plea in support of the right of the Assembly to exclude members for their political views, Mr. Littleton excused himself from further participation in the trial because of a previous engagement to defend United States Senator Newberry in Michigan. Mr. Newberry's seat was contested on charges of bribery and corruption in his election. Mr. Littleton was retained to invoke the sacred rights of representative government in his behalf.

Mr. Martin gracefully excused him without the slightest sign of appreciating the irony of the situation.

The preliminary skirmishes consumed two full days, and now the decks were cleared for the introduction of evidence against the accused Assemblymen.

The air was thick with eager expectations. In the course of the opening arguments, counsel for the Committee had repeatedly and impatiently asked for an opportunity to present their "proof," and the newspapers were promised sensational revelations. They were to be sorely disappointed.

Through tedious days and weeks, counsel for the prosecution read into the record all sorts of ancient and modern documents, relevant and irrelevant, pertaining to the Socialist movement and not pertaining to it, documents that had been openly circulated by the thousands and were matters of common knowledge. Among these "sensational" documents were platforms, declarations, and proclamations of the Socialist Party; constitutions of the national, state, and local organizations of the party; manifestoes of the Communist International; the Constitution of Soviet Russia; excerpts from testimony before the Lusk Committee, and from the trials under the Espionage Law of Scott Nearing, Victor Berger, and the Rand School; long-forgotten articles published in Socialist newspapers and magazines and collected in anti-Socialist handbooks; stenographic transcripts of public speeches made by some of the defendants; the votes of Socialist Assemblymen in previous sessions of the Assembly on certain measures and bills unsuccessfully introduced by them (to prove that they had attempted to put through "measures of an offensive character"); alleged utterances of Eugene V. Debs, Lenin, Trotzky, and hosts of unknown soap-box orators.

Alongside the "documentary evidence," oral testimony was introduced in ample volume. There were witnesses who recounted from memory harrowing statements made years ago at street meetings by the accused Assemblymen or by unidentified Socialists.

The theory upon which this motley assortment of "evidence" was indiscriminately admitted was formulated by Mr. Stanchfield in this unmistakable language:

"Every pamphlet, every declaration, every speech, every statement of every man who is affiliated with or belongs to that party, not necessarily in a technical sense of belonging to it, but everybody who upholds those claims, who supports those principles, who stands upon that platform, is bound by the speeches, the sentiments, the writings, the books, the publications of every other man affiliated with that association, whether they were present at the time when it was made or when they were uttered, or whether they were absent."

As I am copying this statement from the official record, I still find it difficult to realize that it was intended not as a heavy satire but as a sober rule of law, and was seriously propounded by a distinguished member of the Bar and adopted by a legislative investigating committee as a guide in its procedure.

Probably the most sensational witness for the prosecution was a young lady of puzzling age, who swore that she was "almost eighteen" years old and that in 1917, i.e., three years earlier, she was "nearly seventeen." Her story was directed against Charles

Solomon and was very simple. As she recalled it, Solomon was making a Socialist speech at a street corner in Brooklyn, sometime after we had entered the war. A detachment of soldiers under the command of an officer came along for recruiting purposes. They asked Solomon for the use of his platform, but he refused with the emphatic statement, "The gutter is good enough for you."

"Was that all he said at the time?" queried the eager Mr. Stanchfield.

No, that was not all. Mr. Solomon had added, by way of explanation: "I would not let you wipe your dirty feet on it."

And then?

Then the defeated army retreated under the strains of "The Star Spangled Banner" and the intrepid Solomon celebrated his victory by spitting on the American flag.

When Maurice Block, a member of the Judiciary Committee, expressed his opinion that the young lady was "romancing," the unjudicial remark was on motion solemnly expunged from the record.

The star witness for the prosecution was one Peter W. Collins, a sort of itinerant professional anti-Socialist propagandist. He was called as an expert on the Socialist philosophy and Socialist practices.

There were then, as there are now, numerous serious authorities on the history, theory, and methods of Socialism in the non-Socialist or even anti-Socialist camp, men of academic training who had specialized in the subject and had made a thorough study of the voluminous Socialist literature. Mr. Collins was not in that class. He was what might be called a "live witness." He had gained his knowledge by talking to "thousands" of Socialists and debating with some of them. His theoretical equipment consisted of a few compiled pamphlets published by anti-Socialist societies. His testimony covered three full sessions, and never were more colossal ignorance and hair-raising absurdities paraded before a more appreciative audience.

Finally, the prosecution closed its case, and the suspended Assemblymen opened their defense.

After the first week of the trial, I went back to the Adirondacks to resume my interrupted cure, leaving the defense in charge of my colleagues under the capable direction of Seymour Stedman.

I now came back in a new rôle. I had left the trial as counsel for the defendants. I returned as a witness.

Louis Waldman describes this phase of the trial in the following language:

"The first witness called by the defense was Morris Hillquit, its chief counsel. Direct examination was conducted by Mr. Stedman.

"Mr. Hillquit's appearance on the witness stand was a surprise to the prosecution. It was highly pleasing to the audience, which by now had become eager to hear something authoritative concerning Socialism. Even counsel for the prosecution appeared deeply interested. They left their accustomed seats and drew up chairs close around Mr. Hillquit, with the intention of not missing a word. In fact, Mr. Hillquit was, by virtual unanimous consent, given the center of the stage. For three days he kept the stand, his testimony becoming more like the remarks of a professor addressing his class than a witness called in a trial involving a political struggle."

I do not know how a professor feels lecturing to his class, but I must confess that I thoroughly enjoyed the opportunity to give a complete exposition of my much distorted and maligned political creed and to tell the country through the assembled press correspondents the real philosophy, aims, programs, and methods of Socialism, particularly after all the ignorant twaddle that had filled the air of the Assembly Chamber for weeks.

Under the skillful questioning of Mr. Stedman, I sketched the history of the international Socialist movement, described the relations of the Socialist Party of the United States to the parties of other countries, its attitude toward Soviet Russia, its stand on war and its economic and political program. The searching and courteous cross-examination of Mr. Conboy gave me an additional opportunity for elaboration and elucidation.

Among the witnesses who followed me on the stand were Algernon Lee, who dwelt mainly on the economic theories of Socialism, and Otto F. Branstetter, the National Secretary of the Socialist Party. Mr. Branstetter, who was called to explain the structure, composition, and methods of the party, surprised the Committee by the information that a census of the party members had show 73 per cent of them to be native American citizens, and that the party was thus more "truly American" than the population of the country as a whole.

To prove that Socialism was not hostile to religion and did not seek to disrupt the family ties, the defense called a young Presbyterian clergyman, Norman Thomas, then a recent convert to Socialism, who deeply impressed the audience by his idealism and candor.

The last witnesses for the defense were the three suspended Assemblymen against whom charges of personal misconduct had been made, Waldman, Solomon, and Claessens.

Mr. Waldman gave an interesting account of the inner workings of the Socialist "caucus" in the Assembly.

As one of their first tasks the Socialist Assemblymen took up the platform planks and pledges upon which they had been elected, in an effort to translate them into concrete legislative proposals. The work was divided among them, and each member undertook to make a special study of the subjects assigned to him with the aid of the published literature, consultation with experts in the particular field, and supplemental original research.

The results of the studies were reported back to the conference, and when the provisions of any proposed measure were agreed on after full discussion, a bill would be drafted and submitted by the author.

Very little time was wasted on refutation of the absurd charges against their personal conduct, but the witnesses were examined and cross-examined on their social, economic, and political beliefs. To the unbiased observer it soon became evident that, intellectually and morally, the accused Socialist Assemblymen towered head and shoulders above their Republican and Democratic colleagues of the House, including their judges.

This concluded the testimony.

The trial was not without humorous incidents.

At one point of the argument, when Mr. Stedman sought to draw an analogy between the Assembly charges and an indictment in a criminal prosecution, the Chairman interrupted him with the somewhat incautious statement: "This is hardly an indictment. . . . We are not claiming these people are criminals."

Quickly perceiving the force of the admission, I rose to inquire: "Does the Chairman desire to have it on the record that there is no claim on the part of the accusers that these five men who have been denied seats in the Assembly are criminals?" And I added, "If they are not charged with crime, what are they charged with, and what are we here for?"

The moment was tense. The Chairman was visibly embarrassed. Mr. Littleton jumped to his aid.

"Mr. Chairman," he queried, "does the gentleman think that everybody who falls short of the criminal statute is eligible for election to a legislative body?"

"Some who do not fall short are sitting in it," was my somewhat irrelevant and irreverent reply.

The *enfant terrible* of the Judiciary Committee was Assemblyman Louis Cuvillier. Having first expressed his conviction of the guilt of the accused, he distinguished himself by proclaiming on the floor of the Assembly that "if the five accused Assemblymen are found guilty, they ought not to be expelled, but taken out and shot."

I challenged his right to sit in judgment over the defendants, maintaining that "a person who holds such an opinion is qualified as an executioner but not as a judge."

My challenge was overruled, and Louis Cuvillier remained judge, the most obnoxious judge it has ever been my ill fortune to encounter. He was irrepressible and had a habit of interrupting the proceedings with most venomous, irrelevant, and unintelligent remarks, much to the annoyance of the chairman and the amusement of the audience.

One of the charges against the Socialist Party was that its nominations for public office were made by a close group of dues-paying party members without participation of the unaffiliated but enrolled Socialists.

Julius Gerber, Secretary of the New York County Committee of the Socialist Party, was on the stand testifying that the party like all other political parties made its nominations in public primary elections at which every enrolled Socialist could vote, and the following colloquy ensued, with questions by myself:

"*Q.* Now, I will ask you, Mr. Gerber: Within your knowledge, has it ever occurred that a person not a member of the dues-paying organization of the Socialist Party has filed a petition for election in the primaries of the Socialist ticket as a candidate of the Socialist Party? *A.* Yes, sir.

"*Q.* Would you name one instance? *A.* Why, the first instance we had was in 1916, when Assemblyman Cuvillier filed a petition as candidate for member of Assembly on the Socialist Party ticket in the Thirtieth District of New York County.

"*Q.* To file such a petition, Mr. Gerber, you say it required 3 per cent. of the enrolled Socialist voters? *A.* Yes, sir.

"*Q*. Did you see the petition which you say was filed in behalf of Assemblyman Cuvillier in 1916. *A*. I did.

"*Q*. How many names of enrolled Socialist voters did it contain? *A*. Fifteen.

"*Q*. And was that a sufficient number? *A*. It was a sufficient number.

"*Q*. And by whom was that petition executed? *A*. I think the young man that collected the signatures acted as a witness. I think his name was Goodman, some name like that. He was a painter by trade, and an enrolled Socialist.

"*Q*. And did the petition contain, in accordance with the requirements of the law, a statement by the candidate, Mr. Cuvillier, to the effect that he knew the person and vouched for him? *A*. Yes, there was a statement to the effect that Mr. Cuvillier knew the gentleman for a certain number of years, as having been a resident of New York County, and of the election district for two years, and a man of good character, and so on.

"*Q*. Now, the law, Mr. Gerber, permits a candidate to resign or decline such a nomination? *A*. Under the rules of the Board of Elections in New York, all candidates for nomination are notified by mail of their designation for public office as soon as the papers are filed, and then they have a certain length of time, five days, to decline.

"*Q*. Did Mr. Cuvillier decline the nomination for the Socialist primaries in that district that year? *A*. He did not.

"*Q*. Did his name appear printed on the primary ballots in the Socialist column? *A*. It did.

"*Q*. As a candidate for the assembly? *A*. It did.

"*Q*. Did Mr. Cuvillier receive any votes on the Socialist ticket? *A*. He had two.

"Assemblyman Cuvillier: Mr. Gerber, you are under oath, aren't you?

"The Witness: I am.

"Assemblyman Cuvillier: You said that my name appeared on the primary ballot as the Socialist candidate for member of the assembly, didn't you?

"The Witness: Yes, sir.

"Assemblyman Cuvillier: That is all I wanted to know.

"Mr. Hillquit: You have known that all along."

The revelation that Louis Cuvillier, the rabid anti-Socialist, who had just announced his patriotic belief that all adherents of Socialism should be shot for the good of the country, had himself sought an endorsement of the Socialist Party and was ready to run on its ticket in furtherance of his political fortunes, was received with Homeric laughter.

Mr. Cuvillier never denied the fact.

The first piece of "documentary evidence" offered by counsel for the Committee was an English translation of an excerpt from a pamphlet printed in Yiddish. The pamphlet had been purchased by a special policeman in Rochester. It was published anonymously, and neither the publisher nor the seller were shown to have any connection with the Socialist Party or any of the accused Assemblymen. The translation was made by an agent of the Lusk Committee, who answered my questions with the following amusing testimony about his literary effort:

"*Q.* Well, what were you told when you got the booklet? *A.* Just simply to look it over. I used my own judgment as to—

"*Q.* As to what? *A.* As to translating what was vital.

"*A.* As to translating what was vital for what purpose? *A.* For the purpose of submitting it as evidence.

"*Q.* For the purpose of submitting as evidence against whom? *A.* Against Socialism.

"*Q.* Then you were given this pamphlet by a representative of the Lusk Committee with the general direction to translate

such portions as would serve as evidence against Socialism?
A. Yes, sir.

"*Q.* By what were you guided about the choice of portions
that you did translate? *A.* I was guided by my own judgment.

"*Q.* As to what? *A.* As to Socialism as it preaches violence.

"*Q.* Then you were looking for such portions as would support the contention that Socialism preaches violence, is that it?
A. Absolutely."

It subsequently appeared that the pamphlet was an academic
discussion of the "Dictatorship of the Proletariat," in which the
anonymous author essayed to summarize the views of the opponents as well as those of the supporters of the theory.

The Yiddish pamphlet and the selective English translation
were admitted in evidence, against the strenuous objections of
the defense, on the broad theory of admissibility which Mr.
Stanchfield had propounded.

Taking advantage of the "liberal" ruling, the defense offered
in evidence a copy of my *Socialism Summed Up,* which was
duly received. It was published at the expense of the State in a
fairly large edition as "Assemblymen's Exhibit 3," and distributed freely by politicians among their friends.

We contemplated following it up by offering in evidence the
three volumes of Marx's *Capital,* but a scrutiny of the faces of
our judges and their counsel deterred us from the execution of
the hardy project.

In the course of my cross-examination by Mr. Conboy, it was
brought out that I was counsel to Mr. Martens, the representative of the Soviet government in the United States. Mr. Conboy
was obviously endeavoring to create the impression that I was
biased in favor of Soviet Russia as its paid agent.

I quote his examination from the record.

"*Q.* Now, you receive compensation for your work in that
connection, do you not? *A.* I do not, Mr. Conboy.

"*Q*. Have you ever received compensation from the Russian Bureau? *A*. Never.

"*Q*. Or Ludwig C. K. Martens? *A*. No, or anybody in his behalf or its behalf.

"*Q*. Wasn't a check drawn to your order for $3,000? *A*. Nothing for $3,000 or 3,000 cents, or any check of any kind.

"*Q*. And I presume it will be a surprise to you if we will produce the check? *A*. It will be a welcome surprise if you hand it to me.

. . . .

"*Q*. It may be that you have never seen any money for the services you have rendered as counsel, and I take it that you want us to understand, without qualification or reservation of any description, that you have never received any money whatever from the Russian Bureau, representing the Russian Soviet Republic, or from Mr. Martens, or from anyone else, in their behalf, either in the sum of $3,000 or any other amount, Mr. Hillquit? *A*. Let us have it quite clearly on the record.

"*Q*. Just as clearly as you want to state it? *A*. I want this Committee to understand that in no capacity, either as counsel or otherwise, have I at any time received any payment of any sum of money, no matter how big or small, from the Soviet government, or from Mr. Martens, or, directly or indirectly, in behalf of the Soviet government, or Mr. Martens, or anybody, or anything connected with either the Soviet government or Mr. Martens. Is that clear enough?"

All during this questioning Mr. Conboy handled a piece of paper conveying the impression that it was the mysterious check to which he alluded.

The next morning the newspapers carried a story to the effect that the prosecution had in its possession a bill for $3,000 rendered by me to the Soviet government for legal services.

On resuming the stand at the next session I made the following statement:

"Before proceeding, Mr. Chairman, if you will permit me, I should like to make for the record a personal explanation on a matter brought out yesterday on cross-examination. I was asked by Mr. Conboy whether I had ever received any compensation for services from the Soviet government or its representative in the United States. I said: 'No, at no time and in no form.' Counsel then implied by his questions, at any rate, that they had a check in their possession—I presume a cancelled check—showing a payment to me by the Soviet government, which I denied. I notice from the morning's papers that counsel for the Committee are alleged to have given out a statement to the effect that they have in their possession a bill rendered by me to the Soviet Bureau for legal services, which bill had been seized, at some time. My recollection of this bill—and it is pretty definite—is as follows: It was never rendered to the Soviet government or to Mr. Martens. It was dated about six months before there was any Soviet government and at least a year before Mr. Martens was appointed. It was rendered not to the Soviet government, but to one Mr. Nuorteva, who at that time represented an entirely different government, namely, the Finnish Socialist government. I had been retained by Mr. Nuorteva as counsel for that government, and in the course of time I rendered a bill, which I believe was for three thousand dollars. Mr. Nuorteva expected large sums of money from this government, and in anticipation of that he paid me one thousand dollars on account. A couple of weeks later the remittance from his government having failed, Mr. Nuorteva asked me whether I would not loan him one thousand dollars for his ambassadorial purposes. I gave him the money and said: 'Do not consider it as a loan, but as a repayment of the fee, and cancel my bill.' That was acceptable to both sides, but later, money still failed to materialize, and my ambassador asked me whether I could not advance him another $250, which I did.

"In the meanwhile the Finnish Socialist Republic was overthrown and still owes me the two hundred and fifty. That is the extent to which I received money from that government. When Mr. Martens was appointed he came to see me and offered me the same post, which I accepted. He asked me: 'How about your compensation?' I said, 'Mr. Martens, from my dealings with the late Finnish Socialist government, I have learned that foreign governments, as paying clients, are not all they are cracked up to be; I would rather serve without compensation.'

"Both sides have since that stuck to that arrangement. I have served, and they have done no compensating. So that my statement stands absolute. I have at no time received any money in any shape, form or manner, as compensation for services or otherwise from the Soviet government or its representative in this country."

In the final phase of the long-protracted trial, counsel for both sides summed up the case.

I opened in behalf of the defense. The speech took between seven and eight hours. It was probably the greatest effort in my professional and public career. I was deeply impressed with the seriousness and importance of the situation. I felt keenly and spoke earnestly.

I subjected the whole proceeding—the charges, the "evidence," and the rulings of the Committee—to a close and critical examination and pointed out its juridical and political monstrosities, its dishonesty and hypocrisy, without mincing words.

I then launched into an explanation and defense of Socialism, its social, economic, and political theories.

Frederick C. Hicks did me the honor of including my summary in his admirable volume *Famous American Jury Speeches,* where it can be read in full by anybody who has enough curiosity and patience; but I cannot refrain from reproducing here a short excerpt on the crucial charge of the prosecution, the alleged Socialist disloyalty during the war.

That accusation ran through the entire proceeding like a red thread. It was the trump card of the prosecution and was reverted to by it again and again on every conceivable occasion and in an endless variety of forms. The record fairly bristled with anti-war proclamations of the Socialist Party and anti-war speeches of the accused Assemblymen and other Socialists.

I knew that the "charges" would be repeated for years to come, and that in the atmosphere of post-war hysteria they would be apt to poison the minds of the uncritical public against our cause.

I determined to state our attitude towards the war fully, frankly, and emphatically.

"We recognized," I said, "that the war was on; that it had been legally declared; and we complied with all concrete enactments of war legislation in every respect. We did not surrender our opinion, our sincere belief that the war was wrong, monstrously wrong, and that every day of its continuance entailed unnecessary misery and privations upon our people. We voiced these sentiments. We voiced them because we maintained, and maintain, Mr. Chairman, that there isn't an act of the highest type of legislative measures, such even as a constitutional enactment, which intends to silence the tongues and stifle the thought of the people, to which the people must bow, not merely in the sense of practical submission, but in the sense of intellectual and moral submission. We say that it was never intended that this doctrine should be tolerated in this country. It was never intended that upon the declaration of war or the happening of any other great national emergency, all thinking in this great Republic should cease, all democratic institutions should come to an end, and the destiny of more than 110,000,000 persons should be placed in the hands of one individual, no matter how exalted. This is not democracy. It is the worst form of autocracy.

"We maintain that it is not only the right, but the duty of every citizen at all times, and in connection with all measures, to use his best judgment, and if he honestly, conscientiously believes that a measure enacted is against the interest of his country and his fellow men, it is his right and duty to do all in his power to have it righted, to have it undone.

"We had ample authority in the precedents of this country for the theory that the greater the crisis the greater the duty to speak, the greater the danger of expressing opposition the higher the call of duty to brave that danger. It is only the arrant political coward who supinely submits to what he in good faith considers a crime.

"Construing our rights as we have stated them, we viewed our entry into the war unhampered by the fear of manufactured public sentiment. We thought it a great calamity. We knew that at the time we were about to enter the war, six million human beings had been slaughtered on the battlefields, a greater number than had ever been killed in any war or wars of any century in the past. We knew that all Europe was in chaos, going to ruin and destruction, and we said: 'What will the entry of the United States in this war mean? It will add to the conflagration; it will subject thousands, hundreds of thousands, and if it continues long enough, millions of our boys to slaughter; make millions of American widows and orphans; destroy this nation industrially and morally; breed hatred in our ranks as it has bred hatred in Europe, and not accomplish anything good, nothing certainly commensurate with the sacrifice required.'

"We did not believe that democracy would be assured as the result of this war. We thought on the contrary that as a result of this war, the classes of war lords, profiteers and reactionaries would set up a reign of terror in almost every country. We did not believe that human civilization would be advanced by this war. We could see nothing in it but a colossal carnage brought on by the commercial rivalries of the capitalist powers of Europe, nothing but a cataclysm of human civilization; and we said, 'Here are we, the United States, about four thousand miles away from the seat of this insane carnage, a powerful people, powerful in wealth and influence, a people that has set out to create a new civilization on this hemisphere, a people that has turned away from the intrigues and machinations of the old world Here is our opportunity; let's stay out of this insane carnage. Let us preserve all our resources, all our strength, in order to render them plentifully to the distracted nations of Europe when the carnage is over and the process of reconstruction and reconciliation and rebuilding sets in.'

"And when we heard what we considered this insane, artificially stimulated cry for participation in this slaughter, we said, 'The men who do that, the men who are pushing this Republic into this European carnage, with which it has no direct vital concern, may mean well, but they are committing or are about to commit, the gravest crime in the annals of history against this nation and against the world.'

"And we said, 'Holding these views as we do, it is our sacred duty as citizens of this country, our sacred duty to our fellow men, to protest against the war, to oppose it with every fibre of our existence, come what may, in the shape of opposition, persecution or suffering,' and we say to you, gentlemen, if any of you had held those convictions, and if you were true to yourselves, true to your country, you couldn't have acted otherwise. We did not. And now that the war is over and the entire world is quivering under the tortures inflicted upon it, now that ten million or more human beings have been directly slaughtered and many more millions killed by the ravages of epidemics, now that all Europe is in mourning, that the greater part of Europe is starving and bringing up a generation of anæmic, undernourished weaklings, now that we helplessly behold the ruins of our civilization and are unable to rebuild the world; now, we Socialists say we have absolutely no reason to repent our stand."

I was followed by Mr. Conboy and Senator Brown, who summed up for the prosecution. The proceeding was terminated with Mr. Stedman's closing address.

On March 30th, almost three months after the suspension of the Socialist Assemblymen, the Judiciary Committee made its report. It favored expulsion by the narrow majority of seven to five. One member of the Committee recommended seating two of the accused and barring the other three.

Then the scene shifted to the Assembly, where the debate lasted for twenty-two hours.

It was a sad and humiliating spectacle. As the discussion went on the legislators worked themselves into a state of frenzied exultation and vied with each other in the use of violent invective. The members of the Assembly turned into a wild, howling and shrieking mob, drunk with "patriotic" fervor and—"Never was there a better irrigated debate," reported the New York *Globe* the next day. "It seemed at times that every man one met had a bottle of old-time whiskey on his hip and was ready to share it. The cloakroom of the Assembly reeked with alcohol, and most of the breaths one encountered in the lobby were redolent of the still."

When the vote was finally taken, it stood 116 to 28 for expulsion.

The intoxicated forces of law and order had secured a decisive victory, but the general indignation which the disgraceful proceeding aroused throughout the country was such that it is safe to assume that for at least some years to come no American legislative body will dare again to disfranchise a legally constituted political party.

BOOK III

THE SWING OF THE PENDULUM

CHAPTER I

THE REVOLUTIONARY FLOOD AND EBB

On November 7, 1917, the world was electrified by the startling news of the Soviet revolution in Russia. The radical wing of the Socialist movement had captured the government of the vast Russian empire and proclaimed the absolute rule of the workers and peasants. With one revolutionary decree it had expropriated the powerful land-owning classes and abolished all private wealth and personal privileges. The old world, the world of class rule and oppression, of hatred and war, was to be changed with one stroke. A new social order, based on equality, coöperation, and peace, was to be instantly inaugurated.

To millions of persons in all lands it seemed that the age-long dream of a reign of reason and justice was about to come true. To them the Russian revolution was not an isolated and fortuitous event. It was the prelude to a world upheaval, the most important outgrowth of the World War, more important than the war itself. The Russian revolution appeared to unfold the real meaning and historic significance of the war.

I quote from an article which I wrote for *Le Populaire*, the newly founded organ of the anti-war faction of the French Socialist Party, edited by Jean Longuet and Léon Blum, towards the end of the war and after the Bolshevik revolution:

"As the gruesome war continues on its fatal course, without let-up or relaxation, we begin to ponder about its deeper and truer meaning. An event of such crushing weight cannot come into human history as a mere accident. It cannot pass out of it without revolutionizing effects. What does this European convulsion import for the progress of the human race?

"We have long been talking about the coming break-up of the so-called capitalist civilization. Is it not possible that this universal orgy of death and destruction presages the beginning of the end? Capitalism has long maintained itself by oppression and violence. Is it not fit and reasonable that in violence it shall perish?

"The war is of capitalist origin but not of the conscious making of the capitalist classes. It was precipitated blindly as capitalism generally works blindly. And blindly may it lead capitalism to its destruction. For no event in history has so clearly demonstrated the instability and insecurity, the folly and inhumanity of capitalist civilization as has this most senseless and criminal of all wars. And gradually the masses of the workers in the trenches and out of them begin to see it. As yet they fight and bleed and kill each other to settle the quarrels of their masters and rulers, but the realization of the horror is finally dawning upon them. The symptoms of revolt are increasing among them. The revolt will grow as the war goes on and momentary intoxication gives way to sober reflection. The end of the war will find a discredited capitalist class and a working class in rebellion. Then perhaps will come the hour of the long-deferred reckoning and the end of capitalist misrule.

"In the vast and dread battlefields of war-ridden Europe, amidst the roar of cannon, the smoke of powder, the groans of the wounded and the sighs of the dying; in the convulsion of death and horror, a new world is perhaps being born. The ghastly war may be the purgatory of blood and fire through which mankind is passing to a better civilization—to a world of brotherhood and good will and peace."

As I read over the somewhat exultant lines after an interval of fifteen years and in the light of the black reaction into which many parts of the world have been precipitated during that period, I find it difficult to realize that they represented the sober belief of large masses of people in every advanced country. Yet, they faithfully reflected the prevailing Socialist sentiment of the time, and the events of the few following years seemed to fully justify it. The period from 1917 to 1920 was one of general revolutionary ferment.

Close upon the heels of the Bolshevik revolution in Russia came the establishment of the "Provisional Government of the People's Republic of Finland," the result of a victorious Socialist rising in January, 1918.

In the same year practically the whole of Central Europe was politically reorganized under Socialist auspices.

The German republic was proclaimed from a window of the Reichstag building by the Social Democratic deputy Philipp Scheidemann as spokesman for this party. A revolutionary government was established under the title of "Council of People's Commissars," composed of six members, all Socialists. The Socialist saddlemaker Friedrich Ebert was elected the first president of the Reich.

In Austria likewise the Socialist Party was godfather to the newly born republic. The first government was largely socialistic. The first president of the republic was Karl Seitz, the popular Socialist mayor of Vienna of later years.

The liberated and reconstructed autonomous republic of Poland began its political career with a prevalently Socialist régime under the leadership of Marshal Pilsudski, then an ardent member of the Socialist Party.

The Czechoslovak government was formed by a coalition of progressive democratic parties with substantial Socialist participation. The venerated president of the republic, Thomas G. Masaryk, who describes himself as a national Socialist, had always worked in sympathetic coöperation with the Social Democratic Party.

In 1919 the Soviet government of Hungary was established under the Communist leadership.

Thus the political complexion of the world was thoroughly revolutionized. The powerful imperial dynasties of the Romanoffs, Hohenzollerns, and Hapsburgs were suddenly and almost simultaneously overthrown. The greater part of Europe was under the political rule of Socialism of one complexion or another.

Nor were the countries with bourgeois governments exempt from the general revolutionary ferment. In Italy the working masses were restive. Their movement grew steadily in extent and aggressiveness, culminating in the famous "occupation" of the factories by the locked-out metal workers in August, 1919. In England and the Scandinavian countries the Socialist and Labor parties made rapid strides towards the conquest of the power of government which they were to achieve a few years later. In France, Belgium, Holland, and Switzerland the revolutionary spirit of Socialism had received a new impulse. Even the peoples of the politically inert and somnolent Far East began to shake off their age-long torpor and to raise their heads in defiance and revolt.

And then the seemingly irresistible and universal revolutionary wave suddenly spent itself. Within the incredibly short period of two or three years the old order again dominated the world. The revolutionary Socialist régime of Finland and the Soviet government of Hungary were violently overthrown by the capitalist "white guards" of these countries with the impartial aid of foreign powers from both camps in the late war. Unmerciful vengeance was wreaked upon the leaders and supporters of the ill-fated working-class rebellions. The incipient Soviet republic of Bavaria was throttled almost at its birth. In Italy, Mussolini's Fascist dictatorship put down the insurgent movements of the proletariat with an iron hand.

In Germany the provisional Socialist government voluntarily relinquished power when the first general elections after the overthrow of the old régime showed that it lacked the support of a clear majority of the people.

In Austria the Socialist movement, probably the strongest in the world in relative numbers, discipline, and organization, deliberately refrained from any attempt to capture and hold the powers of government as a minority party. Poland began its fatal evolution from a democratic republic into a semi-military dictatorship following the tortuous political leadership of its erratic idol Jan Pilsudski, and in Czechoslovakia the Socialists, weakened by the Communist split, voluntarily withdrew from the government.

To the thinker of the romantic school it will always remain a subject of fascinating speculation whether German Social Democracy, which led in the retreat, did not commit a fatal historical blunder in yielding the reins of government to its bourgeois opponents at a time when it seemed to hold them so firmly in hand. The Socialist movement has been violently divided on that interesting question for fifteen years: dictatorship or democracy, bold revolutionary *coups d'état* or gradual building up of a Socialist world and Socialist mind on the solid foundation of voluntary popular support—which is the better and surer road to the coöperative commonwealth?

In this connection the political fates of Russia and Germany are inevitably contrasted. The Bolshevik revolution was accomplished by a comparatively small group of radical and determined Socialists without the support of an organized and trained labor movement and in the practical absence of an industrial proletariat. The Soviet government has maintained itself in power by a policy of systematic repression and political terror.

The country has never emerged from a condition of universal and chronic poverty and privation. Yet the Communist régime is still going strong, and the people are struggling and hoping and finding comfort and solace in the never dying vision of better things to come.

The German Socialists acquired power almost automatically. The catastrophic termination of the disastrous war left the political institutions and economic organization of the country in a state of utter chaos. The Socialist parties with their network of local organizations, supported by the powerful trade unions and coöperative societies with millions of members, emerged as the only cohesive social force. Government fell into their lap, easily and unresistingly. They refused to cling to their fortuitous and precarious political victory, and took their stand on a program of gradual social development, which, they were convinced, would eventually lead to a voluntary acceptance of their economic, political, and moral creed by a substantial majority of the whole people and to a peaceful and ordered transition to a permanent Socialist régime. They threw the whole weight of their influence into the task of building a democratic and progressive republic based on an enlightened written constitution as the most reliable instrument of lasting social regeneration, and for fifteen years they struggled desperately for the preservation of that republic and that constitution. This was the aim uppermost in their minds in all the kaleidoscopically changing political situations of that agitated period, in the course of which they headed or participated in governments or supported minority governments of opposition parties. No sacrifice was too great, no humiliation too deep for them in their efforts to save their newly conquered democracy, and after fifteen years of convulsive struggles they found their country ruled by the crudest, most ruthless and brutal dictatorship that ever disgraced a great nation in modern times. Russia is still governed by the iron hand of Joseph Stalin, and Germany is groveling in moral and spiritual dust before the puny figure of the sinister Adolf Hitler.

On the face of it the methods of Russian Bolshevism have, to date, scored a clear victory over those of German Social Democracy. Still it may be rash to venture a final historic judgment on the much mooted question. The Russian revolution has not yet run its full course or matured its final meaning and form, nor has Germany reached its ultimate political and economic destiny through its tortuous and thorny post-war path.

But all this is rather idle speculation born of after-acquired knowledge of developments unforeseen and largely unforeseeable at the time. As a rule the course of history is determined not so much by the conscious volition of man as by the blind forces of the compelling social and economic conditions as they evolve from day to day.

In 1918 the highly industrialized and politically advanced countries of Central Europe, defeated in the war and mercilessly penalized by their victors, were in an entirely different situation from Russia of 1917, with its demoralized ruling classes, its leaderless insurgent army, its predominant land-hungry peasant population, its political disorganization and industrial backwardness.

In 1920 Europe again presented a different picture. Two important factors developing within that brief period were mainly responsible for the weakening or collapse of the European revolutionary currents. The breathing spell allowed to the harassed bourgeoisie afforded them an opportunity to collect their waning forces, to reform their broken lines and to raise their heads again. In this process of moral, economic, and political recovery, they were generously assisted by their class allies in the recent enemy countries, who were scared by the specter of the many-headed revolutionary hydra, menacing the foundations of the whole capitalist world.

But even more determining for the triumph of the counter revolution was the fatal division within the ranks of the Socialist movement itself. Sharing the tragic fate of so many great revolutionary movements in the past, it broke up in internal dissensions and factional quarrels just when victory seemed within certain reach, and when unity of purpose, strategy, and leadership was needed as never before. Oddly enough the main source of discord sprang from a point which should have been expected to be the inspiring and unifying center of the whole movement—Soviet Russia.

Until the October revolution the "Bolsheviks" were nothing but a wing of the Russian Social Democratic Party. They held somewhat more authoritarian and militant views on more or less theoretical questions of methods and tactics than their comrades of the "Menshevik" wing, and under the leadership of Nicolai Lenin they had obtained the support of a majority of the party membership. In fact the terms "Bolshevik" and "Menshevik," which were subsequently to gain such general currency and misinterpretation in the political literature and journalism of all countries, are nothing more than the Russian rendering of "majority faction" and "minority faction." But they were Social Democrats and a regular component part of the international Socialist movement and organization. It was only during the Russian revolution set in motion by the establishment of the Provisional Government, when the question of methods of gaining and holding political power ceased to be one of abstract theory and became a practical problem of immediate and vital importance, that the factional disagreements between the two wings widened into bitter and irreconcilable party antagonisms.

With aggressive ostentation the Bolsheviks broke away from the rest of the Socialist movement in and out of Russia. To emphasize the finality of the separation they changed their party name from "Social Democratic" to "Communist."

The new name was not arbitrarily chosen, but was intended to symbolize a new direction of the movement, a direction best described by the slogan "Back to Marx!"

In the early part of the last century the incipient Socialist movement of Europe, known by that name, was represented by a variety of schools, of French, English, and German origin, mostly of nebulous philosophic concepts and utopian programs. It was the historical achievement of Karl Marx and his followers that they lifted the movement out of the sterile field of metaphysical speculation and sentimental appeal and planted it on the solid ground of economic necessity and political struggle as an international movement of the working classes. To avoid confusion with the utopian "Socialist" movements of the time, the founders of the Marxian school adopted the somewhat inaccurate and misleading designation of Communism to distinguish their political creed. It was thus that the first international organization of Marxian or "scientific" Socialism was named the "Communist League," and that its famous declaration of principles and statement of program were published under the title of "Communist Manifesto" in 1848.

In later years, when the Marxian creed ceased to be a mere philosophic system and became the theoretical basis of an organized political movement dealing with practical everyday social problems, and when its competing early schools of Socialism had sunk into oblivion, the movement again assumed the more appropriate and expressive name of Socialism or Social Democracy.

In 1917 Nicolai Lenin and his followers conceived themselves to be facing a situation similar to that which confronted Karl Marx in 1848, and accordingly resurrected the discarded Communist label for their reorganized movement.

With the change of name the Bolsheviks not only signalized

their complete break with international Social Democracy, but proclaimed relentless war upon it. Social Democracy henceforward was declared to be totally unrelated to true Socialism or Communism. It was its foe; it was the most formidable impediment to the success of the proletarian revolution and was to be combated even more energetically than the direct forces of capitalism.

At first blush such an attitude would seem to be absurd, if not suicidal, even from a narrow partisan Bolshevik point of view. Soviet Russia was surrounded by an iron ring of hostile capitalist powers, who shrank from no measure of overt or covert attack, including economic blockades, unsanctioned warfare, and lavish support of all counter-revolutionary intrigues within the Russian borders. The popular elements in the foreign countries upon which sympathies and support the Soviet government could rely, were the workers in those countries, mostly under Social Democratic leadership. The forces of organized labor and Social Democracy were strong enough to exert effective pressure on the policies of some of the most important governments and were strenuously opposing any foreign interference with the Soviet régime. Why then should the Bolshevik leaders have chosen to antagonize their only possible allies in the desperate struggle?

The answer to the seemingly puzzling question lay in the deep-rooted Bolshevik conviction of the imminence of a world revolution.

With a total and stubborn misunderstanding of Western sentiment and conditions, the Russian Communists naïvely believed that the "workers and peasants" of the leading countries, including Germany, France, England, and even the United States, were ready for an immediate overthrow of capitalism, and that nothing held them back from a revolution after the Russian pattern except the cowardice and treachery of their

Socialist leadership. To a large extent also the wish was probably the father of the thought, for at that period even the most sanguine of the Bolshevik leaders did not believe that the Soviet government could survive unless speedily reinforced by a proletarian world revolution. The culminating point of the intra-Socialist feud was the formation of the Communist International in March, 1919, in opposition and expected succession to the organizational pre-war center of world Socialism, generally known in historic sequence as the "Second International."

The latter, after a brilliant career of twenty-five years of almost uninterrupted growth and achievements, was badly crippled by the antagonistic war stands of its principal affiliated national parties. Numerically it was still the largest international organization of Socialism, including in its membership such important bodies as the British Labor Party, the Social Democratic Majority Party of Germany and the Socialist organizations of most of the countries that had remained neutral during the war. But morally it was bankrupt. It had lost prestige and authority and had forever ceased to be a directing and inspiring force in the world of Socialism.

In this new political line-up a number of national Socialist organizations, including those of France, Austria, Switzerland, and the United States, and minority parties, such as the Independent Social Democratic Party of Germany, the Independent Labor Party of England, the Russian Mensheviks and Italian "Unitary" Socialists, found themselves without international affiliation. They could not subscribe to the unrealistic conceptions and fantastic program of the Communist International, nor could they acquiesce in the passive and sterile conservatism of the Second International. They were eventually driven to form an international organization of their own, known as the International Workers' Union, with the avowed purpose of reëstablishing Socialist unity in the world.

Thus the Socialist movement was divided into three distinct groups, nationally and internationally, expending its energies on mutual criticism and recrimination and missing the greatest historic opportunity of its career.

CHAPTER II

THE BREAK-UP OF AMERICAN SOCIALISM

THE events in Europe had an immediate and direct effect on the Socialist movement in the United States. There was little similarity between the political atmosphere and popular temper of this country, just emerged from a victorious war and embarking on an era of unparalleled national prosperity, and the ruined, desperate, and strife-torn countries of Central and Eastern Europe. The American people were about to elect to the Presidency of the republic that most typical personification of middle-class complacency and capitalist "normalcy," Warren Gamaliel Harding. The American workers were, as always, poorly organized and conservative to the bone to the extent that they were organized. The only evidence of a "revolutionary atmosphere" was the hysterical fear of the ghost of a mysterious and lurking radicalism, which haunted the editorial offices of certain sensational newspapers, largely stimulated by ignorant or ambitious politicians. The chief manifestations of "civil war" were the lawless raids on liberal, Socialist, and Communist institutions under the intrepid leadership of Attorney General A. Mitchell Palmer and lesser political satellites in several states.

But Socialists are internationally minded and are more apt to think in terms of general world problems than the more conservative political groups.

This was particularly true of the American Socialists of that period, not only because they found greater comfort and encouragement in the struggles and victories of their comrades across the ocean than in their own insignificant achievements, but also because of the character and racial composition of the movement at the time.

Normally the Socialist movement in this country, contrary to prevailing popular impressions, is predominantly American. In 1908, when the Socialist party undertook a census of its dues-paying members by the countries of their birth, it appeared that no fewer than 71 per cent were natives, while 4 per cent had been born in Great Britain, 8½ per cent in Germany and 5 per cent in the Scandinavian countries, other nationalities accounting for the remaining 11½ per cent. The Socialist Party was quite as "American" as the country's population at large, and it remained such until the closing years of the war.

For the convenience of transacting business and carrying on the Socialist propaganda among their countrymen the non-English-speaking members were organized into "foreign language federations." In 1912, when the party reached the zenith of its organizational strength with a dues-paying membership in excess of 118,000, only 16,000, or about 13 per cent of the total, were in the foreign federations. . . . By 1918 the party membership had dropped to 81,000, and of these no fewer than 25,000, or about 30 per cent, were composed of members in the non-English-speaking groups.

The next year witnessed another astounding change in the make-up of the party. Its dues-paying membership jumped to 108,000, and practically the entire increase was furnished by recent arrivals from Russia and its border states. The membership in the foreign-language federations rose to 57,000, or 53 per cent of the total, and the bulk of it was represented by Russian, Ukrainian, South Slavic, Finnish, Lithuanian, and Lettish organizations. It was the Soviet revolution that had primarily stimulated the interest of the workers of these countries in the Socialist movement at home and in the foreign centers of their emigration, and these new recruits were Bolsheviks to the core. They accepted everything emanating from Moscow unquestioningly and uncritically and urged the complete and immediate adoption of the Bolshevik program and methods by the Socialist Party of the United States.

They were by no means alone in their enthusiasm for Soviet Russia. The sentiment in favor of the revolutionary government of the workers and peasants was practically unanimous in all party ranks. But the older members with a more sober appreciation of the realities of the situation refused to be carried away by their enthusiasm to the extent of disregarding the fundamental social, economic, political, and psychological differences between Russia and the United States and attempting to apply one stereotyped revolutionary formula to both countries.

The opposing conceptions found expression in continuous controversies at party meetings and in the party press, and, as is customary in the ardent atmosphere of the Socialist movement, they waxed sharp, bitter, and personal. Inevitably the theoretical discussion developed into antagonistic action. The "left-wing" faction organized its forces in open opposition to the official party administration and the latter retaliated by suspending seven foreign-language federations and three "left-wing" state organizations.

The break became final and complete in August, 1919, when the party split into three distinct and separate organizations.

The formal separation was accomplished in three conventions simultaneously held in Chicago by the main contending factions. The first of these was called by the regular party administration to submit its suspension of the "left-wing" organizations for the ratification and to take an authoritative stand on the controversial questions of program and policies.

The convention, largely in control of the "right-wing" or "centrist" elements, reaffirmed the traditional position of international Social Democracy with generous concessions to the altered world conditions after the war and the radical revolutionary spirit of the time. It flatly rejected the new Communist creed as applicable to the United States.

Another convention was held in the same city by the suspended "left-wing" organizations, who had abandoned their fight for the control of the party and refused to carry the controversy about the propriety of their suspension to the floor of the regular convention. It was at this gathering that the "Communist Party" of the United States was launched.

The new party endorsed the regulation Communist program in full and proclaimed itself the American section of the Communist International.

Between these two bodies with sharply defined differences there stood an intermediate group of party members, who held a convention of their own and formed the "Communist Labor Party." This body was Communistic in principle, but with a somewhat more American orientation than the Simon-pure Communist Party.

The organized Socialist movement of the United States was thus effectively crippled. The Socialist Party emerged from the conflict as a mere organizational skeleton of its former self. Its membership had shrunk to a mere 25,000. Its press, educational institutions, and other services and activities were badly disorganized. The Communist Labor Party claimed a somewhat similar membership, while the Communist Party boasted of no fewer than 50,000 organized adherents. Between the three parties there was unremitting warfare all along the line.

During all these agitated times I was away from the active field of battle, secluded in a distant mountain village, where I was impatiently "taking the cure" for a long-standing ailment. I followed the disheartening developments within the Socialist movement through the party press and such private information as was furnished to me from time to time by my closer party friends. Anxiously and helplessly I watched the rapid disintegration of the movement that meant so much to me.

Occasionally I would intervene in the raging controversies by an expression of opinion in the columns of the party papers. Often I was consulted by the party leadership on particularly critical situations. I was asked to and did prepare the "manifesto" adopted by the party at its emergency convention in 1919. But such spasmodic long-distance activities only brought home to me more poignantly the realization of the tantalizing handicaps my enforced idleness imposed on me in these most critical hours in the history of American Socialism. It was not until the summer of 1920 that I was allowed to go home and to resume normal work.

Almost the first thing that confronted me was the Convention of the Socialist Party held in New York that year. It was a regular nominating convention ostensibly called for the purpose of designating candidates for President and Vice President of the United States. It was a foregone conclusion that Eugene V. Debs would be the party's choice for President. The nomination of the prisoner of Atlanta, Convict No. 9653, was not only a tribute of love for the aged warrior, but a challenge to the reactionary powers that held him captive as a prisoner of war almost two years after the armistice. It was unanimous and was acclaimed with fervid enthusiasm.

But the real attention of the delegates was engrossed in an entirely different subject on the order of business—the determination of the party's international affiliations. This had become a question of burning interest not so much on account of its intrinsic importance as because it was bound to bring to the surface the sharp theoretical and tactical differences which still divided the American Socialists in spite of the regrouping and repeated "purgings" of the party. The formal choice was between the discredited survival of the old pre-war International and the recently organized Moscow International under Communist leadership, or, as they were popularly known, the Second and Third Internationals. The so-called Vienna Union of parties of the Socialist center was not yet in existence. Nobody seriously advocated affiliation with the Second International. The general sentiment was in favor of the Third, and the real question was, to join or not to join.

In its original declaration of principles the Moscow International had defined the paramount task of Socialism as "the immediate universal dictatorship of the proletariat in view of the present dissolution of the capitalist régime of the whole world."

The practical steps for attaining this simple objective were outlined as "the seizure of governmental power, the disarming of the bourgeoisie, the general arming of the proletariat, and the suppression of private property," and the method of struggle prescribed was "mass action of the proletariat as far as open conflict of arms against the governmental power of capitalism."

In the early part of 1919 the program did not lack some element of realism for the few European countries in the center of the revolutionary whirlpool. It was a rather stiff dose for a handful of American Socialists by the middle of 1920. But even if the slight difficulties in the way of an immediate seizure of the governmental power in the United States were to be overlooked, as some enthusiastic delegates thought they might be, there were other serious questions of a practical nature to be considered.

The Communist International was not any too hospitable to strangers at its gates. "Our International is not an hotel, where every wayfarer can stop," Gregory Zinovieff, its secretary and moving spirit (who has since been disgraced), had declared. And indeed, the Moscow International was rather an exclusive club than a public hotel. Its rules of admission were strict from the outset. They were made more stringent and explicit in the famous "Twenty-one Points" promulgated in its second convention, held in August, 1920.

The "points," which covered the admission of new parties as well as the rules of conduct of affiliated organizations, reiterated the fundamental original declaration of the Communist International and added some specific practical directions, such as the creation by all parties of "parallel illegal organization machines, which at the decisive moment will be helpful to the party in fulfilling its duty to the revolution," carrying on a vigorous propaganda in the army, organizing Communist nuclei within the trade unions, submitting unquestioningly to the rulings of the International and expulsion of all members who disagreed with any part of the Twenty-one Points. One of these points, the famous Seventh, was of particular personal interest to me. It read: "The parties wishing to belong to the Communist International are obligated to proclaim a clean break with reformism and with the policy of the center and to propagate this break throughout the ranks of the entire party membership. Without this a logical communist policy is impossible.

"The Communist International demands unconditionally and in the form of an ultimatum the execution of this break within a very brief period. The Communist International cannot reconcile itself to a condition that would allow notorious opportunists, such as are now represented by Turati, Kautsky, Hilferding, Hillquit, Longuet, MacDonald, Modigliani, *et al.,* to have the right to be counted as members of the Third International. That could only lead to the Third International resembling to a high degree the dead Second International.

I was in good company.

Filippo Turati, one of the pioneers and leaders of Italian Socialism, was among the noblest figures of the international Socialist movement. A poet of great lyric depth, an orator of rare eloquence, a trenchant writer and clear thinker, he had since early manhood placed his time, means, and talents at the service of the poor and humble among his countrymen, who idolized him. In the constantly changing moods of the temperamental Italian movement between flights of emotional revolutionary enthusiasm and policies of crass opportunism, he always held a firm hand on the balance wheel of realistic working-class Socialism and stuck courageously to his course, regardless of popular approval and heedless of personal consequences. He consistently opposed Italy's entry into the war and was one of the most outspoken and effective opponents of Fascism before and after it had come into power. When the iron grip of Benito Mussolini tightened around Italy, Filippo Turati, the former comrade and teacher of the apostate dictator, was held a virtual prisoner in the country. After a sensational rescue by a group of daring young anti-Fascists, he landed in Paris and resumed his struggles for the liberty of his country in very straitened circumstances but with unabated faith and enthusiasm. He died in exile in 1933, at the age of seventy-one years, deeply mourned by the whole world of Socialism.

Karl Kautsky is the leading theoretician and philosopher of international Socialism and the recognized spiritual successor to Karl Marx and Friedrich Engels. Although an Austrian, or, to be more exact, a Bohemian by birth, he early identified himself with the struggles of German Social Democracy. During the twelve-year period of the Bismarck Exceptional Laws he lived in Zurich and London, furnishing much of the underground Socialist literature that found its way to Germany through the well-organized secret "red-express" service. From 1890 he was the editor-in-chief of the foremost international organ of Socialist opinion, *Die neue Zeit*. He was not only the recognized exponent of the Socialist philosophy but the valued guide and adviser of the organized movement in all countries. After the death of Friedrich Engels in 1895, he assumed the burden of international correspondence and personal contacts. Socialist refugees and visitors of many lands and Socialist workers and students seeking advice and direction always found a cordial welcome and a word of cheer in the simple and hospitable home of Karl Kautsky and his charming and cultured wife Luise. During the war he stood with the left-wing antiwar faction of German Social Democracy. In later years he removed to Vienna, but he still remains the intellectual head and beloved teacher of international Socialism.

Rudolf Hilferding was the leading Socialist economist of the younger generation. His famous book *Das Finanzkapital* was considered in Socialist circles as a monumental work and a worthy supplement to Marx's *Capital*. He held the portfolio of the Treasury in the coalition government of Chancellor Hermann Müller and is credited with substantial and lasting reforms of the financial system of the Reich. After the split within the ranks of German Social Democracy he was the recognized spokesman of the insurgent Independent Socialist Party.

Jean Longuet came by his Socialism through legitimate inheritance. A grandson of Karl Marx, the founder of the modern Socialist movement, and son of Charles Longuet, the noted Communard, he was born and bred in the atmosphere of Socialist struggle, and to that struggle he has remained true all his life.

He was one of the first, if not the very first, amongst the leaders of French Socialism to take a public stand against the irreconcilable *jusqu'-au-bout* war policy of his country and to advocate a peace of reconciliation, a "peace without victory" in the subsequent phrasing of President Wilson. His views eventually prevailed and became the dominant policy of French Socialism towards the close of the war, but it took unusual moral courage to advocate them in the midst of the conflict and in the teeth of the hysterical chauvinism of his suffering and enraged country.

J. Ramsay MacDonald was the only avowed "right winger" in the proscribed group of "notorious opportunists." At the date of the Moscow edict he was the Secretary of the Second International. He had not yet attained the preëminent position among the statesmen of Europe that was to come to him in later years, nor had he made the sad renunciation of his life work in favor of a narrow nationalistic ambition that was to cloud the evening of his otherwise unblemished career in the Socialist and Labor movement. In 1920 he was just emerging from the most heroic period of his public life. He was above everything else a passionate pacifist and had consistently opposed the war in spite of all ignominy and persecution to which the unpopular stand subjected him and, in spite of the heartbreaking isolation among his own comrades at arms. At the time of his excommunication by the Moscow synod the war fever had largely abated among the workers of Great Britain, and Ramsay MacDonald and the small but valiant group of his anti-war supporters were again coming into favor.

Emanuele Modigliani, brother of Amadeo, the famous painter of tragic fate, and the last man on the list of proscripts, was a lawyer of note, a close friend and co-worker of Turati and next to him probably the most influential leader of the Unitary Socialist Party of Italy. He too had been a decided opponent of the war and an aggressive foe of Fascism. After the Mussolini dictatorship outlawed all forms of Socialist propaganda and labor activities, Modigliani forsook his home and career and chose voluntary exile in Paris, where he leads a precarious existence of hardship and privation, devoting his great abilities and indefatigable energies to the defeat of Fascism.

These then were the types of persons who were to be excluded from the new International for fear that their presence might contaminate the pure spirit of sacred Communism. It was characteristic of the peculiar Communist psychology that it directed its most vicious attacks not against the avowed "right-wing" leaders of the Socialist parties in all countries who had betrayed the principles of peace and international working-class solidarity, but against those of more radical orientation who had courageously struggled against the tidal wave of war intoxication.

Of the two alternatives which were thus open to the Socialist Party Convention in 1920, the Second International, which it did not want, and the Third International, where it was not wanted, the delegates chose neither. After a protracted and heated debate, the convention by a majority vote adopted a resolution, which I had proposed, in this language:

"The Socialist Party of the United States considers that its paramount duty is to build a powerful, revolutionary socialist organization in this country. It is, therefore, resolved to devote all of its energy and resources to this task, believing it to be the most valuable service it can render to the cause of international socialism."

It is significant of the temper prevailing within the Socialist Party of the United States at the time that the convention resolution was rejected by the body of membership when it was submitted to it for approval, and the National Executive Committee of the party was directed to apply for affiliation to the Moscow International in spite of the obvious absurdities of its program as applied to the United States and in spite of the utterly impossible character of its conditions. The application was duly made and rejected.

In the meantime, however, the International Union of the Socialist parties of the center was organized with headquarters in Vienna and the Socialist Party of the United States associated itself with the new body, thus avoiding the Scylla of the Second International's opportunism and the Charybdis of Communist impossibilities.

CHAPTER III

THE LA FOLLETTE INTERMEZZO

In the election of 1920 Eugene V. Debs polled a vote in excess of 915,000, thus beating the best previous record of the Socialist Party.

The relatively big vote was the last flicker of the dying candle and did not deceive the Socialists. It was due in large measure to the personal popularity of the Socialist standard bearer and the dramatic element of his challenge to the powers that be from a prison cell.

The Socialist Party as such continued to decline catastrophically. It was completely wiped out in a number of states, and all that was left of the erstwhile vigorous and promising movement was a small band of stubborn die-hards, largely concentrated in a few Eastern and Midwestern states, not exceeding 10,000 in all.

Under the circumstances, it was inevitable that the American Socialists should turn to a critical reëxamination of the theoretical foundations and organizational structure of their movement. American Socialism had failed in the face of the striking progress of the identical movements in practically all other advanced countries. The obvious cause of the failure was the lack of working-class support. Was there anything organically wrong in the methods of Socialist approach to American labor?

There are two distinct organizational forms within the international Socialist movement. One, of which German Social

Democracy may be considered the historical and classical prototype, is based on individual dues-paying membership. Such organizations are primarily, if not exclusively, political in character. They leave the economic struggles in the hands of the trade unions and coöperative societies, with whom they work in close harmony on the basis of mutual support in their respective fields.

The other type is best exemplified by the British Labor Party. The party, properly speaking, has no independent existence of its own. Rather is it in the nature of a joint political committee of the trade unions, coöperative societies and Socialist organizations, coöperating for the sole purpose of electing public officers and shaping or influencing the policies of their countries along the lines of Socialist and labor programs.

As a rule the former type originated in countries in which the Socialist movement historically preceded the trade unions and largely prevails in continental Europe, while the labor party form of organization springs up in countries of reverse historic development, principally those denominated as Anglo-Saxon, such as Great Britain and Australia.

In the United States the Socialists from the first adopted the system of individual dues-paying membership, to some extent undoubtedly because the founders of the movement were in the main Social Democratic immigrants from Germany and almost automatically fell into the ways of their native country.

Whether that form of organization was best suited to American political institutions and customs always was a much debated question within the Socialist movement. It still is, and the chances are that it never will be solved through aprioristic theoretical reasoning. In itself the form of organization rarely, if ever, determines the character or success of a movement. A Socialist party by that name may be as effective in the United States as it is or was in the principal countries of continental

Europe, if it gains sufficient working-class political support. An American labor party may serve the purpose just as well if it is permeated by a Socialist spirit and Socialist ideals. The ultimate form of the movement in the United States will probably be determined by some important future political or economic development, now unforeseen and unforeseeable.

In 1921, however, the question was one of practical and immediate moment to the Socialists of America. Not only had their own organization apparently failed, but a distinct tendency seemed to be discernible on the political horizon towards the birth of an independent political labor movement.

The year 1919 was one of widespread labor unrest. It was marked by a series of prolonged and embittered struggles in the coal and steel industries and the sensational general strike in Seattle.

The railway workers of the country were also in an unusual state of mental ferment and political agitation. The brief period of war-time operation of the railroads by the government had given the workers an improved status and secured full recognition of their unions, and now that it was proposed "to return the railroads to their owners," *i.e.,* restore their control to the bankers, the employees strenuously objected and for the first time in history formulated a clear-cut program of government ownership with adequate representation of the workers and the public in the management.

The United Mine Workers' of America, with a membership of 400,000, at its national convention in 1919 declared itself in favor of the immediate formation of an independent labor party and instructed its officers to take practical steps in that direction. The next year its example was followed by the powerful Brotherhood of Painters, Decorators and Paperhangers of America.

Resolutions favoring the principle of working-class political action were adopted by the State Federations of Labor in Penn-

sylvania and Indiana and by a number of city central labor
bodies and local unions.

A somewhat similar development had sprung up among the
wheat-growing farmers of the West and Middle West under the
leadership of the Nonpartisan League. This organization was
first formed in North Dakota in 1915 and rapidly spread to
South Dakota, Minnesota, Idaho, Montana, Nebraska, Colorado,
and Washington. As the name indicates, the Nonpartisan League
was not, properly speaking, a political party. It did not enter the
field of politics in opposition to the old parties and did not nominate candidates for public office. Its mode of operation was to
concentrate its forces in support of the friendliest candidate running in either the Republican or Democratic primaries and to
bring about his nomination and election. The father of the new
idea and the moving spirit of the organization was Arthur C.
Townley, a farmer with a wonderful genius for organization,
who had received his political education and training in the
ranks of the Socialist Party. The League was maintained by
rather substantial annual dues paid by its members. Around
1920 it reached the zenith of its strength. It had elected United
States senators, members of the House of Representatives, and
governors, state legislators and local officials in several states. It
had the support of a hundred newspapers, operated a bank and
several coöperative societies, and was a formidable political power
in the centers of its activity.

One of the most significant and lasting outgrowths of the
movement was the organization of the Farmer-Labor Party of
Minnesota. In that state, as in most other strongholds of the
League, it was soon found that the Townley plan was ineffec-
tive in the long run. The old-party political machines, at first
caught by surprise, rapidly adjusted themselves to the new situation and re-formed their broken lines. Where the usual political
machinations did not suffice, they resorted to the simple expedi-

ent of repealing the primary laws and restoring the system of party nominating conventions. This was the situation in Minnesota in 1919, when the leaders of the Nonpartisan League in that state, recognizing the futility of further attempts to capture the old-party primaries, organized a party of their own under the somewhat paradoxical name of Nonpartisan Party. The novel feature of the organization was that it represented an equal political partnership between the farmers in the country and the workers in the city. In the following year the party name was changed to Farmer-Labor Party, thus formally linking the political interests of the farmer and the industrial worker. The advantages of such a combination between the American producers in field and factory were quite obvious. The insurgent political movements of farmers in the past had been short-lived and barren of lasting results largely because they were confined to limited sections of the country, mostly the Western and Midwestern states. On the other hand a political movement resting solely or very preponderatingly on city workers did not by far offer the same chances of success on a national scale as did such movements in the smaller and highly industrialized countries of Europe.

As a matter of fact some of the most significant political revolts in recent American history, such as those represented by the Greenback and Populist movements, have sprung up among the farmers, and even the modern "progressive" bloc in Congress is in great part a species of agrarian radicalism.

The "farmer-labor party" has thus become the ideal form of the much courted and evanescent third-party movements in the minds of their American advocates.

Towards the end of 1919 the National Labor Party, later known as the Farmer-Labor Party, was born at a memorable national convention held in Chicago. The moving spirits behind it were mainly Socialists who in some way or other had become disassociated from the Socialist Party during the multiple factional splits earlier in the year. The convention was unexpectedly well attended. Local unions, district councils, and city central labor bodies from forty states were represented by several hundred enthusiastic delegates. A radical platform, strongly influenced by the Socialist philosophy, was adopted, and a permanent party on national scale with provisions for state and local organizations was created. Some of the latter, notably the state organizations in Illinois and Pennsylvania, seemed to be giving promise of solid development.

In 1920 the party nominated candidates for President and Vice-President of the United States and polled about 250,000 votes.

In these circumstances the Socialist Party, whose attitude to the incipient and sporadic "third-party" movements had theretofore been largely negative, could no longer ignore their possible significance. In 1921 it adopted a resolution instructing its National Executive Committee to make a careful survey of the field with a view of ascertaining the chances of a political alliance between the party and other radical and labor organizations.

The survey was soon made. Within two years from the first appearance of its promising manifestations the third-party movements had practically died out. The National Farmer-Labor Party rapidly disintegrated under the opposition of the conservative leadership of the national unions and the American Federation of Labor. The organization was subsequently "captured" by the Communists, who renamed it Federated Farmer-Labor Party and in due course quietly consigned it to its political grave.

Of the numerous local labor parties only the Chicago body retained some vitality, while the elaborate organization of the Nonpartisan League melted away as quickly as it had been built up. The only survivor in the political wreck was the Farmer-Labor Party of Minnesota, but that organization confined itself strictly to the politics of its own state and evinced no desire or intention to extend its operations into the nation.

At this juncture, however, a new impulse to revive the movement came from an unexpected source.

Towards the end of 1921 I received a communication from William H. Johnston, General President of the Machinists' Union, inviting me to attend a close and confidential conference to consider the chances of organizing an effective political party on the model of the British Labor Party. I accepted the invitation with alacrity. The Machinists' Union was one of the most important labor organizations in the country and held a key position in the trade-union movement through its affiliation with the American Federation of Labor on the one hand and with the powerful Brotherhoods of the railway workers on the other.

Johnston himself represented the highest type of trade-union official. He had been a member of the Socialist Party and was elected to his office in a vigorous fight between the insurgent "progressive" wing, which he headed, and the conservative old-line leadership of the union. In the ten years of his incumbency in office he had retained the complete confidence of the rank and file of the union and had established an enviable reputation for integrity and capacity in the world of organized labor. His initiation of the new movement was a guaranty of its solid prospects, good faith, and progressive character. Several months elapsed and I heard nothing more about the proposed conference. I took it for granted that the plan had been abandoned for lack of sufficient support, until I received a new invitation to attend "a conference of Progressives" in Chicago on February 20, 1922. This time the call was formal and, greatly to my astonishment, it was issued over the signature not only of William H. Johnston, but also of Martin F. Ryan, General President of the Brotherhood of Railway Carmen; W. S. Stone, Grand Chief of the Brotherhood of Locomotive Engineers; E. J. Manion, President of the Order of Railroad Telegraphers; Timothy Healy, President of the International Brotherhood of Stationary Firemen and Oilers, and L. E. Sheppard, President of the Order of Railway Conductors.

Those were names to conjure with in the American labor movement. They stood for six of the largest and most solid labor organizations in the railway industry and occupied a position of recognized spiritual leadership within the whole group of allied unions, whose members were wholly or partly employed on the roads and who were collectively known as the Sixteen Standard Railway Labor Unions.

The move was officially authorized by these organizations, which were ordinarily rated as among the most conservative in the labor movement. Their aggregate membership was no less than 1,500,000.

From the Socialist point of view the unexpected change was not an unmixed blessing. The numerical gain was largely offset by a corresponding loss in clarity of purpose and harmony of views. The letter of invitation was couched in careful and cautious language. The object of the conference was stated to be "to discuss and adopt a fundamental economic program designed to restore to the people the sovereignty that is rightly theirs, to make effective the purpose for which our government is established, to secure to all men the enjoyment of the gains which their industry produces." The invited conferees were expressly warned or reassured that "this is not an attempt to form a New Political Party." The most promising feature of the experiment was its unlimited possibility of development. The invitation was not confined to trade unions but was extended to all "progressive elements in the industrial and political life of the nation," and, what seemed to me most important, it expressly included the Socialist Party. Whenever we Socialists contemplated the possibility of a political party springing up independently within the body of the trade-union movement, we dreaded the prospect of being excluded from active participation. A labor party composed solely of conservative American trade unions offered scant promise of virile and aggressive political progress and would besides place the Socialist movement of the country in a most awkward predicament. With a "pure and simple" but bona fide political organization of the trade unions permanently in the field it might be just as suicidal for the Socialist Party to function in opposition to it as to obliterate itself in its favor.

On the other hand we were not unduly worried by the absence of a clear program and a consistent political philosophy in the initial stages of the movement.

We firmly believed that any considerable body of workers united for their common political interests would in the long run be led by the logic of economic and political development, and by their experience in the struggle, to accept the fundamental basis of the Socialist philosophy, particularly if the Socialists were with them to point out the meaning of such developments and the lessons of their experience. This view was supported not only by aprioristic theoretical reasoning but by the living example of the British Labor Party. It is a curious and oft-forgotten fact that the latter started on its spectacular political career without as much as an attempt to formulate a program or statement of principles. The historic resolution of the Trade Union Congress in 1899 which set in motion the creation of the Labor Party invited the coöperation "of all Coöperative, Socialist, Trade-Union and other working-class organizations to devise ways and means for the securing of an increased number of Labor members in the next Parliament." And that was all. For eighteen years the new party continued its existence blissfully forgetful of programs and formulations of general principles but steadily growing in membership, parliamentary representation, and clarity of aim.

It was not until 1917 that the party deemed it expedient to

incorporate in its constitution a statement of its objective, and this was couched in the following clear and unambiguous language: "The object of the Labor Party is to secure for the producers by hand and brain the full fruits of their industry, and the most equitable distribution thereof that may be possible, upon the basis of common ownership of the means of production and the best obtainable system of popular administration and control of each industry or service."

The British Labor Party, which had entered the arena with a political mentality quite similar to that of the present American trade-union movement, had quietly, naturally, and irresistibly evolved into a full-fledged Socialist body.

It was largely because of these considerations that the Socialists invited to the conference decided to attend. The Socialist group consisted of six persons: Victor L. Berger, Daniel W. Hoan, mayor of Milwaukee; James Oneal, editor of the party paper; Otto Branstetter, member of the party's National Executive Committee; Bertha Hale White, its secretary, and myself.

The total number of conference delegates was about 150. It was a truly representative gathering. Besides the sixteen standard railway unions there were in attendance accredited delegates from the United Mine Workers of America, several important national organizations in the needle-trade industries, always classed as "progressives," representatives of the Farmer-Labor Party, the National Nonpartisan League, the Farmers' National Council, the Women's Trade Union League and several minor organizations. At a conservative estimate the conference had a constituency of 2,000,000 members, the overwhelming majority of whom were organized workers.

It was the first time in history that American Socialists had sat in with such a formidable body of organized labor to discuss common political action.

The conference opened in a somewhat strained atmosphere.

The labor men were not free from a certain feeling of suspicion and distrust of the Socialists, with whom they had never come into close contact, and whom they were inclined to regard as unpractical intellectual theorists.

It was not until the conference had been in session several hours that the ice was broken. The discussion had been ambling along rather aimlessly for some time, when Edward F. Keating, putting his hand on my shoulder in a gesture of paternal benevolence, asked me the bland question: "Brother Hillquit, are you Socialists here in the hope of forming an independent political labor party?"

Mr. Keating was one of the important men in the conference. As a member of the House of Representatives from Colorado he had consistently, ably, and aggressively espoused the cause of the workers, and as editor of *Labor,* the official weekly paper of the railway workers, with a circulation of 400,000 copies, he exerted a powerful influence in the councils of their unions. The question was aimed at the very heart of the differences between the Socialists and trade unionists in the conference. The latter still clung to the "nonpartisan" policy of supporting the most friendly candidates on either of the old-party tickets. In their view the main object of the body about to be created was to make the support more telling and effective, thus spurring on both parties to nominate progressive candidates, and to keep elected representatives in line with an eye to reëlection.

I welcomed the question because it afforded me an opportunity for a full statement of the Socialist position. "We Socialists," I replied in substance, "have come to this conference in the frank hope and with the confident expectation that the movement initiated here will ultimately lead to the formation of a labor party in direct and consistent opposition to the Republican and Democratic parties alike. We have no faith whatever in the slogan of 'rewarding our friends and punishing our enemies' within the old parties. We are convinced that this policy tends to dissipate and fritter away the potential political forces of labor instead of mobilizing them effectively for a consistent objective, and that it is bound to result in disappointment and deception. We reserve the right to voice our views in your councils without obstreperousness or obstruction. We hope our arguments and your experiences will eventually convince you that we are right. But we have no intention to attempt to 'capture' the conference by intrigue, maneuvers, or machinations. We have no personal stakes in the movement and are here solely to serve the interests of the working class as we see them. In the meantime, we shall be ready to coöperate with you in good faith to the extent that such coöperation is consistent with the fundamental principles and policies of our party."

The declaration seemed to satisfy the conferees, and gradually the atmosphere of suspicion was dissipated. It was touching and inspiring to watch the growing confidence of the labor men in the Socialist group. Before the notable meeting was adjourned a permanent National Committee of fifteen was chosen, on which I held membership as representative of the Socialist Party, and a statement of principle and plan of organization were formulated with active Socialist participation. Even the name of the permanent organization—Conference for Progressive Political Action—was adopted on my suggestion.

The next two years were years of activity and progress. Within that period two more national conferences were held, and each registered a successive growth in organizational strength and political vitality. The second conference, held in Cleveland in December, 1922, was attended not only by representatives of its original constituent bodies, but also by delegates from thirty-two state organizations that had been created within the first nine months after the formation of the national body. The third conference, held in St. Louis in February, 1924, was an even more representative gathering, having all the characteristics of a well-knit and solid permanent organization.

But what was infinitely more encouraging to the Socialist participants in the movement was its gradual but seemingly unmistakable trend towards ever more progressive political views and independent policies.

Already in the first "Call to Action" issued immediately after the initial Chicago conference, the National Committee largely modified its uncompromising stand against independent labor politics and summed up the position of the conference on the vital question in this language: "The Conference agreed that the time was ripe for progressive political action, but that the organization of a new party should await developments."

The instructions of the National Committee to state organizations contained explicit directions for the use of the old-party primaries in support of progressive candidates but concluded with this significant advice:

"Better still, nominate and elect farmers and workers of your own choosing.

"When action within the old parties is futile, organize independently. It is often better to lose as independents with a square-cut issue, than to lose as you have lost in the past by wasting ballots on men who cannot be trusted."

In the Cleveland conference I was appointed chairman of the important Committee on Organization and Finance, and as such was largely instrumental in formulating the first complete constitution of the newly formed body.

The constitution, which was adopted unanimously, limited the political support of the conference to such candidates for public office as "are pledged to the interests of the producing classes and to the principles of genuine democracy in agriculture, industry and government." It left the state conferences free to follow the nonpartisan policy through the old-party primaries or to organize for independent political action, and added the direction to make independent nominations when both old parties failed to name progressive candidates.

Thus the conference moved cautiously around the delicate conflict of principle between nonpartisan and independent politics, with the latter slowly but steadily gaining. The time, however, approached when a definite choice seemed inevitable, for 1924 was a year of Presidential elections. While it was possible though not necessarily consistent to support a Republican here, a Democrat there and to nominate an independent candidate elsewhere, in congressional, state, and local elections, a contest for the Presidency of the United States did not offer a similar convenient situation. In the election of 1924 the Conference for Progressive Political Action was confronted with the narrow alternative of throwing its forces behind the candidate of one of the old parties and thus being practically absorbed by it; supporting no Presidential candidate and largely abdicating its fundamental functions, or nominating a Presidential ticket of its own and committing itself definitely to the policy of independent politics.

The St. Louis conference adopted a temporizing resolution to call a national convention of workers, farmers, and progressives "for the purpose of taking action on nomination of candidates for the offices of President and Vice-President of the United States," thus leaving the vital question of difference open for the time being. But the issue could not be avoided much longer. The convention was called for July 4th in Cleveland, and the conference would be forced to take a clear and definite stand by that time.

The approaching convention threw the whole world of radical and "progressive" politics into a turmoil of excitement. Labor unions, Socialists, progressive farmers and third-party advocates of all stripes were busily preparing for participation, choosing delegates and discussing programs and tactics. It was felt that the Cleveland gathering would be an event of prime if not revolutionary importance in the political history of the United States, and many hoped that July 4, 1924, would signalize the dawn of a new day for American labor.

An important element in the situation, and one that largely enhanced its complexity and interest, was the fact that Robert M. La Follette had definitely declared war to the finish against the national machines of both old parties and was commonly understood not to be disinclined to head an insurgent campaign on a radical platform.

The senior Senator from Wisconsin was a unique figure in American politics. For years he had been its stormy petrel. Entering the field of practical politics as a young man of twenty-five, he had successively ascended the rungs of the political ladder from district attorney in an upstate county to member of the House of Representatives, Governor of his state, and United States Senator. In no case was his promotion due to favors of the political machine. It was always conquered in open fight against the party bosses and in the teeth of bitter opposition. His method invariably consisted of a direct appeal to the people. Whether his constituency was limited to a county or congressional district or whether it extended to the whole of the state, Robert La Follette made it his business to reach as nearly all of them as possible by personal contact, by means of public meetings or through literature. He was a powerful speaker, clear, concise, and impressive, and a careful student with a rare mastery of the material facts and figures underlying any political controversy in which he found himself engaged. Small in stature, stocky in build, and vigorous in manner, he conducted his campaigns and controversies with almost physical intensity and earnestness. His attacks were straight, direct, and heavy. He did not spare his opponents. In battle he disdained social ameni-

ties and "senatorial courtesies." "Fighting Bob" was the affectionate sobriquet he earned early in his career, and it clung to him to
the end of his days.

He spoke and voted against America's entry in the World
War, and his pacifist stand earned for him the intense hatred and
petty persecution of the war-crazed patriots, including those of
his own state. He was burnt in effigy and expelled from social
clubs. The Wisconsin state legislature passed a resolution of
condemnation against him and the faculty of the state university,
to whose upbuilding he had so largely contributed, subjected
him to official public denunciation. In domestic politics he consistently took the side of the underdog and was the recognized
and trusted champion of the farmer and the worker as against
"vested interests" and the "power of privilege."

Although he had no social philosophy beyond the immediate
and specific problems of the day, and his political conception
moved wholly within the orbit of the existing economic system,
he was in the eyes of most of the men in the Conference for
Progressive Political Action the ideal leader of a movement
such as they envisaged.

The convention opened with a larger representation and
keener public interest than was anticipated by its initiators.
About six hundred accredited delegates presented credentials,
and an even larger number of interested and eager visitors
thronged the vast convention hall hours before the formal opening. They came from all parts of the country and from all walks
of life with workers and farmers heavily predominating. A
tense atmosphere of expectation hung over the gathering, while
the prospects and proposed methods of the campaign were
animatedly discussed by eager groups.

In the meantime the fate of the movement was being decided
behind closed doors by the National Committee. The range
of discussion was rather narrow. It was at this time a foregone

conclusion that an independent candidate would be named for the Presidency, and that Senator La Follette would be the choice. The sole question was whether the convention would constitute itself into a permanent political party. The conservative leaders of the Conference for Progressive Political Action had for some time been considering a plan to limit the convention action to a personal endorsement of Mr. La Follette's candidacy and to maintain the "nonpartisan" political principle in congressional, state, and local elections as the permanent policy. The idea was quietly spread among the principal railway unions, much to the dismay of the Socialists and other third-party advocates. I do not know to this day whether the strange notion originated with the Senator and was acquiesced in by the Brotherhood chiefs or, what seems to me more likely, the reverse was the fact. In either event it struck me as a case of deliberate sabotage or monumental folly. About three weeks before the date set for the opening of the convention I prepared a confidential memorandum of my views on the subject at the request of Gilbert E. Roe, former law partner and at all times confidential adviser of Senator La Follette, for submission to the latter.

I quote the cogent paragraphs of the memorandum:

"If a movement is set on foot for the sole purpose of electing Senator La Follette, it will succeed if the Senator is elected, and will fail, at least for all immediate practical purposes, if he is defeated. If a third party is created as a permanent party of opposition to the two reactionary old parties, the Senator's chances of election will not be diminished, but if he fails of election, a new, fruitful, and powerful instrument will have been created under his leadership to fight for the rights of the people at all times.

"What better and more lasting service could a man of the type and record of Senator La Follette render to the cause of political progress?

"As a purely practical proposition, moreover, it seems to me that the other course proposed, *i.e.*, uniting all progressive elements on the presidential ticket, but leaving them to work within the old parties in congressional, state, and local campaigns, would take the very soul out of the movement. To be successful our campaign must be in the nature of a crusade born of a popular revolt against the iniquities of the old parties. How can we expect an effective campaign if we arraign the Republican and Democratic parties in the presidential fight and support the same parties in local contests? Such tactics would besides invite all kinds of political deals in which the presidential ticket may sometimes be sacrificed."

It was these and other arguments that I urged upon the National Committee with all the earnestness at my command. I was warmly supported by the representatives of a few national labor unions and the spokesmen for practically all other component elements of the conference. But the railroad men stubbornly adhered to their evasive plan of action. The discussion was heated and prolonged, and the body of delegates and visitors became restive. Rumors of what was going on in the committee room had spread among them, causing apprehension and consternation. At one point, when the gathering grew tired of the "inspirational" speeches delivered to bridge over the hours of suspense, and began to show loud and unmistakable signs of impatience, I was sent out to speak to them in behalf of the National Committee in an effort to allay their ruffled feelings.

My appearance on the stage was the signal for a spontaneous and lusty ovation, such as I had seldom, if ever, witnessed. Delegates and visitors stood on chairs, waved and cheered and shouted for many minutes, until I succeeded in establishing a semblance of order and was able to make myself heard.

Neither I nor my opponents in the committee were deceived about the nature and meaning of the demonstration. It was not a personal tribute. It was generally known that I was desperately fighting in the committee for the formation of an independent political party, and the popular acclaim was an endorsement of my stand as clearly as articulate language could have expressed it. Had I at that moment proposed the immediate organization of a new party the proposal would have been carried by an overwhelming vote.

The temptation was great, but one to be resisted. The National Committee was still debating the crucial point, and some acceptable compromise seemed possible. It would manifestly have been an act of disloyalty for me to attempt to force a decision from the floor of the convention before the committee had reached a conclusion, especially when I was acting as emissary of the committee. A snap convention decision to form a new party would moreover have been a Pyrrhic victory. The great majority of the delegates were undoubtedly ready for such a step, but the majority of the delegates did not represent the majority of the constituents. The railroad workers, who were the backbone of the movement and constituted the bulk of its adherents, stood behind their leaders, and these were not yet ready to sever all ties from the old political parties. Even while their negotiations with Senator La Follette were in active progress, some of them were busily lobbying the Democratic convention in behalf of the candidacy of William G. McAdoo. As war-time railway administrator President Wilson's Secretary of the Treasury and son-in-law had shown himself exceedingly friendly and helpful to the workers on the roads, and the latter were now out to reward him according to the accepted formula. Had Mr. McAdoo been nominated by the Democrats instead of the conservative John W. Davis, there would have been no La Follette campaign in 1924 or, at any rate, it would not have had the support of the organized railway workers or for that matter of the American Federation of Labor. The American labor leaders still attached greater importance to the person than to the cause; the rank and file generally followed them, and it seemed ludicrous to think that after years of patient maneuvering and hard educational work we would only arrive at a "labor party" without labor.

I allayed the impatience of the crowd as best I could pending the arrival of an expected message from the Senator on the vital question.

The message finally came in the form of a multigraphed typewritten statement, which was distributed among the delegates and read by the candidate's son, Robert M. La Follette, Jr.

It was a long and disappointing document, uninspired and uninspiring. It was replete with well-worn phrases about the "predatory interests in control of the American government," the necessity of destroying the combined power of private monopoly over the political and economic life of the nation, and other familiar expressions from the middle-class political vocabulary of the congressional Progressive or Insurgent bloc. On the vital question that kept the convention in a fever heat of expectancy there was nothing beyond the somewhat ambiguous declaration that the time had come "for a militant political movement, independent of the two old-party organizations," offset by the rather inconsistent and historically inexact assertion that "permanent political parties have been born in this country after, and not before, national campaigns."

The effect of the message on the convention was depressing.

Between Senator La Follette's obvious support of the position of the railway workers' leadership and the manifest desire of the convention majority for the immediate formation of a full-fledged and permanent party, the National Committee found a way out in a compromise recommendation, which provided for an endorsement of the La Follette candidacy and the creation of a unified and country-wide organization to function during the campaign. Tacked on to the recommendations and forming their most important part was this resolution:

"On the 29th day of November, 1924, the National Committee shall meet and issue a call for a special National Convention, to be held in the latter part of January, 1925, at such place and such definite date as the Committee may decide.

"The object of the Convention shall be to consider and pass upon the question of forming a permanent independent political party for National and local elections, upon the basis of the general principles laid down in the platform adopted by this Convention."

To the "third-party" advocates of all shades, including the Socialists, the concession seemed quite substantial. It was their expectation that in the four months of common work and campaigning ahead of the movement, its divers component elements would be automatically fused into a harmonious whole, that the sentiment in favor of a new party would inevitably grow in extent and intensity, and that a national convention held after the election, for the sole and express purpose of deciding on the formation of such a party, could not possibly fail to launch one on a solid and permanent basis.

It was with this confident expectation that the recommendations of the Committee were adopted, and it was with this expectation in mind that the Socialist Party subsequently endorsed the candidacy of Robert M. La Follette, thus for the first time in its history departing from its established custom and supporting a non-Socialist candidate for public office.

Senator La Follette polled five million votes in round numbers. Taking into account all the handicaps that beset his campaign, its hasty, often haphazard and fragmentary organization, paucity of funds, the heavy pressure exerted by many employers to coerce their workers into voting for "Coolidge and Prosperity," the confusion resulting from the ambiguous politi-

cal "nonpartisan" alliances in several states, the lack of supporting local tickets and campaigns, and finally the lukewarmness
and even open betrayal by certain sections of organized labor,
it was a splendid showing. If a regularly organized and permanent political party had achieved similar results in its début,
it would have left a deep imprint on the political history of
the United States. It would have beaten the record of the best
performance of any third party in the past; it would have given
the new party control of at least one state (Wisconsin) and
advanced it to second position in a number of other states;
it would have elected some United States senators and a sizable
group of congressmen and local officials; it would have given
the party a solid foundation for growth and expansion.

But it had been a one-man campaign, and the "practical"
labor politicians viewed its results solely from the point of view
of concrete achievement. They had staked their political all
on one card and had lost. Senator La Follette was defeated,
and gloom reigned in their camps.

The special convention was held, with a month's delay, in
Chicago, February 21-22, 1925. It was a vastly different gathering from that which had assembled in Cleveland on the preceding 4th of July.

This time the delegates had come to bury Cæsar, not to
praise him. The railway brotherhood chiefs frankly declared
their intention to withdraw from the movement. Other organizations of workers and farmers had also lost much of their enthusiasm for it. The two opposing currents within the Conference for Progressive Political Action had come to a definite
parting of the ways.

There was no acrimony or bitterness about it. More as a
matter of form and record than with any hope of success, the
Socialists made a supreme effort to save the situation by a last-
hour plea for straight working-class politics. It was a tense,

solemn, and sad day as their spokesmen, one after another, made their final pleas and exhortations. It was a particularly moving moment when the aged Eugene V. Debs rose to address the gathering. He had taken a leading part in the organization of the railroad workers during the early period of their struggles. He had worked for them unselfishly and untiringly in the days of their weakness and poverty and had suffered persecution and imprisonment in their behalf. And now, as he stood there, tall, guant, earnest, and ascetic, before the well-groomed and comfortably situated leaders of a new generation, he seemed like a ghost of reproach risen from their past and calling them back to the glorious days of struggle, suffering, and idealism.

He was listened to with close attention. But the railroad men were not moved from their position. In the course of three years of coöperation the Socialists had earned their confidence and respect. They did not wish to put any obstacles in the way of organizing a new party, but they were not ready to participate in such a movement.

To save appearances and feelings it was arranged that the convention of the Conference for Progressive Political Action should formally adjourn, but that the delegates individually should be free to reconvene for the formation of a labor party. A resolution to form such a party was thereupon adopted by the reconstituted convention; but the Socialists, following the example of the labor unions, refused to take part in it. Without organized labor the "convention" was little more than a motley array of advocates of heterogeneous political nostrums with a sprinkling of dubious farmers' organizations and liberal progressive groups without constituencies. There was little common ground between them and the Socialists and no prospect for fruitful political coöperation. The new political party, nominally formed in Chicago on the 2nd day of February, 1925, never functioned.

Thus closed one of the most promising and most tragic chapters in the history of the American labor movement.

The Socialist Party, disappointed but not dismayed, reverted to its traditional policy of playing a lone hand in politics. In the years immediately following, it was a difficult, often disheartening, task to maintain a semblance of life in the dismembered, discouraged, and seemingly hopeless organization. In 1928 the party touched the lowest point in its downward career, when Norman Thomas, its candidate for President, running against the popular Alfred E. Smith, received less than 300,000 votes in the whole country.

Paradoxically, however, the party's standing and prestige did not wane with the loss of its organizational and electoral strength. Its persistent struggles against heavy odds and its unshakable faith in its political doctrine won a certain measure of respect from its opponents, a respect which was largely enhanced, when the catastrophic business crisis of the last few years demonstrated to many thoughtful citizens in all walks of life the utter inadequacy of the prevailing capitalist system.

In 1932 Mr. Thomas, again heading the Socialist ticket, trebled his former vote.

The Socialist Party has almost regained the high point of political strength in its history, and has entered on a promising upward course in all directions. The pendulum has again swung clearly around.

CHAPTER IV

HAS IT BEEN WORTH WHILE?

An After-Dinner Speech *

It is forty years, almost to a day, since the first Socialist candidate for the Presidency of the United States was named. The Socialist Party was not yet in existence. The nomination was made by its political predecessor, the Socialist Labor Party.

This party was organized in 1878, the year when the Imperial German government under the régime of its Iron Chancellor, Otto von Bismarck, adopted the infamous "Exceptional Laws" and inaugurated a campaign of extermination against everybody and everything Socialistic. German Social Democrats by the tens of thousands sought a haven of refuge in the United States, and for many years they constituted the main body of the new party's support.

In its earlier years the party confined its efforts to the work of propaganda with only occasional incursions into the field of practical local politics; but in 1892 the leaders deemed the time ripe for an experiment on a national scale.

A convention was called, of eight delegates from five Eastern states, and Simon Wing of Massachusetts was named candidate for President of the United States.

Mr. Wing was not a member of the party, and his Socialist views and sympathies were rather vague, but he possessed cer-

* Delivered on the occasion of the Socialist State Convention of New York, July, 1932.

tain personal qualifications which far outweighed his doctrinal deficiencies. He measured up to the Constitutional requirement of American birth, a status which few, if any, party members could claim for themselves. He was the proud possessor of a long gray beard and outspoken Yankee features, looking to all the world like the conventional image of Uncle Sam, and, last but not least, he was ready to lend his name to the ticket.

Hopes ran high in Socialist breasts. Up to that time the American workers had had practically no opportunity to express themselves politically. Except for a few sporadic and unintelligent political revolts represented by the Greenback and Populist movements, the choice had always been confined to the two major parties, both dominated by capitalist interests.

For the first time in the history of the country a political party presented to the people a clear-cut working-class program with a demand for the complete abolition of the oppressive system of capitalist exploitation and the establishment of a Socialist commonwealth based on coöperative labor and collective enjoyment. The party platform expounded the Socialist philosophy fully, elaborately and scientifically. It was bound to convince every worker who took the trouble to read it. While the Socialists were not so sanguine as to expect to carry the election, they confidently hoped to pile up an impressive vote and to lay the foundation for an effective party of labor.

Many meetings were held, and many speeches were made, mostly in German, but some also in English. A vigorous campaign was conducted, and when the returns slowly drifted in after election day, it was found that the Socialist Labor Party, with Simon Wing as its standard bearer, had polled a total of about 21,500 votes.

Eight years later we were in a new flutter of political hopes and excitement.

The Socialist Party had just been formed. Unlike the old

Socialist Labor Party, it was made up largely of indigenous elements of the American population with strong support in the Middle West. The Party's nominee for President was Eugene V. Debs, one of the most popular and beloved labor leaders, and a man of rare eloquence and personal magnetism. The Socialist Party set itself the modest goal of one to two million votes in its first onslaught on the political citadel of capitalism; but when the smoke of the electoral battle had cleared and the votes were counted, somewhat less than one hundred thousand were credited to Mr. Debs.

With this inauspicious début the Socialist Party entered its political career of the next thirty-two years. It has been a checkered and hectic career of alternating ups and downs, of slow progress and frequent recessions, of few victories and many disappointments.

In the zenith of its power the party polled in the neighborhood of one million votes and had one hundred and twenty thousand dues-paying members. It was well organized in every state of the Union and commanded the support of more than a hundred newspapers, dailies and weeklies, in English and in practically all the multifarious tongues spoken and read in our great country of composite nationalities.

Then came our entry into the World War, the government persecution and suppression of all radical movements, the division between pro-war and anti-war Socialists, the Communist split and the long period of economic prosperity, spiritual materialism, and political apathy. For ten years the Socialist movement of America was virtually dormant. The membership and activities of the Party dwindled down to the point of insignificance. Four years ago its candidates on the Presidential ticket polled less than three hundred thousand votes.

And now, we are apparently facing a new Socialist uplift. The spirit of narrow-minded intolerance which was engendered during the war and carefully cultivated and intensified for years after, is fast yielding to the normal and more tolerant psychology in a political democracy. The feverish period of expansion and prosperity has been followed by a catastrophic collapse of our industrial system with an appalling trail of misery and suffering in its wake. Political complacency and economic optimism have received a rude shock. The American people are beginning to doubt and to question. Old economic theories and political beliefs are subjected to a critical reëxamination. New views and creeds receive an attentive and sympathetic hearing.

The Socialist Party is getting a new lease of life. Its membership, vote, and political influence are again in the ascendant, although it has not yet made up for its losses in the past dozen years.

And so we begin once more.

Has it all been worth while?

I have taken an active part in the Socialist movement throughout the entire period under review. To me Socialism has never been a mere abstract philosophy or intellectual pastime. It has been my ideal and religion and one of my principal interests in life. I have given my whole adult existence to the service of the cause.

Has it been worth while?

I would not be candid if I did not confess that in the periods of heavy defeats I had moments of disappointment and discouragement, black moments of doubt and misgiving, when I asked myself the tantalizing question.

I always emerged from the soul-searching quest with an abiding conviction that my course was right and that my work was not in vain. I realize, of course, the psychological temptation of self-justification, the protective instinct which rebels against an avowal of a misspent life, but I am quite certain that my conclusions were arrived at honestly.

I utterly reject the opinion that the Socialist movement has been a failure. What is failure, what is success in the struggle for a high humanitarian cause or, for that matter, in the life of the individual?

I have never considered Socialism as purely or even mainly as a political movement. Socialism is above all a philosophy of life and civilization. It aims at a saner, higher and nobler social order. Its concrete task is to prepare and to develop the economic, intellectual and moral foundations of a better world to come. The progress of such a movement cannot be measured by any concrete tests. It can hardly be measured at all. Who can be so bold as to say that the Socialist propaganda has not left a deep imprint on American thought and mind?

Forty years ago theory and policy of our government was rampantly individualistic. The dominant article of the American political creed was the principle of noninterference with the struggles of the rich and the poor, the strong and the weak. The government kept studiously aloof from the assumption of economic or social functions. Today the principle of individualism in government is largely an outworn political fiction. Our statute books are replete with restrictive and protective measures of social legislation, and our administrative structure is honeycombed with agencies and institutions to regulate, control, and supervise economic activities and social relations. The spirit of Socialism, which places the welfare of society above the selfish interests of the individual, clearly characterizes the whole modern trend of American governmental policy, and much of it is directly traceable to the work of Socialist propaganda.

It is interesting to note how many reform measures first formulated as political planks by the Socialists have been enacted into law by the old parties under pressure of economic necessity and public clamor.

The Socialist vote and party membership are no index to the

extent to which Socialistic thought has permeated the population of the country.

In the last forty years hundreds of thousands of men and women have held membership in the Socialist Party, coming and going. Millions have at one time or another voted the Socialist ticket, and many more have listened to Socialist speeches or read Socialist literature and passed on splinters of Socialist thought to others. All these accumulated and imponderable factors leaven the political thought of the American masses, all this is the unharvested fruit of the Socialist propaganda.

Some day the hidden and uncrystallized forces of Socialist sentiment may spring forth into a powerful movement, suddenly and spontaneously. Such has been the course of all great social and political upheavals. Abolitionism seemed to be making little or no headway for many years, but all the time its ideal was silently and imperceptibly germinating under the political surface, and when its inevitable triumph came it seemed rapid and sudden to the superficial observer. The propaganda of the French encyclopedists and libertarians was for years seemingly confined to small circles of choice spirits. Few persons appreciated the extent of its hold on the public mind until the "sudden" outbreak of the great Revolution. In Russia the pathetic struggle for Socialism was carried on for half a century by a small band of heroic propagandists and scattered groups of émigrés. Except for a brief period during the régime of the czar's dumas, it seemed to make no headway among the Russian people; but when the Constituent Assembly was convoked in 1917 and the masses of the peasants and workers had their first chance to cast a free and untrammeled vote, the overwhelming majority of the elected representatives consisted of Socialists of the various schools.

It is a mistake to assume that because the Socialist movement in the United States has made no appreciable and visible progress in the last forty years it may not prove victorious in the course of the next twenty years, and it is equally false to infer that when the movement resumes its growth, it will necessarily be regular and gradual, and that it may not proceed by leaps and bounds.

I am hopeful of seeing a great and powerful, perhaps even a triumphant Socialist movement in this country in my own days.

But whether I live to see the realization of the Socialist goal or not is after all not a matter of prime importance.

There is, strictly speaking, no such thing as a final social goal. The social horizon, like the physical horizon, is only an illusory line marking our visual limitation.

To the person who does not move from the spot it remains at a stationary and fixed distance. To the traveler who proceeds on his onward path it is a shifting and unattainable goal. As he advances towards the horizon, it recedes from him, uncovering ever new stretches ahead of him, unfolding ever new vistas before his eyes. What had been the horizon yesterday is left far in the rear today, and new elusive horizons appear before him with every minute of his progress.

A century and a half ago the social horizon of the forward-looking men did not extend beyond the vision of political democracy and national government. Today we can envisage a social order of industrial democracy, world organization, and world peace. The ideal Socialist commonwealth is projected on the horizon of the twentieth century. Some day it will be reached and passed, and new and higher goals will confront the human race in the never-ceasing process of social progress and betterment. Satisfaction does not lie so much in attainment as in effort, not so much in "victories" as in aspiration and struggle. Our supreme justification as Socialists is that we have been going and are going in the right direction.

But even while I am attempting to rationalize my social philosophy and political creed I cannot help feeling that it is an unprofitable and largely irrelevant task. Our inclinations and sympathies, our convictions and actions are not determined by free and deliberate choice but by a complexity of factors, physical, psychological, and social, individualistic and environmental, which inexorably shape our lives.

I am a Socialist because I cannot be anything else. I cannot accept the ugly world of capitalism, with its brutal struggles and needless suffering, its archaic and irrational economic structure, its cruel social contrasts, its moral callousness and spiritual degradation.

If there were no organized Socialist movement or Socialist party, if I were alone, all alone in the whole country and the whole world, I could not help opposing capitalism and pleading for a better and saner order, pleading for Socialism.

By violating my conscience, I might have made peace with the existing order of things and found a comfortable place among the beneficiaries of the system. I might have joined one of the political parties of power and plunder and perhaps attained to a position of influence and "honor." I might have devoted my life to the acquisition of wealth and possibly accumulated a large fortune. But my apparent success would have been dismal failure. I should have felt dissatisfied and mean. I should have been deprived of all the joys of life that only an inspiring social ideal can impart, of the pleasure and comradeship of the best minds and noblest hearts in all lands, and, above all, of my own self-respect.

Having chosen and followed the unpopular course of a Socialist propagandist, I am entirely at peace with myself. I have nothing to regret, nothing to apologize for.

If, forty years ago, I could have foreseen all phases of the tortuous course of the Socialist movement in this country and in the world, I would have done exactly as I did. If I had forty more years of life in me I would continue spending them in the

Socialist movement, without regard to its "practical" prospects or immediate accomplishments.

To me the Socialist movement with its enthusiasm and idealism, its comradeship and struggles, its hopes and disappointments, its victories and defeats, has been the best that life has had to offer.

INDEX

333